THE GLOBAL EXPERIENCE

D1015995

THE GLOBAL EXPERIENCE:

Readings In World History

Volume I

Stuart B. Schwartz
Yale University

Linda R. Wimmer
Bridgewater State College

Robert S. Wolff
University of Connecticut

College of the Rockies
Library

 **LONGMAN**

An imprint of Addison Wesley Longman, Inc.

New York • Reading, Massachusetts • Menlo Park, California • Harlow, England
Don Mills, Ontario • Sydney • Mexico City • Madrid • Amsterdam

Executive Editor: Bruce Borland
Developmental Editor: Jessica Bayne
Project Coordination: Electronic Publishing Services Inc.
Cover Designer: Kay Petronio
Cover Illustration/Photo: Mesoamerican Sculpture, Courtesy Stuart Schwartz
Art Studio: Electronic Publishing Services Inc.
Photo Researcher: Judy Feldman
Electronic Production Manager: Angel Gonzalez, Jr.
Manufacturing Manager: Willie Lane
Electronic Page Makeup: Americomp
Printer and Binder: R. R. Donnelley & Sons Company
Cover Printer: The Lehigh Press, Inc.

For permission to use copyrighted material, grateful acknowledgment is made to the copyright holders on pp. 259–264, which are hereby made part of this copyright page.

Library of Congress Cataloging-in-Publication Data

The global experience : readings in world history / Stuart B.
   Schwartz, Linda R. Wimmer, Robert S. Wolff.
        p.   cm.
   ISBN 0-673-99380-9 (v. 1)
      1. World history.   I. Schwartz, Stuart B.   II. Wimmer , Linda R.
   III. Wolff, Robert S., 1966–   .
   D23.G58   1996   96-30731
   909—dc20   CIP

Copyright © 1997 by Stuart B. Schwartz, Linda R. Wimmer, Robert S. Wolff

All rights reserved. No part of this publication may be reproduced, stored in a retrieval system, or transmitted, in any form or by any means, electronic, mechanical, photocopying, recording, or otherwise, without the prior written permission of the publisher. Printed in the United States.

ISBN 0-673-99380-9

12345678910—DOC—99989796

Contents

PART FOUR
THE WORLD SHRINKS: 1450 CE TO 1750 CE   237

Chapter 14
The Changing World Balance   239

Preface

*T*his anthology presents a selection of documents and secondary readings that introduce students to the study of world history. It is the result of our common experience of teaching world history to large numbers of undergraduates and trying to convey to them the variety, complexity, and accomplishments of peoples in the past, across the globe. We have found that the understanding of that story is greatly helped by students' direct contact with primary sources wherever possible and by their practice in trying to relate primary sources of different types to the varieties of historical opinion and analysis. We have tried to concentrate on issues that are global in nature and that provoke historical comparisons because we feel that these are essential aspects of the study of world history. Our collection is thematic and was developed to be used along with lectures and a textbook or other readings. Although it was created specifically to accompany Stearns, Adas, and Schwartz, *World Civilizations: The Global Experience* (Longman), it can be used with any narrative text.

This anthology emphasizes social and cultural history; its goals are simple. We hope first of all to have students develop a sense that history is more than names and dates, but also to understand that interpretations are based upon historical evidence. Reading primary sources gives students an opening to the worlds of the past and some direct contact with different cultural traditions. The problems of interpreting these sources should also make them aware of the difficulties that historians, or anyone else for that matter, face when trying to make sense of the past.

There are a number of features that distinguish this anthology from many others. First, it emphasizes the social fabric of daily life in a wide range of societies. Rather than concentrating only on "great civilizations," "great leaders," and "great ideas," we have mixed traditional themes such as state-building, the rise of civilizations, the spread of universal religions, colonialism, and nationalism, with the themes of livelihood, identity, and community as they have been articulated within different societies in the past.

The primary documents we have chosen tend to be short and have been selected because of their potential to convey a sense of the past in different cultures and to provoke students to question and compare. Because of our thematic organization, not every culture will be represented within every theme, but the larger questions raised should stimulate students to think about parallels and contrasts across societies. We have included a great variety of sources including iconographic images and documents drawn from oral literatures. These challenge students to use historical materials in an imaginative way and to be aware that a historical source need not be an "official," written document in order to provide insights into the past. Our brief introductions to the sources are designed to set the context for the material but not to interpret the source. That challenge is reserved for the student. To assist students and instructors, each chapter contains a brief set of questions that can be used as the basis for written assignments or class discussions.

Another distinguishing feature of this anthology is the inclusion of some secondary readings and analyses along with the primary sources. We have done this especially when dealing with periods or peoples for whom few written records exist or when such analyses can show students the complexities of interpretation. By including these studies, we also introduce students to the contributions that archaeology, anthropology, linguistic studies, and other disciplines can make to historical analysis.

Although we have incorporated important texts from the "great civilizations" of ancient Egypt, China, Greece, and Rome, we have consciously sought to expand the geographical boundaries and the variety of cultures usually represented in anthologies such as this. Admittedly, some of these texts will demand greater sophistication from the readers, but they also demonstrate the problems that historians constantly confront. All of the texts included here—primary documents, images, and secondary studies—demand that students question them. Who created them and for what audience? Why were they written or created? and, why at this particular place and time?

In another vein, students of World History must acknowledge the complexities of creating a "global history" from within Western tradition. We recognize that certain themes such as "progress" or "industrialization" tend to emphasize the West and dichotomize history in an ethnocentric way between those who are "advanced," and those who are seen as "backward" or "traditional." Given our own cultural heritage in which writing and technology have been seen as the keys to civilization, it is easy to understand this tendency. We have tried to be careful about such definitions and about the selection of themes and terminology that tend to reinforce the idea that the West is the measure of all else. Readers will also note that we have tried to avoid depending too heavily on the great wealth of European observation by travelers, explorers, conquerors, and diplomats as the best way to describe non-Western societies. As rich as those materials are, they often convey images and interpretations that are essentially European in nature. We have tried to use such materials sparingly and to include wherever possible primary sources generated by the indigenous societies themselves. This has created some problems because such sources are not always easy to find, but it is here that iconographic materials or images, and secondary studies have been particularly helpful. We believe that discussing the role of the West in world history, incorporating non-Western views into our understanding of the past, and appreciating the history of cultures without a written tradition, are all essential aspects of a world history course.

In selecting the sources included here we have received suggestions and help from a number of colleagues and friends. We wish to thank the following: Michael Adas, Carlos Aguirre, Jean Allman, Pradip Bhaumik, Pete Burkholder, J. Wendel Cox, Jennifer Downs, Caesar Farah, Ted Farmer, Michelle Mouton, Jean O'Brien-Kehoe, Helena Pohlandt-McCormick, Kay Reyerson, Peter Stearns, Guy Thompson, Jacob Tropp, and Ann Waltner. At Longman, we wish to thank Bruce Borland and Jessica Bayne. We also wish to express our appreciation for the thoughtful comments provided to us by the following reviewers: Tim Keirn, California State University, Long Beach; Pier Larsen, Penn State University; David Smith, California State Polytechnic University, Pomona; and Malcolm Thompson.

Introduction

*T*o some extent each generation writes its own history, or more precisely, it looks at the past from a different viewpoint, seeking to find the roots or explanations of those things it finds important in the present. World history has been around for a long time (as some of the selections here will show). However, as the world has become increasingly integrated by communication and transportation, by international commerce, and by cultural contacts, world history has increasingly become a focus and concern as we have all become part of a global system. What happens today in Tehran, Tokyo, and Rio de Janeiro will have effects on people in Paris and Johannesburg as well as in rural Maine and Mexico. Realizing this makes us all potential students of, and participants in, world history.

Whose history is *world history?* World history must deal with the variety and the interconnections of the human past: if it excludes the historical experience of any people or region, it cannot truly be a global history. This is not to say that everyone's history is the same. Of course people who have different national, religious, ethnic, gender, or class experiences will have a different understanding of what the past means to them. *The Global Experience* tries—where possible—to reflect this diversity of opinion and interpretation. The problem in the study of world history is not who should be included, but how to tell an inclusive story.

World history seeks to find connections, comparisons, and parallels on a global scale. Such a search raises interesting but difficult questions. Does human history have some grand themes like the rise of the state, or the struggle for political power, that cross geographical and cultural boundaries? Why do different societies display similar or contrasting developments? How have cultures interacted and influenced each other over the course of history? These global developments, linkages, and comparisons have preoccupied men and women for centuries. Ibn Khaldun, the great North African historian of the fourteenth century, and Georg Wilhelm Friedrich Hegel, the nineteenth-century German philosopher, both sought to find the underlying patterns in the human past. Today, as e-mail, fax and the

Concorde have brought societies into increasing contact, a knowledge of global connections has become increasingly important for understanding others as well as ourselves. Yet while changes in our world have brought societies closer together, those changes also make explaining the interconnections and parallels between peoples correspondingly more difficult.

Historians are not in agreement about how to address these issues. The French historian Fernand Braudel thought that the events of history, such as battles, kings, treaties, politics, and personalities, were like the foam on the top of an ocean wave and that the real forces of history, including family patterns, the use of the land, or the nature of political rule, were much deeper and often moved slowly and imperceptibly. He thought that these deeper patterns should be the historian's primary focus. This is part of an old debate among historians. Did Napoleon make the "Age of Napoleon" or was he created by the events and possibilities of his time? Do people make their own history, or is it made for them by forces beyond their own control? The debate between a history shaped primarily by human agency, or one shaped by the structures of human society and the natural world, remains unresolved.

This anthology seeks to present a selection of sources and readings that reflect the variety of human experiences and which reveal the complexity and creativity of people in the past. This collection does not emphasize Western civilization, but it certainly does not ignore it either. Our objective is not to see history as essentially divided between "us" and "them," but rather to emphasize mutual interactions, contacts, and parallels across cultural and political boundaries. Western civilization is viewed here as an important aspect of world history to be understood and appreciated in the context of its importance in that global story. We have concentrated on social and cultural history and in many sections we have used readings which draw on archaeology, linguistic studies, and religious studies in order to present a fuller picture of the past. Also, we have sought to present materials that reflect the lives of ordinary people rather than concentrating only on leaders or on documents written by elites. To do this, we have used the themes of identity, livelihood, and community to guide our selection of sources. Exploring how peoples in the past made their living, formed their families, celebrated and mourned, dreamed and despaired, decided who they were and were not, and how they organized themselves as communities from village to nation, has been our principal aim.

THEMES IN WORLD HISTORY

This volume stresses three themes in world history—*identity, livelihood,* and *community*. The readings have been carefully chosen to explore these themes as they affect the social fabric of people's lives in the past. Identity, livelihood, and community are building blocks of societies that are shared by peoples throughout the world. Through these themes, it is possible to think about the history of the world in a global fashion without privileging one region over another. The project of world history is a comparative one: in each chapter, readers will compare and contrast the experiences of peoples in different regions of the world on particular issues or during specific epochs in human history. Unlike most textbooks in world history that are organized geographically, this reader is organized thematically around a series of issues such as the agricultural revolution, the spread of peoples and cultures, the impact of industrialization, and global conflict.

Within this reader, a "civilization" is defined as a particular kind of society that produces a surplus of food large enough to permit differentiation within that society. When people found ways to produce a surplus of food, it was possible for a more varied division of labor to emerge with increasing numbers of people occupied in activities not directly related to immediate survival. The success of the agricultural revolution—the knowledge of sedentary farming—made it possible for men and women to specialize in crafts and trades, as well as laid the foundations for cities and empires. Put simply, the neolithic or agricultural revolution created the circumstances in which dense populations could exist.

By drawing examples from a wide variety of societies, including some from societies that do not meet this definition of "civilization," we hope to achieve a reader that is both representative of world history and one that allows students to examine themes in different settings. We believe that students will benefit from a reader that makes the definitions of historical terminology themselves a topic for discussion and debate. Where a textbook must define and standardize historical terminology for the purposes of writing a narrative account, a documentary reader can throw those definitions open to question, encouraging students to become more perceptive readers of history.

Within the global history narrative, the aim of the authors is to examine the social and economic fabric of daily life and the construction of identity. By "social fabric of daily life," we mean the intertwining of relationships between and among individuals, families, and communities in everyday activities including subsistence production, commodity production and trade, and social reproduction including the creation of families and maintenance of community organization.

Identity

People's identity, the construction of one's self in relation to others in society, is historically variable. Identities are not static, but rather change over time as they come to be imbued with different meanings. Identity both shapes and is shaped by people's experiences. What are the facets of identity? Scholars usually include gender, age, race, ethnicity, sexuality and social class or status as components of identity. Simply put, a person's identity is the answer she or he gives when confronted with the question, "Who are you?" When reading primary and secondary sources, ask yourself what components of the author's identity are most prominent. How are the societies that you explore organized in terms of identity? Is, for example, the category of gender—the social and cultural meaning of being female or male— particularly revealing for understanding how peoples organize the daily work that they do? How did ethnic and racial differences shape the ways in which Europeans understood peoples in Africa, Asia, and the Americas during the periods of colonization and imperialism?

Livelihood

The livelihood of a society is the basis of individual existence as well as community and social organization. How a society, or a community, manages those tasks necessary for the reproduction and continued well-being of the people—their livelihood—is a fundamental theme of this reader. What are the tasks needed to maintain communities and ensure their continuity? These tasks include the provision of food, fuel, and water, care of both the very young and the very old, and the protection of society from predators or invaders. The livelihood of a community is shaped by powerful forces such as the environment (including timely and adequate rainfall, days of sunshine during the growing season, extremes of heat and cold, as well as plagues, floods, and other disasters). Indeed the environment is often a powerful influence that determines many of the possibilities available to human communities. Fertile river valleys can support large populations; deserts, tropical rain forests, and arid mountains cannot. The livelihood of communities has changed over time, and varies geographically as well. Rural and urban communities provide for themselves in different ways. In sedentary communities, not all people are engaged in the production or collection of food, fuel, and water. In these societies, the livelihood of a particular family is ensured through other means. Workers earn wages or barter their skills for goods. The wealthy obtain their livelihood by controlling peasants, workers, and slaves, or, in more recent times, through their investments in the global economy. How the livelihood of people and their communities is arranged provides important clues into the values of the societies you will study.

Community

Identity and livelihood are examined within the context of particular communities. Rather than focus upon nations or empires, we have chosen to explore (when possible) the daily life of communities throughout the past. There are certainly examples drawn from empires as well as readings that explore traditional issues such as imperialism. However, the community level is important for two reasons. First, at the level of the community it is possible to describe the daily life of the people whose work and efforts supports all societies, whether they live in hunter-gatherer groups in southern Africa, coastal fishing villages in Indonesia, or in an empire in the central valley of Mexico. At this level it is possible to examine identity and livelihood in all of their complexity without resorting to generalizations about particular nations or peoples. Second, by studying communities it is possible to compare societies thematically while remaining aware of the differences that exist within societies along, for example, ethnic or religious lines.

READING HISTORICAL SOURCES

What Are Historical Sources?

A historical source is anything that tells the historian about events that happened in the past. Conventionally, historians use written records, and certainly these are important. Diaries, letters, newspapers, government correspondence and even shopping lists are historical sources that can provide answers to historians' questions and help to explain events in the past. However, the sources available to scholars are by no means limited to written records. Nonwritten sources such as oral memory and tradition, archaeological findings, ethnographic studies, and linguistic research can provide information about societies, both past and present, for which written sources are unavailable. Nonwritten sources provide a valuable complement to written records as well.

Sources that provide a firsthand, or contemporary, perspective on events in the past are called *primary* sources. These sources form the foundation of all historical research and writing. This reader contains many such primary sources: These include not only written documents like the Code of Hammurabi, but also the findings of archaeological research. In the latter case, the primary source material are the findings of the archaeological dig, and might include bone fragments, arrowheads, or city walls. How the historian or the archaeologist interprets the primary source material, however, is what is called a *secondary* source. In other words, the original data of historical research, whether it is a bone fragment, written document, or photograph, are primary sources. The articles and books written by scholars are secondary sources because they interpret primary source material.

Primary Sources

In order to use primary sources, historians often ask the following general questions about the source they are using. The first set of questions helps to establish the context in which the document was created. The second set helps you to establish some critical questions you should ask yourself about the veracity and significance of the source.

Establishing Context

What is the actual source?　There are many different kinds of sources. Letters, diaries, newspaper stories, merchants' account books, and other written forms of evidence are the most commonly used by historians but there are others as well. Physical evidence (other than written sources) might include materials from a burial site, fortification, or a garbage heap. For the purposes of this introduction to working with documents, we'll talk about three different, hypothetical sources: a letter, a tax law, and a photograph. Each source can tell you different kinds of information: each has strengths and limitations. Letters (and diaries) often provide detailed information about events that are happening at the time the letter was written, yet at the same time offer no information about the correspondents other than their names. A tax law can explain how a society generates revenues, and through its clauses one can usually discern some information about that society such as what, and who, is taxed. A weakness of all legal evidence is that you as a scholar have no way of knowing whether the laws are enforced. Photographs, and more recently film footage, are graphic sources that provide vivid detail. For example, a photograph of an elite Javanese couple taken in the late nineteenth century would show how indigenous clothing and customs had become interwoven with

European ones. Yet photographs, especially older ones, were not "candid," but rather posed because of the tremendous expense involved. Finally, all of the documents mentioned so far are typical of most historical sources in that alone they tell us only about that moment in time when they were produced. They may suggest what has occurred previously in this society, but they certainly cannot say anything about what happened afterwards. For this reason, whenever possible, historians try to accumulate as many sources as possible to observe historical change over time.

Who created the source?   Knowing who produced this source may tell you a great deal about why the letter was written, the tax code enacted, and the photograph taken. Sources do not produce themselves; they are made by people in the course of their day-to-day activities. In the example of the letter, it would certainly be helpful to know who both author and recipient were. Is the letter from a political leader, merchant, laborer, or priest? Was it written by a woman or a man? Or is the letter perhaps written by a group of people? Documents like tax laws are usually the work of more than one person. Was the law promulgated by a king or queen, or passed by a council or legislature? Photographs usually are presented without any information about the person who took the photograph, why the photograph was taken, and even the identity of the people in it. However, knowing such information, or even making general inferences will help you to better understand this iconographic source.

Why was the source produced?   What do you know about the motivations of those who produced the source? What do you know about the society from which the source comes? Looking at the specific examples, why was the letter written? Is it part of a larger correspondence, or is it a single letter about a particular event in someone's life? Did the author feel compelled to relate her or his experience to a friend? Or perhaps the letter is a formal one, from a political leader to a subordinate far away containing vital instructions. What made the leader send those instructions at this time? The motivations behind tax codes are both simple and complex. The simple reasoning behind any tax is to generate revenue for the state, however other, and deeper motivations, certainly exist. Who will be taxed? Who will be most, and least, affected by taxes on particular goods? Questions such as these that probe more deeply into the motivations behind the laws can bring the reader more information about how a society is structured in terms of class, gender, ethnicity, and race. Photographs are obviously taken to record a particular moment for posterity, but they, too, have other motivations as well. Perhaps a ruler wishes to show himself, or herself, to be healthy and vigorous. A photograph of the aging Chinese Communist leader Mao Zedong swimming in a river was once published for this very reason.

Asking Critical Questions
Once the more basic information about the source has been established, other in-depth historical questions should be asked.

Is the source believable?   How well do you trust the information presented to you in your source? Do you believe it to be accurate, or not? When all is said and done, no source can ever be completely accurate in every respect, but it is the case that some sources are more accurate than others. Presuming that your source is not a forgery, you might still have reasons to mistrust the information presented within it. The contents of a letter may seem wholly accurate but it is possible that the author either lied, or (as more often happens) that the author was mistaken about information presented in the letter as the "truth." In order to test the veracity of the information in a letter, historians often search for confirmation from another source. Is the tax code believable? Probably the tax code accurately reflects what the leaders of the society wish to do, but the contents of the law may not accurately reflect the daily life of the community. A tax on land ownership does not imply that everyone owns land. Harsh punishments for failure to pay taxes does not mean that such punishments are always, or even often, imposed. Photographs are often assumed to be accurate but for this reason great caution must be exercised. A picture of a bustling urban market may mask famine in the countryside.

In practice, historians are rarely faced with an outright forgery although they do exist. A German periodical published excerpts from the diary of Adolf Hitler: the diary was later proven to be a fake. Traditionally historians have placed their greatest faith in the written word. Only recently have some of the other sources mentioned so far—photographs, archaeological remains, oral traditions about the past, etc.—become accepted within the historical profession, and it is still the case that these nonwritten sources are treated with great caution. However, all sources have their strengths and limitations: these must be explored one source at a time.

Of what significance is the source?   After answering all of the above questions, only one question remains but it is the most important: what does the source tell you about the past? A letter might reveal critical information about a past event, or describe the personal feelings of one individual toward another. If, however, this letter is roughly identical to many others you have read, then its significance is minimal. A tax code may provide information about how a society is structured, or it may prove to have information too superficial from which to make any inferences at all. A photograph of peasants in a field might explain the division of labor between women and men in a particular society.

Determining significance is perhaps the hardest task of all, for you must decide this by yourself: there is no absolute standard against which your personal answer can be measured. In order to determine the significance of a particular primary source, you need to first think about what theme, or themes, the material might describe or explain. Historical data are like pieces of a puzzle: you must decide whether, and where, they fit in the broader patterns of world history. While there is no photograph of the puzzle to guide you, there are both the introductory passages before each reading and your textbook to act as guides.

Secondary Sources

History is more than "just the facts." There was a time when historians believed that their job was simply to present the facts for their readers: historical monographs—and textbooks in particular—deluged the reader with events, names, and dates. Most historians now see their job as both *descriptive* and *explanatory*. The essentials of description, drawn from primary sources, are the events, names, dates, etc., so familiar to students everywhere. It is this information that historians weave together to tell a story about the past. The second aspect of history is explanatory in that historians seek to explain past events. Rather than simply describe events, scholars ask why they happened, and what consequences events had for the people who experienced them. For this reason, it is often said that there are no completely "right" answers in history because history is a matter of interpretation. It is the case, however, that some answers are more "right" than others because they more accurately reflect the material available to the scholar.

Although we have discussed mainly primary documents to this point, secondary sources must also be read with the same critical eye. These sources are one scholar's interpretation of a subject based on his or her reading of primary sources. However, this does not mean that he or she has the final, definitive word on the topic. Interpretation, argument, and debate characterize the historical profession. Consequently, in the case of secondary sources, the reader must assess the author's argument in terms of the evidence presented, and in conjunction with evidence or arguments by other scholars, to decide whether or not it is a convincing historical argument. The following questions will assist you in reading secondary sources.

Is it a primary or secondary source?   The easiest way to ascertain whether or not a written source is primary is to ask yourself if the author was present at the events described. Someone who is an eyewitness to events will provide you with primary source information. Of course there are other kinds of *primary* sources, such as photographs and archaeological remains, and many of these pose special problems. Any historical account that does not possess firsthand knowledge of events is a *secondary* source. A historical narrative of events, even though it is certain to contain primary source information as evidence, is the most common kind of secondary source you will encounter. The Greek historian Herodotus, who lived during the fifth-century BCE, wrote a historical narrative of ancient Egypt: This narrative is a secondary source because it describes many events in the Mediterranean world that occurred before his lifetime. The most common secondary source in most high school and collegiate history courses is the textbook, but historians have written about an almost infinite variety of topics in world and comparative history: the impact of European disease on indigenous populations in the Americas following the voyage of Columbus, the causes of the Second World War, the influence of economic growth on the natural environment, just to name a few. You will also encounter more specific studies as well, such as Basil Davidson's survey of the kingdom of Meroe and John W. Dower's analysis of racism in the Second World War.

However, a word of caution is in order. Some forms of secondary sources—such as the archaeological reports mentioned above—are very much like primary sources. While your instructors can reproduce the Code of Hammurabi, the Mayan *Popul Vuh*, and the United Nations Charter for you to read, it is not practical to provide each student with bone fragments from early hominids or glass beads from excavations at Great Zimbabwe. Yet the objects found in those excavations are certainly primary source material, even though they appear in a secondary source article written by an archaeologist. Conversely oral traditions are often treated as primary sources even though the person who preserves the memory of past events might not even have been born at the time. These two examples suggest that the line between primary and secondary is often blurred. When this appears to be the case, you are best off approaching the material with a combination of questions to explore both the primary and secondary aspects of the source.

The following questions will help you to understand secondary sources and how they are used by historians.

What is the author's thesis?   In a secondary source, authors interpret the primary source material for you. Authors will have a particular point that they wish to convey: this point is called the *thesis*. Do not confuse the thesis, which is an interpretation or argument, with the *topic* which is merely the subject matter. For example, historian Janet Lippman Abu-Lughod has studied extensively the rise of Islam between the seventh and thirteenth centuries CE and its connections to the growth of western European commercial power beginning in the fourteenth century. That subject matter is the topic of her work, but her thesis, or interpretation, of those connections is that, "Europe's rise was substantially assisted by what it learned from other, more advanced cultures—at least until Europe overtook and subdued them."[*]

Fortunately for readers, finding the thesis is usually easy. It appears at the end, and sometimes the beginning, of the essay, and usually is phrased in a straightforward manner. Either in the thesis or in the paragraphs that surround it, you will learn what other scholars have said about the same events. In this way you can place the thesis you have read in the context of historical debates about the past. Of course, once you understand where the author's thesis "fits" within the larger picture, you still need to decide whether it is plausible.

How would you evaluate this thesis?   When reading primary sources, you answered two critical questions: *Is the source believable?* and *Of what significance is the source?* Here you must ask yourself a similar set of critical questions. In order to evaluate the thesis, you must judge its clarity and assess how well this thesis explains the material you have studied. Did the author include all relevant information? Does the thesis provide a comprehensive explanation of the material? Is the essay factually accurate? Most importantly, do you agree with the author? Why, or why not? It is all too easy to accept what a professional scholar says as "the truth": you should approach each secondary source as a skeptic who demands that the author prove his or her point. Regardless of whether you agree or disagree with the author's thesis, you should be prepared to explain your reasons for doing so. Finally, within the context of a global history course, you should ask yourself how this thesis affects your understanding of the human past.

---

[*]Janet Lippman Abu-Lughod, "The World System in the Thirteenth Century: Dead-End or Precursor?" in *Islamic & European Expansion: The Forging of a Global Order,* ed. Michael Adas (Philadelphia: Temple University Press, 1993), 75.

PART One

FROM HUMAN ORIGINS TO THE GREAT RIVER VALLEY CIVILIZATIONS

When does human history begin? How can scholars study the earliest years of human society? These fundamental questions in the study of world history can only be answered by first understanding how that history has been understood in the past. Not that long ago, it was common to distinguish—either explicitly or implicitly—between the "civilized" and "uncivilized" peoples of the world. In the Western world, the origins of civilization were to be found exclusively in the so-called "classical" societies of Greece and Rome, and to a lesser extent in ancient Egypt. To other societies, Western intellectuals and scholars applied a simple test to determine the level of civilization—those peoples that possessed traits similar to Europeans were "civilized" and others were not. As Europeans made contact with other peoples through exploration, trade, and conquest after the fifteenth century, the most important traits they sought in other societies were a written language, metal tools, use of the wheel, and proper dress. To these traits was later added the willingness to adhere, at least on the surface, to Christianity. This distinction between the "civilized" and the "uncivilized" was further complicated in the nineteenth century by theories about supposed biological, or genetic, differences between the races. Using these theories, Western writers created elaborate hierarchies of the races, usually with African and Native American peoples near the bottom of the ladder and Europeans always at the top.

Condescension toward other societies reinforced by racial and ethnic prejudice made the study of world history a narrow one indeed. One example will suffice: in their explorations of southern Africa, Europeans in the nineteenth century discovered a great stone compound located in present-day Zimbabwe. Refusing to believe that Africans could have built the massive enclosure with walls in some places 17 feet thick and 32 feet high, they speculated that it was a Phoenician ruin. Or perhaps, some thought, it was the ruined kingdom of Prester John, a mythic

Christian king in Africa. Later archaeological research confirmed what the indigenous population always knew—Great Zimbabwe was an African trading center that peaked in the fourteenth and fifteenth centuries.

In choosing the starting point for human history, it is important to remember that this uniquely Western, or Eurocentric, narrative of the past was, and is, tremendously influential. To offer a different perspective, this section begins with a collection of creation stories that describe how different peoples understand the origins of the earth and human society. The second chapter introduces the archaeological past and shows how the past of human communities can be reconstructed from clues left behind by people who produced no written record of their lives. The third, and final, chapter of this section explores the growth of the great river valley civilizations in China, Mesopotamia, Egypt, and India. In these chapters, many different kinds of sources are used to introduce readers to the complexities of understanding the human past. Throughout these chapters, and the ones that follow, the readings are designed to provide a history that is both global in scope and comparative in nature, without privileging one society's past over another's.

Chapter 1

In the Beginning

*T*ales of the world's creation exist in many cultures. These diverse "creation myths," as they are often labelled by scholars, contain a wealth of information about how different people understand the origins not only of humankind, but of the earth as well. Why do these stories persist to the present day? One answer to this question is that the information, or lessons, contained within these tales is believed to be important even now. If this is the case, then they can also provide you with information about what each society feels is important about its culture. Are these stories "myths" or "history"? This question you must answer for yourself as you read the excerpts in this section. However, you should consider the proposition that one person's "myth" may well be another person's "history." It is impossible to label one story as more authentic, or more accurate, than any other because you have no other evidence before you.

The first selection recounts an Australian aboriginal tale of the origins of life on Earth. "In the Dreamtime," the story begins, "all the Earth lay sleeping." In contrast with other creation stories, the individual who starts the process of creation is neither a god nor a person, but an animal. The second excerpt tells the Japanese story of Izanagi and Izanami, the man and woman whose children become the islands of the Japanese nation. The third creation story is taken from Genesis in which a god creates the world in seven days, and then creates people to populate it. The fourth story is taken from a North American people, the Huron, and begins with the fall of a woman from the sky. Anticipating her fall, animals on the water-covered planet below try to create a place for her to land. The fifth creation tale is taken from the Yoruba, a West African people who live in Nigeria and Dahomey. In it, the earth is created when a god from the sky decides to displace the waters and marshes below.

1   Australia: The Beginning of Life

Oodgeroo Nunukul. *Stadbroke Dreamtime.* Pymble, Australia: Angus & Robertson, 1992. 59–61.

This aboriginal creation myth is from Stadbroke Island, off Australia's Queensland Coast. At the center of the tale is the Rainbow Serpent, who beckons other animals to come forth and assist in the creation of the earth. As the animals increase, some grow quarrelsome and are turned to stone. Others are turned into humans as a reward for obeying the laws of the Serpent.

In the Dreamtime all the Earth lay sleeping. Nothing moved. Everything was quiet and still. The animals, birds and reptiles lay sleeping under the earth's crust.

Then one day the Rainbow Serpent awoke from her slumber and pushed her way through the earth's crust, moving the stones that lay in her way. When she emerged, she looked about her and then travelled over the land, going in all directions. She travelled far and wide, and when she grew tired she curled herself into a heap and slept. Upon the earth she left her winding tracks and the imprint of her sleeping body. When she had travelled all the earth, she returned to the place where she had first appeared and called to the frogs, "Come out!"

The frogs were very slow to come from below the earth's crust, for their bellies were heavy with water which they had stored in their sleep. The Rainbow Serpent tickled their stomachs, and when the frogs laughed, the water ran all over the earth to fill the tracks of the Rainbow Serpent's wanderings—and that is how the lakes and rivers were formed. Then the grass began to grow, and trees sprang up, and so life began on earth.

All the animals, birds, and reptiles awoke and followed the Rainbow Serpent, the Mother of Life, across the land. They were happy on earth, and each lived and hunted for food with his own tribe. The kangaroo, wallaby and emu tribes lived on the plains. The reptile tribes lived among the rocks and stones, and the bird tribes flew through the air and lived in the trees.

The Rainbow Serpent made laws that all were asked to obey, but some grew quarrelsome and were troublemakers. The Rainbow Serpent scolded them, saying, "Those who keep my laws I shall reward well. I shall give to them a human form. They and their children and their children's children shall roam this earth for ever. This shall be their land. Those who break my laws I shall punish. They shall be turned to stone, never to walk the earth again."

So the law-breakers were turned to stone, and became mountains and hills, to stand for ever and watch over the tribes hunting for food at their feet.

But those who kept her laws she turned into human form, and gave each of them his own totem of the animal, bird or reptile whence they came. So the tribes knew themselves by their own totems: the kangaroo, the emu, the carpet snake, and many, many more. And in order that none should starve, she ruled that no man should eat of his own totem, but only of other totems. In this way there was food for all.

So the tribes lived together in the land given to them by the Mother of Life, the Rainbow Serpent; and they knew that the land would always be theirs, and that no one should ever take it from them.

2   Japan: Izanagi and Izanami

Juliet Piggott. *Japanese Mythology*. London: Paul Hamlyn, 1969. 13–14.

In this brief Japanese creation story, Izanagi and Izanami are gods who descend from heaven to create land in the sea. Their offspring become the islands of the Japanese archipelago, as well as the natural features of those islands. The female god, Izanami, dies giving birth to a final child, fire, and departs for the underworld. Despite her protests, Izanagi follows her to the underworld where they quarrel bitterly.

Out of the primeval oily ocean mass, a reed-like substance emerged. This became a deity, and at the same time two other divine creatures, male and female, came into being. Little is told of this original trio, but they did produce generations of gods and goddesses in their celestial land, and after a period of unmeasured time a pair of gods were finally created called Izanagi and Izanami. Their names in translation are "Male-who-invites" and "Female-who-invites" respectively. They came down from their heaven to the oily mass by a bridge, generally accepted to have been a rainbow. Izanagi disturbed the primeval ocean with his spear and the drops from its tip congealed and, in falling, formed the island of Ono-koro or "self coagulating". . . . Although Izanagi and Izanami were supposedly brother and sister, they married on Ono-koro. They learned the art of love-making by watching a pair of wagtails, and these water birds are still associated with the couple. Even the god of Scarecrows cannot frighten wagtails, a blessing given the birds at their creation.

Among the offspring of Izanagi and Izanami were geographical landmarks, including the rest of the Japanese islands, waterfalls, and mountains, trees, herbs and the wind. The wind completed the creation of Japan, for he it was who blew away the hazy mists and revealed the scattered islands for the first time. The first child of the two gods was miscarried (supposedly through a misdemeanor on Izanami's part at the marriage ceremony) and this jellyfish-like creature was, not surprisingly, put into the sea.

All their other children survived. The last to be born after the string of islands had been formed and populated was the cause of his mother's death. He was the god of fire. After his birth, Izanami became ill with a burning fever which finally killed her. She went to the Underworld—Yomi, the Land of Gloom—but Izanagi followed her there in spite of her protests. She chased him, aided by hideous female spirits, in order to punish him for pursuing her, but he just managed to escape back to the world. At the entrance of Yomi, she screamed after him that in revenge she would denude the world of its inhabitants by destroying a thousand daily. However, Izanagi replied that he would create fifteen hundred each day.

In this story not only did the pair, through their marriage and progeny, establish the pattern of nature for all time, but through their "divorce" they created mortal life and death.

Izanagi kept his word, and after undergoing a ritual purification to wash away the effects of his descent into the Underworld, he gave birth to the Sun goddess, the Moon god and to Susano the Storm god.

3 West Asia: Monotheism

Genesis 1:1–2:9, 2:15–24. *The New English Bible.* Oxford and Cambridge, England: Oxford and Cambridge University Presses, 1970.

In Judeo-Christian tradition, the creation of the earth and its population by animals and plants was accomplished by a deity over seven days. Beginning with the simple command, "Let there be light," the god proceeds to create different aspects of the world one day at a time. At first the god makes the planet, then the plants and animals, and finally a man to till the earth. To provide a companion for him in the garden of Eden, a woman is fashioned from the rib of man. In this rendition of creation, people are made to "rule" the earth.

In the beginning of creation, when God made heaven and earth, the earth was without form and void, with darkness over the face of the abyss, and a mighty wind that swept over the surface of the waters. God said, "Let there be light," and there was light; and God saw that the light was good, and he separated light from darkness. He called the light day, and the darkness night. So evening came, and morning came, the first day.

God said, "Let there be a vault between the waters, to separate water from water." So God made the vault, and separated the water under the vault from the water above it, and so it was; and God called the vault heaven. Evening came, and morning came, a second day.

God said, "Let the waters under heaven be gathered into one place, so that dry land may appear"; and so it was. God called the dry land earth, and the gathering of the waters he called seas; and God saw that it was good. Then God said, "Let the earth produce fresh growth, let there be on the earth plants bearing seed, fruit trees bearing fruit each with seed according to its kind." So it was; the earth yielded fresh growth, plants bearing seed according to their kind and trees bearing fruit each with seed according to its kind; and God saw that it was good. Evening came, morning came, a third day.

God said, "Let there be lights in the vault of heaven to separate day from night, and let them serve as signs both for festivals and for seasons and years. Let them also shine in the vault of heaven to give light on earth." So it was; God made the two great lights, and the greater to govern the day and the lesser to govern the night; and with them he made the stars. God put these lights in the vault of heaven to give light on earth, to govern day and night, and to separate light from darkness; and God saw that it was good. Evening came, morning came, a fourth day.

God said, "Let the waters teem with countless living creatures, and let birds fly above the earth across the vault of heaven." God then created the great sea-monsters and all living creatures that move and swarm in the waters, according to their kind, and every kind of bird; and God saw that it was good. So he blessed them and said, "Be fruitful and increase, fill the waters of the seas; and let the birds increase on the land." Evening came, and morning came, a fifth day.

God said, "Let the earth bring forth living creatures, according to their kind: cattle, reptiles, and wild animals, all according to their kind." So it was; God made wild animals, cattle, and all reptiles, each according to its kind; and he saw that it was good. Then God said, "Let us make man in our image and likeness to rule the fish in the sea, the birds of heaven, the cattle, all wild animals on earth, and all reptiles that crawl upon the earth." So God created man in his own image; in the image of God he created him; male and female he created them. God blessed them and said to them, "Be fruitful and increase, fill the earth and subdue it, rule over the fish in the sea, the birds of heaven, and every living thing that moves upon the earth." God also said, "I give you all plants that bear seed everywhere on the earth, and every tree bearing fruit which yields seed: they shall be yours for food. All green plants I give for food to wild animals, to all the birds of heaven, and to all reptiles on earth, every living creature." So it was; and God saw all that he had made, and it was very good. Evening came, and morning came, a sixth day.

Thus heaven and earth were completed with all their mighty throng. On the sixth day God completed all the work he had been doing, on the seventh day he ceased from all his work. God blessed the seventh day and made it holy, because on that day he ceased from all the work he had set himself to do.

This is the story of the making of heaven and earth when they were created.

When the Lord God made earth and heaven, there was neither shrub nor plant growing wild on the earth; nor was there any man to till the ground. A flood used to rise out of the earth and water all the surface of the ground. Then the Lord God formed a man from the dust of the ground and breathed into his nostrils the breath of life. Thus the man became a living creature. Then the Lord God planted a garden in Eden away to the east, and there he put the man whom he had formed. The Lord God made trees soaring from the ground, all trees pleasant to look at and good for food; and in the middle of the garden he set the tree of life and the tree of the knowledge of good and evil.

The Lord God took the man and put him in the garden of Eden to till it and care for it. He told the man, "You may eat from every tree in the garden, but not from the tree of the knowledge of good and evil; for on the day that you eat from it, you will certainly die." The Lord God said, "It is not good for the man to be alone. I will provide a partner for him." So God formed out of the ground all the wild animals and all the birds of heaven. He brought them to the man to see what he would call them, and whatever the man called each living creature, that was its name. Thus the man gave names to all cattle, to the birds of heaven, and to every wild animal; but for the man himself no partner had yet been found. And so the Lord God put the man into a trance, and while he slept, he took one of his ribs and closed the flesh over the place. The Lord God then built up the rib, which he had taken out of the man, into a woman. He brought her to the man, and the man said:

"Now this, at last
bone from my bones,
flesh from my flesh!
this shall be called woman,
for from man was this taken."

4   North America:
The Woman Who Fell
From the Sky

Horatio Hale. "Huron Folklore." *The Journal of American Folk-Lore.* Vol. 1, No. 3 (October–December 1888). 180–182.

In Huron tradition in North America, the creation of land on earth began when a woman fell from the sky. Hoping to prevent her from drowning in the endless sea, different animals each try to dive to the ocean floor in order to bring some dirt to the surface to make an island. Many die in the attempt but one finally succeeds. After arriving on the land, the woman dies giving birth to twin brothers—one good, and the other evil. From her body spring forth plants like maize [corn]. Each son creates animals to populate the land according to his own vision of the world, until finally they fight a duel to the death.

In the beginning there was nothing but the water, a wide sea, which was peopled by various animals of the kind that live in and upon the water. It happened then that a woman fell down from the upper world. Two loons, which were flying over the water, happened to look up and see her falling. To save her from drowning they hastened to place themselves beneath her, joining their bodies together so as to form a cushion for her to rest on. In this way they held her up, while they cried with a loud voice to summon the other animals to their aid. The cry of the loon can be heard a great distance, and the other creatures of the sea heard it, and assembled to learn the cause of the summons. Then came the tortoise . . . , a mighty animal, which consented to relieve the loons of their burden. They placed the woman on the back of the tortoise, charging him to take care of her. The tortoise then called the other animals to a grand council, to determine what should be done to preserve the life of the woman. They decided that she must have earth to live on. The tortoise directed them all to dive to the bottom of the sea and endeavor to bring up some earth. Many attempted it—the beaver, the muskrat . . . , and others—but without success. Some remained so long below that when they rose they were dead. The tortoise searched their mouths, but could find no trace of earth. At last the toad went down, and after remaining a long time rose, exhausted and nearly dead. On searching his mouth the tortoise found in it some earth, which he gave to the woman. She took it and placed it carefully around the edge of the tortoise's shell. When thus placed, it became the beginning of dry land. The land grew and extended on every side, forming at last a great country, fit for vegetation. All was sustained by the tortoise, which still supports the earth.

When the woman fell she was pregnant with twins. When these came forth they evinced opposite dispositions, the one good, the other evil. Even before they were born the same characters were manifested. They struggled together, and their mother heard them disputing. The one declared his willingness to be born in the usual manner, while the other malignantly refused, and, breaking through his mother's side, killed her. She was buried, and from her body sprang the various vegetable productions which the new earth required to fit it for the habitation of man. From her head grew the pumpkin-vine; from her breasts the maize; from her limbs the bean. Meanwhile the twins grew up, showing in all they did their opposing inclinations. The name of the good one was Tijuskeha, which means . . . something like . . . good man. The evil brother was Tawiskarong, meaning flinty, an allusion probably to his hard and cruel nature. They were not men, but supernatural beings, who were to prepare the world to be the abode of men. Finding that they could not live together, they separated, each taking his own portion of the earth. Their first act was to create animals of various kinds. The bad brother made fierce and monstrous creatures, proper to terrify and destroy mankind—serpents, panthers, wolves, bears, all of enormous size, and huge mosquitoes, "as large as turkeys." Among other things he made an immense toad, which drank up all the fresh water that was on the earth. In the meantime the good brother, in his province, was creating the innocent and useful animals. Among the rest he made the partridge. To his surprise, the bird rose in the air and flew toward the territory of Tawiskarong. Tijuskeha asked him were he was going. The bird replied that he was going to look for water, as there was none left in that land, and he heard there was some in the dominion of Tawiskarong. Tijuskeha then began to suspect mischief. He followed the course which the partridge had taken and presently reached the land of his evil brother. Here he encountered the snakes, ferocious brutes, and enormous insects which his brother had made, and overcame them. Finally he came to the monstrous toad, which he cut open, letting the water flow forth. He did not destroy the evil animals—perhaps had not the power to do so—but he reduced them in size, so that men would be able to master them.

The spirit of his mother warned him in a dream to beware of his evil brother, who would endeavor to destroy him by treachery. Finally they encountered [one another], and as it was evident that they could not live together on the earth, they determined to decide by a formal combat . . . which of them should remain master of the world. It was further agreed that each should make known to the other the only weapon by which he could be overcome. This extraordinary article of their agreement was probably made necessary by the fact that without such a disclosure the contest would have lasted forever. The good brother declared that he could be destroyed only by being beaten to death with a bag full of corn, beans, or some other product of the bread kind; the evil brother rejoined that he could be killed only by the horn of a deer or of some other wild animal. . . . Tawiskarong [. . .] set upon his brother with a bag of corn [and] chased him about the ground, and pounded him until he was nearly lifeless and lay as if dead. He revived, however, and recovering his strength, pursued in turn his evil brother, beating him with a deer's horn until he killed him. But the slain combatant was not utterly destroyed. He reappeared after death to his brother, and told him that he had gone to the far west, and that thenceforth all the races of men after death would go to the west, like him.

5   West Africa: Yoruba Creation

"The Descent from the Sky." In Harold Courlander, *A Treasury of African Folklore: The Oral Literature, Traditions, Myths, Legends, Epics, Tales, Recollections, Wisdom, Sayings, and Humor of Africa.* New York: Crown Publishers, Inc., 1975. 189–192.

In Yoruba (West Africa) tradition, there was no land at the beginning of time, only the sky above and water below. The sky was ruled by a male god, Olorun, and the water by a female god, Olokun. When the lesser gods in the sky suggest creating land below to hold "fields and forests," Olorun agrees. With the help of a goldsmith, land is created, displacing Olokun's oceans and marshes.

In ancient days, at the beginning of time, there was no solid land here where people now dwell. There was only outer space and the sky, and, far below, an endless stretch of water and wild marshes. Supreme in the domain of the sky was the orisha, or god, called Olorun, also known as Olodumare and designated by many praise names. Also living in that place were numerous other orishas, each having attributes of his own, but none of whom had knowledge or powers equal to those of Olorun. Among them was Orunmila, also called Ifa, the eldest son of Olorun. To this orisha Olorun had given the power to read the future, to understand the secret of existence and to divine the processes of fate. There was the orisha Obatala, King of the White Cloth, whom Olorun trusted as though he also were a son. There was the orisha Eshu, whose character was neither good nor bad. He was compounded out of the elements of chance and accident, and his nature was unpredictability. He understood the principles of speech and language, and because of this gift he was Olorun's linguist. These and other orishas living in the domain of the sky acknowledged Olorun as the owner of everything and as the highest authority in all matters. Also living there was Agemo, the chameleon, who served Olorun as a trusted servant.

Down below, it was the female deity Olokun who ruled over the vast expanses of water and wild marshes, a grey region with no living things in it, either creatures of the bush or vegetation. This is the way it was, Olorun's living sky above and Olokun's domain of water below. Neither kingdom troubled the other. They were separate and apart. The orishas of the sky lived on, hardly noticing what lay below them.

All except Obatala, King of the White Cloth. He alone looked down on the domain of Olokun and pondered on it, saying to himself: "Everything down there is a great wet monotony. It does not have the mark of any inspiration or living thing." And at last he went to Olorun and said: "The place ruled by Olokun is nothing but sea, marsh and mist. If there were solid land in that domain, fields and forests, hills and valleys, surely it could be populated by orishas and other living things."

Olorun answered: "Yes, it would be a good thing to cover the water with land. But it is an ambitious enterprise. Who is to do the work? And how should it be done?"

Obatala said: "I will undertake it. I will do whatever is required."

He left Olorun and went to the house of Orunmila, who understood the secrets of existence, and said to him: "Your father has instructed me to go down below and make land where now there is nothing but marsh and sea, so that living beings will have a place to build their towns and grow their crops. You, Orunmila, who can divine the meanings of all things, instruct me further. How may this work be begun?" Orunmila brought out his divining tray and cast sixteen palm nuts on it. He read their meanings by the way they fell. He gathered them up and cast again, again reading their meanings. And when he had cast many times he added meanings to meanings, and said: "These are the things you must do: Descend to the watery wastes on a chain of gold, taking with you a snail shell full of sand, a white hen to disperse the sand, a black cat to be your companion, and a palm nut. That is what the divining figures tell us."

Obatala went next to the goldsmith and asked for a chain of gold long enough to reach from the sky to the surface of the water.

The goldsmith asked, "Is there enough gold in the sky to make such a chain?"

Obatala answered: "Yes, begin your work. I will gather the gold." Departing from the forge of the goldsmith, Obatala went then to Orunmila, Eshu and the other orishas, asking each of them for gold. They gave him whatever they had. Some gave gold dust, some gave rings, bracelets or pendants. Obatala collected gold from everywhere and took it to the goldsmith.

The goldsmith said, "More gold is needed."

So Obatala continued seeking gold, and after that he again returned to the goldsmith, saying, "Here is more metal for your chain."

The goldsmith said, "More gold is needed."

Obatala said, "There is no more gold in the sky."

The goldsmith said, "The chain will not reach the water."

Obatala answered: "Nevertheless, make the chain. We shall see."

The goldsmith went to work. When the chain was finished he took it to Obatala. Obatala said, "It must have a hook at the end."

"There is no gold remaining," the goldsmith said.

Obatala replied, "Take some of the links and melt them down."

The goldsmith removed some of the links, and out of them he fashioned a hook for the chain. It was finished. He took the chain to Obatala.

Obatala said, "Now I am ready." He fastened the hook on the edge of the sky and lowered the chain. Orunmila gave him the things that were needed—a snail shell of sand, a white hen, a black cat, and a palm nut. Then Obatala gripped the chain with his hands and feet and began the descent. The chain was very long. When he had descended only half its length Obatala saw that he was leaving the realm of light and entering the region of greyness. A time came when he heard the wash of waves and felt the damp mists rising from Olokun's domain. He reached the end of the golden chain, but he was not yet at the bottom, and he clung there, thinking, "If I let go I will fall into the sea."

While he remained at the chain's end thinking such things, he heard Orunmila's voice from above, saying, "The sand."

So Obatala took out the snail shell from the knapsack at his side and poured out the sand.

Again he heard Orunmila call to him, saying this time, "The hen."

Obatala dropped the hen where he had poured the sand. The hen began at once to scratch at the sand and scatter it in all directions. Wherever the sand was scattered it became dry land. Because it was scattered unevenly the sand formed hills and valleys. When this was accomplished, Obatala let go of the chain and came down and walked on the solid earth that had been created. The land extended in all directions, but still it was barren of life.

Obatala named the place where he had come down Ife. He built a house there. He planted his palm nut and a palm tree sprang out of the earth. It matured and dropped its palm seeds. More palm trees came into being. Thus there was vegetation at Ife. Obatala lived on, with only his black cat as a companion.

After some time had passed, Olorun the Sky God wanted to know how Obatala's expedition was progressing. He instructed Agemo the chameleon to descend the golden chain. Agemo went down. He found Obatala living in his house at Ife. He said: "Olorun instructed me this way: He said, 'Go down, discover for me how things are with Obatala.' That is why I am here."

Obatala answered, "As you can see, the land has been created, and palm groves are plentiful. But there is too much greyness. The land should be illuminated."

Agemo returned to the sky and reported to Olorun what he had seen and heard. Olorun agreed that there should be light down below. So he made the sun and set it moving. After that there was warmth and light in what had once been Olokun's exclusive domain.

Obatala lived on, with only his black cat for a companion. He thought, "Surely it would be better if many people were living here." He decided to create people. He dug clay from the ground, and out of the clay he shaped human figures which he then laid out to dry in the sun. He worked without resting. He became tired and thirsty. He said to himself, "There should be palm wine in this place to help a person go on working." So he put aside the making of humans and went to the palm trees to draw their inner fluid, out of which he made palm wine. When it was fermented he drank. He drank for a long while. When he felt everything around him softening he put aside his gourd cup and went back to modelling human figures. But because Obatala had drunk so much wine his fingers grew clumsy, and some of the figures were misshapen. Some had crooked backs or crooked legs, or arms that were too short. Some did not have enough fingers, some were bent instead of being straight. Because of the palm wine inside him, Obatala did not notice these things. And when he had made enough figures to begin the populating of Ife he called out to Olorun the Sky god, saying, "I have made human beings to live with me here in Ife, but only you can give them the breath of life." Olorun heard Obatala's request, and he put breath in the clay figures. They were no longer clay, but people of blood, sinews, and flesh. They arose and began to do the things that humans do. They built houses for themselves near Obatala's house, and in this way the place Obatala named Ife became the city of Ife.

But when the effects of the palm wine had worn off Obatala saw that some of the humans he had made were misshapen, and remorse filled his heart. He said: "Never again will I drink palm wine. From this time on I will be the special protector of all humans who have deformed limbs or who have otherwise been created imperfectly." Because of Obatala's pledge, humans who later came to serve him also avoided palm wine, and the lame, the blind and those who had no pigment in their skin invoked his help when they were in need.

Now that humans were living on the earth, Obatala gave people the tools they needed to perform their work. As yet there was no iron in the world, and so each man received a wooden hoe and a copper bush knife. The people planted and began the growing of millet and yams, and, like the palm tree, they procreated. Ife became a growing city and Obatala ruled as its Oba or Paramount Chief. But a time came when Obatala grew lonesome for the sky. He ascended by the golden chain, and there was a festival on the occasion of his return. The orishas heard him describe the land that had been created below, and many of them decided to go down and live among the newly created human beings. Thus many orishas departed from the sky, but not before Olorun instructed them on their obligations. "When you settle on the earth," he said, "never forget your duties to humans. Whenever you are supplicated for help, listen to what is being asked of you. You are the protectors of the human race. Obatala, who first descended the chain and dried up the waters, he is my deputy in earthly affairs. But each of you will have a special responsibility to fulfill down below." . . .

But Olokun, the orisha of the sea, on whose domain land had been created, was angry and humiliated. And so one time when Obatala was resting in the sky Olokun decided to destroy the land and replace it again with water. She sent great waves rushing against the shores and flooded the low ground everywhere, causing marshes to reappear on every side. She inundated the fields where humans were growing their crops and drowned many of the people of Ife. All that Obatala had created was disappearing, and mankind was suffering. The people called for help from Obatala, but he did not hear them. So they went to the orisha Eshu, who now lived on earth, and begged him to carry to Obatala word of the disaster that was overwhelming them.

Eshu said to them, "Where is the sacrifice that should accompany the message?"

They brought a goat and sacrificed it, saying, "This is the food for Obatala."

But Eshu did not move. He said, "Where is the rest?"

The people said: "We do not understand you. Have we not brought a sacrifice for Obatala?"

Eshu answered: "You ask me to make a great journey. You ask me to be your linguist. Does not a person make a gift to the lowliest of messengers? Give me my part, then I will go."

So the people gave a sacrifice to Eshu, after which he left them and went up to the sky to tell Obatala what was happening to the land and the people over which he ruled.

Obatala was troubled. He was not certain how to deal with Olokun. He went to the orisha Orunmila to ask for advice. Orunmila consulted his divining nuts, and at last he said to Obatala: "Wait here in the sky. Rest yourself. I will go down this time. I will turn back the water and make the land rise again." So it was Orunmila instead of Obatala who went down to Ife. As Orunmila was the oldest son of Olorun, he had the knowledge of medicine, and he had many other powers as well. He used his powers in Ife, causing Olokun's waves to weaken and the marshes to dry up. The waters of the sea were turned back, and at last Olokun's attempt to reclaim her territory came to an end.

DISCUSSION QUESTIONS

1. What images or themes are common to the different tales you have read? What motivations might people have had for preserving these stories?

2. Do you think any one of them, or perhaps all of them, are authentic history? What makes some stories seem more historical than others to you or other students in your class?

3. What is the relationship between the earth and humankind in each of the stories? What might this tell you about the beliefs of the people who first created these tales, as well as about the ideas of those who have carefully preserved them?

4. How would you characterize the relationship between women and men in each myth?

5. Do you feel that these stories tell you more about the past, or about today's world?

Chapter
2

The Archaeology of Early Peoples

O ne distinction that is commonly made in studies of this early period is that of "history" versus "prehistory." The historical period is traditionally considered to have begun with the invention of writing. One of the problems with this definition, however, is that it limits historical enquiry to societies, eras, and topics for which writing not only existed but also has survived to the present. The invention of writing in different societies also varied widely in time. Furthermore, the types of information that can be gathered are limited to those that were set down in writing, often by a society's leaders, priests, or merchants: in other words, the elites of society who could preserve their thoughts and actions in writing.

Archaeology provides a means to push historical enquiry farther back in time, and to include sectors within societies, as well as entire societies, that were not literate. By using material evidence of human habitation, archaeologists can deduce forms of organization of a society, the lifestyle of its members, and their livelihood. In this chapter, we will examine archaeological sites and evidence of societies in what are now Australia, Turkey, China, Brazil, and Kenya. In each selection, archaeologists use evidence in novel ways to report societal organization, economy, gender roles, and other facets of the human past. But archaeological evidence, like any historical evidence, needs to be interpreted, and often more than one interpretation is possible.

6   Human Origins

Maeve Leakey. "The Dawn of Humans." *National Geographic.*
Vol. 188, No. 3 (September 1995). 40–51.

Fossils discovered in the Lake Turkana region in eastern Africa, an area that
encompasses the nations of Ethiopia, Kenya, and the Sudan, shed new light
on human origins. It is here that early representatives of humankind have
been discovered in the volcanic sediment of the East African Rift. Although
the famous "Lucy" skeleton, actually *Australopithecus afarensis,* was
discovered in northern Ethiopia by David Johanson in 1974, for decades
paleoanthropologists have concentrated on the Lake Turkana region as well,
locating fossils which date back over 3 million years. In this excerpt, Maeve
Leakey describes the discovery of a new hominid species at Kanapoi which
dates back 4.1 million years.*

"Surely this is where we came from," Kamoya whispered as he gazed in awe at
three strange-looking teeth that he held delicately in his hands. I knew exactly
what he meant. Looking very ape-like, but at the same time vaguely human, the
teeth had come from sediments four million years old at a place called Kanapoi in
northern Kenya. That made them significantly older than the most ancient evidence of the human lineage then known. Were the teeth from a new species? If
so, could they have belonged to humanity's earliest ancestor? Such questions
raced through my mind.

When our associate Peter Nzube Mutiwa found the teeth a few days earlier, I
was back in Nairobi, tending to commitments as head of the paleontology depart-
ment at the National Museums of Kenya. Then Kamoya called me on the radio
telephone. Kamoya Kimeu leads the museums' team of fossil hunters we call the
Hominid Gang. Hominids are animals on the human family tree—ourselves and
all our ancestors or close relatives since we diverged from the apes—and over the
past three decades Kamoya's men have unearthed some of the most important
specimens.

"We have something for you," Kamoya had said.

I made the daylong drive back to Kanapoi as quickly as the rutted roads and
tracks allowed. After I congratulated Nzube, who had discovered the teeth among
a carpet of lava pebbles, we began planning how to recover more. We marked out
a large area and removed the bigger stones. Then we passed the loose soil and
smaller rocks through a sieve.

Gradually we collected an almost complete set of this mysterious animal's
lower teeth, in all but perfect condition. We also found tooth fragments from

---

*As this research progressed, Tim White of the University of California at Berkeley discovered even
older fossils of a new genus, *Ardipithecus.*

another individual. My hunch that Kanapoi would produce some remarkably early hominids seemed to be right.

The site lies about 30 miles southwest of Lake Turkana, an immense jade green inland sea. Although crocodiles bask on the lakeshore, the Turkana Basin quickly turns to desert as one travels inland. The earth here bakes all year in heat well above a hundred degrees.

Yet I feel at home. Since 1969 I have worked in the Turkana Basin with teams led by my husband, Richard Leakey, a paleoanthropologist. Almost certainly our first apelike ancestors emerged in Africa, and few places offer as rich a fossil record as this region. Tectonic activity has uplifted ancient sediments, exposing to rapid erosion the soils in which the early hominids' bones were fossilized. Thus each rainstorm can bring new fossils to light. In addition, volcanism over the eons has deposited many layers of ash. Radioactive materials in the ash decay at known rates, letting us date each layer and the fossils in between. . . .

Until the 1994 season scientists had only the scantiest evidence for hominids older than 3.6 million years. Our earliest known ancestor was a short, apelike creature called *Australopithecus afarensis,* whose most famous representative is Lucy, a partial female skeleton discovered by Donald Johanson in 1974 at Hadar in Ethiopia.

Lucy had long arms like an ape, but her pelvic and leg bones indicate that she walked on two legs. She lived about 3.18 million years ago, yet we know she had older relatives. Footprints left in volcanic ash by three earlier members of her species were found by my mother-in-law, Mary Leakey, at Laetoli in Tanzania in 1978. They have been dated to 3.56 million years ago.

Hominids and African apes share a common ancestor. No one knows what that animal looked like, but we can guess that, like our closest living relatives, chimpanzees and gorillas, it lived in forests and moved through the trees, swinging from its arms and climbing on all fours. At some point one group of those ancestors took the critical first step on the road to modern humans: They began developing the habit of walking on two legs. We do not know why they became bipedal, but over time that adaptation required such profound anatomical changes—especially in the limbs and pelvis—that it marks the separation of the hominid lineage from the apes.

• • •

One day, while I was recording details about two pig jaws we had found, one of the Hominid Gang, Wambua Mangao, called out excitedly. I followed him to a spot where I could see five small areas of bluish tooth enamel embedded in a rock. I turned the rock over to find that it held half of the upper jaw of a hominid. It was from an animal about the size of a chimpanzee—an old individual because the teeth were quite worn. I shook Wambua's hand enthusiastically.

A few days later Kamoya discovered the upper part of a tibia, the main bone of the lower leg. Slightly bigger than that of the largest *afarensis* yet found, its size surprised us—especially since the jaw nearby was chimpanzee.

Soon Kamoya, Wambua, and Samuel Ngui, another Hominid Gang member, found the lower end of the tibia. It closely resembled that of *afarensis,* strongly suggesting that this hominid was also bipedal.

These were major discoveries, and I returned to Nairobi reluctantly—only to receive Kamoya's phone call about the teeth unearthed by Nzube. The more I studied the teeth, the more they convinced me that this animal was strikingly different from later hominids and from all known fossil apes. Indeed, it appeared that the Hominid Gang had found an altogether new species, with some features found in both chimpanzee and *afarensis* and others that were unique.

What did this blend mean? About the diet, for instance. Was the large canine for breaking nuts or hard fruits? Or was it for display or defense? Were our specimens male or female?

Back at Wambua's site we began recovering the teeth of a second, very young individual as well as the rest of the upper jaw of the first. Thus we had a complete upper jaw with most of the teeth. Now we hoped to find a complete skull, but the season was ending.

On the last weekend Richard [Leakey] flew up to join us. The previous year he had lost both his legs following an airplane accident. He walks now with artificial legs, but his enthusiasm for fossils is undiminished. We were applying a protective coat of plaster to a large elephant skull found earlier. Nzube was with us, even though he was supposed to be overseeing work at another site nearby. He was enjoying having Richard around so much that he hesitated to leave his side. Finally I insisted Nzube go, and he headed off.

It was a walk he had taken often, but this time his route, or perhaps the angle of the light, might have differed slightly. A few minutes after he left, Nzube ran back, shouting in Swahili, "Come quickly. It is wonderful."

I couldn't believe what I saw sticking out of the sediment—a complete lower jaw and right next to it a piece of the ear region of the skull. I hurried back to Richard and asked him if he would excavate a hominid for me.

Nzube's fossils resembled those we had already found that season, showing the same mixture of chimp, *afarensis,* and unique features. The smaller canines suggested that this individual might be female.

The part of the lower jaw that in humans forms our chins sloped sharply backward. *Afarensis's* lower jaw slopes also, but much less so than this individual's. Nzube almost immediately recovered a lower molar of another individual. This was the third site in which we had found the remains of more than one hominid. Perhaps they were the leftovers from some carnivore's meals.

Returning to Nairobi, I was thrilled with the finds we would report—the most complete known specimens of a hominid of this age, and almost certainly a new species older than Lucy. Moreover, we could argue convincingly that this animal was bipedal.

Then came the news that my colleague Tim White, a paleoanthropologist at the University of California, Berkeley, was also about to announce a new hominid species from a site called Aramis in Ethiopia that was even older—4.4 million years. He had found teeth and arm bones of an animal he believed was bipedal. His descriptions and photographs indicated that it might be the same animal as we had at Kanapoi. He had tentatively named it *Australopithecus ramidus,* the species name coming from the Afar word for "root."

Tim and his European colleague Berhane Asfaw generously invited me to Addis Ababa last January to see the Aramis fossils for myself. Tim had just returned from his latest field season with more surprises. Another of his Ethiopian collaborators, Yohannes Haile Selassie, had found a partial skeleton of *ramidus,* including the pelvis and a tibia—critical in understanding this animal's degree of bipedalism. By spring Tim would conclude that the fossils were sufficiently different from previous finds to warrant placing them in a new genus—*Ardipithecus,* or "ground ape." . . .

The search continues, and slowly we will accumulate enough . . . to begin to understand our oldest ancestors.

7   The First Boat People

Josephine Flood. *Archaeology of the Dreamtime: The Story of Prehistoric Australia and Its People,* revised edition. New Haven, Conn., and London: Yale University Press, 1990. 29–37.

Archaeologist Josephine Flood studied the earliest history of the Australian Aborigines by comparing their oral traditions of the past—the "dreamtime"— with artifacts collected at various sites throughout the continent. In the section below, she begins with a lengthy quotation from a dreamtime story about how the first people arrived in Australia and argues that the archaeological record supports oral history traditions that are thousands of years old.

"The truth is, of course, that my own people, the Riratjingu, are descended from the great Djankawu who came from the island of Baralku far across the sea. Our spirits return to Baralku when we die. Djankawu came in his canoe with his two sisters, following the morning star which guided them to the shores of Yelangbara on the eastern coast of Arnhem Land. They walked far across the country following the rain clouds. When they wanted water they plunged their digging stick into the ground and fresh water flowed. From them we learned the names of all the creatures on the land and they taught us all our Law.

That is just a little bit of the truth. Aboriginal people in other parts of Australia have different origins and will tell you their own stories of how the mountains came to be, and the rivers, and how the tribes grew and followed the way of life of their Spirit Ancestors.

The huge Wandjina, maker of thunder, rain and lightning, soared over the sea to Western Australia. Their faces stare at us from the cave walls of the Kimberley Ranges and the spears that fought their giant battles are still in the sands on the coast north of Derby. The giant Rainbow Serpent emerged from beneath the earth and as she moved, winding from side to side, she forced her way through the soil and rocks, making the great rivers flow in her path, and carving through mountains she made the gorges of northern Australia. From the Rainbow Serpent sprang many tribes, and tales about her are told all over Arnhem Land—over to Western Australia, in central Australia and even to New South Wales. Our paintings on rocks illustrate this true story of our ancestors. . . .

In Queensland Giroo Gurrll, part man and part eel, rose out of the water near Hinchinbrook Island and named the animals, birds and all the places there, while the great Ancestor Chivaree the Seagull paddled his canoe from the Torres Islands down the western coast of Cape York to Sandy beach where his canoe turned to stone."

Some aborigines have always believed that their ancestors came from across the sea in the Dreamtime, and now scientists have come to the same conclusion from archaeological and other evidence. In the same way that archaeology has revealed the material traces of the oral traditions enshrined in Homer's *Iliad* and *Odyssey* or the Old Testament stories of the Bible, it has uncovered evidence for some of the historic events remembered in the rich body of Aboriginal myths.

The human history of Australia encompasses the time since the first migrant stepped ashore—which we now know from archaeological evidence was well in excess of 40,000 years ago. To begin at the beginning of prehistory (the whole period before 1788), there is no possibility that human evolution occurred in Australia independently of the rest of the world, for the ape-like ancestors from which *Homo sapiens*—the modern human race—developed in Africa have never been present in Australia. Where, then, did the Australian Aboriginal race originate? The first migrants could not have walked to Australia but must have come across the sea. Since people have been in South-East Asia for more than a million years, it would theoretically have been possible for Australia to have been colonized any time during this period. There was, however, one serious barrier to cross—water.

At no time during the last three millions years has there been a complete land bridge between the Asian and Australian continents. And before then the gulf was even wider. We know from geological evidence that until some fifty million years ago, Australia was part of the great southern continent of Antarctica, well removed from the Asian mainland. It had by then evolved a marsupial fauna. About thirty-five million years ago, the Australian continent drifted northward, acting as a Noah's Ark for the marsupials. Australia was isolated until about twenty-five to fifteen million years ago, when it approached the southern fringes of the island chain of the East Indies. Australia is still in fact a continental raft drifting northwards, but it will take some time to reach Asia at the current rate of less than 5 centimetres a year.

The lack of Asian animals in Australia is evidence that for many millions of years there has been a significant sea barrier between Asia and Australia, which prevented them from spreading southward. For the last two million years (the Pleistocene or ice age), the sea gap isolating Australia from Asia is thought to have never been less than 50 kilometres wide.

We tend to think that the first migrants would have taken the shortest and most logical route from Asia to Australia, but we must constantly remind ourselves that the shape of the continent was different then and that these people had no maps, did not know that Australia existed, and even after arrival would have had no idea that they had reached a continent rather than another small island. It is likely that there was nothing deliberate or planned about the first settlement of Australia. Planned long-distance voyages, such as those that colonized the Pacific Islands, are probably a phenomenon of only the last few thousand years.

The routes by which the first migrants may have arrived in Australia have been examined in great detail by distinguished American anthropologist Professor Joseph Birdsell. Although the landfalls in Australia must have been chance events, assessing the comparative likelihood of each possible route gives the archaeologists clues as to which are the islands most worth searching for evidence of early human occupation.

Birdsell analysed the distance to be travelled, whether the island destination is visible from the point of departure, and the general size of the target island. His conclusions are that at the time of *lowest* sea level, the shortest route across the ocean-deep of Wallacea still involved eight sea voyages. There are two routes most likely to have been used by human migrants. The first, via a series of islands from Sulawesi to the Sahul shelf near north-western New Guinea, was in eight stages, none greater than 70 kilometres. The second is a shorter route through Timor. This also has eight stages, all less than 30 kilometres, except for the last crossing of 87 kilometres from Timor to the Kimberley coast.

Distant smoke from natural bush fires on the Sahul shelf should have been visible from some Indonesian islands, providing an incentive for deliberate voyages to Australia. The vegetation on the shelf at the time is likely to have been semi-arid

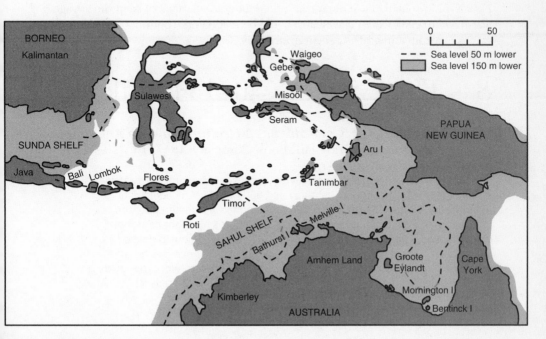

Figure 2.1 Migration routes from Indonesia to Timor and the Sunda and Sahul shelves to Australia.

savanna woodland, which is prone to fires caused by lightning. Even small fires of this type of vegetation produce billows of smoke rising to 1000 metres or more above the sea level, and smoke from large bush fires commonly reaches 5000 metres. Smoke plumes 1000 metres high could have been seen by people standing at sea level up to 110 kilometres away. When the sea was at its lowest level, smoke could have been visible ahead on any route to Australia. And at any time during the ice age the smoke and glare of bush fires on the Australian shore should occasionally have been visible on such Indonesian islands as Timor, Roti, Tanimbar, Seram and Gebe.

The founding population might have been only a few castaways making landfall on the Sahul shelf from time to time. Such landfalls would have become much less likely, although still just possible, when sea level rose to its present height at the end of the last glacial period. Given the sea barriers already described, the number of migrants must in any case have been relatively small, whether they arrived as castaways or by boat.

It is possible that the earliest colonists were tide-riders, using rafts like the *kalum,* a light, triangular, mangrove-wood raft of durable construction, used until recently by four tribal groups on the north-western coast of Australia. This raft was paddled and was normally used over a distance of 8 to 16 kilometres along the coast, one of the most dangerous and inhospitable in the world.

As well as appropriate raw materials, such sea voyages require a high level of technology to fabricate a suitably sturdy craft. Recent archaeological discoveries in Australia and New Guinea indicate that there was the necessary technical skill; for example, it is known that ground stone axes were in use at least 20,000 years ago. Fire would probably have been taken on deliberate voyages to keep the voyagers warm and to cook fish. A clay hearth could be made in the bottom of the boat; this was the custom among Tasmanian Aborigines.

8   The City of Çatal Hüyük

James Mellaart. *Çatal Hüyük: A Neolithic Town in Anatolia.* New York: McGraw-Hill Book Company, 1967. 15, 210–221.

Situated in southern Turkey, Çatal Hüyük was a sizeable community founded around 7000 BCE inhabited by as many as 6000 people. Archaeologists excavated the region beginning in 1961, hoping to understand how the cultivation of crops spread into Europe. The city was a vibrant center of economic development, with extensive cultural and religious practices as well. Social stratification within the city—possible only because the agricultural revolution meant that not all people needed to work to provide food—was visible in the size of houses and the number of material possessions.

Outside the ring of professional archaeology, Çatal Hüyük is still a name of little meaning. But the . . . excavation of the site—still far from complete—has in fact given it an importance of an outstanding kind. . . . Already, after a mere three seasons' work (1961–63), the results may fairly be described as a spectacular addition to our knowledge of the earlier phases of human achievement in terms of urban settlement. For already Çatal Hüyük ranks, with Jericho in Jordan, as one of man's first known assays in the development of town-life. Before 6000 BC Çatal Hüyük was a town, or even a city, of a remarkable and developed kind.

. . .

A great number of objects used in everyday life have been recovered at Çatal Hüyük, abandoned on the floors of houses as successive settlements burnt, broken or thrown away with the swept-out domestic rubbish. Owing to the many fires from which people fled for their lives, the abandoned material is rich and varied, but one specific conflagration, that in which [a settlement] perished c. 5880 BC, fiercer than most, led to the preservation of a quantity of perishable materials, such as cloth, fur, leather, and wood, which are not normally preserved. The terrific heat generated by the burning town, which must have smouldered for a long time, penetrated to a depth of about a metre or more below the level of the floors, carbonising the earth, the bones of the dead, and their burial-gifts and arrested all bacterial decay. The scorching heat was enough to destroy most of the cloth in which the dead were wrapped, but it has survived intact below the skeletons.

As a result of this fire much perishable material is available for study and as the fire came at a period in the history of Çatal Hüyük which marked the transition from a society still largely relying on wood and basketry for its vessels instead of pottery (which becomes common only after the fire . . .), this unique evidence is extremely valuable. Far too often the archaeologist is forced to evaluate a culture from a few broken pots, and tools and weapons of stone and bone, which may conceivably present a false or incomplete picture. At Çatal Hüyük it is clear that the crafts of the weaver and the woodworker were much more highly esteemed than those of the potter or the bone-carver, and one may well wonder whether these two crafts have not been generally underrated or at least inadequately represented among the achievements of the Neolithic period. . . .

One of the most fascinating tasks is the location of the sources tapped by Çatal Hüyük for its raw materials, for with the exception of clay, reeds and wood, nearly everything used was made from materials not locally available. Even timber for building (oak and juniper) does not grow in the plain, but was brought from the hills and probably floated down the river. Fir, used for carving wooden bowls, was brought from the forests in the Taurus Mountains, so were numbers of foodstuffs. Greenstone and volcanic rocks could be found somewhat nearer, the first on a low ridge between Çumra and Karaman, the latter on the Karadağ, the prominent mountain which dominates the center of the Konya Plain. In its foothills limestone is still available. Further east lies a set of volcanoes, still active in the Neolithic period; Mekke Dağ, Karaca Dağ, the twin peaked cone of Hasan Dağ, and farthest away to the north-east, the giant Erciyes Dağ. Obsidian [, used to make chipping tools and weapons,] was obtained from some of these volcanoes and it is definitely known to occur on the Karaca and Hasan Dağ, and near the crater lake of Agicöl (Topada). A red obsidian with black streaks occurs in the deposit on the Nevşehir road. . . .

The common use of all of the rocks and minerals clearly shows that prospecting and trade formed a most important item of the city's economy and undoubtedly contributed appreciably to its wealth and prosperity.

• • •

It is clear from the pottery shapes that throughout the Neolithic period at Çatal Hüyük pottery occupied a secondary position and was unable to free itself completely from hitherto current shapes in wood and basketry. As late as [c. 5750–5700 BCE] a fair number of pottery shapes are angular and wooden, imitate wooden boxes or have wooden feet. This shows conclusively that wooden vessels continued to be made side by side with the pottery until the end of the settlement, and there is no *a priori* no reason why woodworking should have declined. Generally the importance of ceramic production in the Neolithic has probably been greatly overrated. It was a technological advance like any other and was no doubt useful for cooking, but it was easily breakable, hard to transport, in these early [years] not so easy to fire well and aesthetically not very attractive.

• • •

The basis for the spectacular development of the Neolithic at Çatal Hüyük was evidently laid by efficiently organized food production and conservation. That the Neolithic people of this site had succesfully established their 'Neolithic Revolution' which meant freedom from hunger, is proved by abundant evidence. In fact, few other sites have preserved such an abundance and variety of foodstuffs and . . . it is reasonable to conjecture that the same sort of conditions which we find from c. 6500 BC.. . . onwards had prevailed for at least a millennium before, if not considerably earlier.

9   Ancient Walls

An Chin-huai. "The Shang City at Cheng-chou and Related Problems." In *Studies of Shang Archaeology: Selected Papers from the International Conference on Shang Civilization*, ed. K.C. Chang. New Haven, Conn., and London: Yale University Press, 1986. 22–26.

Archaeological explorations in China have provided scholars with clues about numerous topics including the origins of Chinese script and the beginnings of settled agriculture. In the selection below, An Chin-huai examines the remains of an earthen wall within the present-day city of Cheng-chou. The "hang-t'u," or "beaten earth," wall stretches some seven kilometers and once enclosed an ancient city. In some areas, the imprint of wood planks used in the construction of the wall is still visible today, some 3,500 years later.

The parts of the Shang *hang-t'u* city walls that are aboveground have been seriously destroyed; what has been preserved is mainly buried underground. Only a part of the east and south walls and fragments of the north and west walls are now visible. . . . At its highest point the remaining wall is 9 meters, whereas at its lowest portion it is about 1 meter high; the greatest width at the base is 22.4 meters, the narrowest 4.8 meters; in some of the corners, the walls are preserved to a thickness of approximately 30 meters. . . .

According to the evidence of the test trenches excavated into the *hang-t'u* walls, two principal methods of construction were employed. One consisted of first leveling the ground a bit and then pounding the earth layers of the so-called main wall directly on the ground. In the other method, after the ground had been leveled, a flat-bottomed foundation trough somewhat wider at the top than at the bottom was first excavated following the outline of the wall to be built, but closer to its inner face. Then *hang-t'u* layers were piled up beginning from the bottom of the foundation trough. When ground level was reached, the construction of the main wall was started at the full width of the wall. . . .

Once the work reached the surface, wooden boards were used to delimit the edges of the wall under construction, forming, so to speak, an above ground foundation trough. A further detail of construction method was observed during excavation of [an] east wall trench . . . : the main wall was constructed in horizontal sections. Wooden planks were erected on both sides so as to delimit the interior and exterior faces of the wall under construction as well as the side where the wall was as yet unfinished. In these moldlike troughs boarded on three sides, the *hang-t'u* layers of the main wall were piled up one by one. When two or three layers of *hang-t'u* had thus been laid within the board troughs, the wooden facings were moved up on all three sides and more layers accumulating therein. In this way the height of the wall steadily grew. When the height reached that of the previously completed section of wall, the next section was commenced according to the same procedure. Each of these sections was about 3.8 meters long. . . .

Moreover, along the base of the wall, adjacent to the boarded inner and outer faces of the main wall, sloping *hang-t'u* layers were discovered; they were highest where they joined the wall, gradually lowering toward the outside. These sloping chunks of *hang-t'u* were perhaps constructed at the same time as the main wall, to support the boards on its two sides. At the same time, they also served the function of a so-called protective wall that protected the bases of the main wall. On the outer face, this protective wall was 4 meters wide, on the inner face 7.25 meters. Furthermore, on the top surface of the sloping protective wall, by the bases of the inner and outer sides of the main wall, an incompletely preserved layer with many pieces of broken "ginger-rock" was found. They had been placed here at the time of construction, apparently with the intention of protecting the *hang-t'u* layers at the bases of the wall from erosion by rainwater.

• • •

Since the *hang-t'u* layers are thin and the pounding impressions are tightly spaced, and moreover since the earth used in the construction of the city wall consists of sticky red loam mixed with sand—both obtainable in the immediate vicinity of the building site—the earthen layers of the city walls are extremely hard. The method of constructing earthen walls of pounded earth with the help of wooden boards was an important technological invention of the Chinese people of antiquity. . . .

10 The First Americans

Paul G. Bahn. "50,000 Year Old Americans of Pedra Furada."
Nature. Vol. 362 (11 March 1993). 114.

The following excerpt describes a recent archaeological watershed in the effort to date the earliest human occupation of the Americas. Scientific estimates have placed the date of human arrival at 12,000 to 15,000 years ago. At that time, scholars believe that people migrated across the Bering Land Bridge (now the Bering Straits) from present-day western Russia to North America. However, new evidence has emerged from the Toca de Boqueirao do Sitio da Pedra Furada, a cave site in Piauí, a state in northeastern Brazil. These findings revise the date of human arrival to at least 50,000 years ago, during the Pleistocene period. This finding has far-reaching implications for the nature and process of human occupation of the Americas.

Long-awaited data from the Brazilian rockshelter of Pedra Furada have at last been made public, and they constitute convincing evidence that human occupation of the New World extends back at least 50,00 years. In defending his doctoral thesis, Fabio Parenti, co-excavator of Pedra Furada with Niede Guidon, publicly presented his analysis of the site and its contents to a jury of examiners in Paris on 15 February. His defence was successful. The upshot will be the opening of a new era of investigation into the "first American."

The sandstone rock shelter of Pedra Furada is one of several hundred painted shelters discovered and studied by Guidon in the Piauí region of northeastern Brazil. In 1978 she began excavations in the site in order to date its rock art, which was confidently assumed to be . . . less than 10,000 years old. When radiocarbon dates . . . extending back more than 30,000 years, started to emerge from the stratigraphy, the site and its excavator were thrust into the forefront of the debate in which one side (primarily North American) insisted that there was no human occupation in the New World before 12,000 or at best 15,000 years ago, and the other accepted far earlier dates from Pedra Furada, or sites at Monte Verde in Chile and elsewhere.

Parenti commenced work at Pedra Furada in 1984, four years of digging being followed by four of analysis and laboratory work. No site had yet met all criteria necessary to convince sceptics that humans had been present in the New World so far back . . . so his task was clear from the outset. It was made all the harder because the sediments of the sandstone shelters of the Piauí region have destroyed all organic materials (other than charcoal fragments) in pre-Holocene levels. In addition, the Pleistocene levels of Pedra Furada contain tools made only of the quartz and quartzite pebbles from a conglomerate layer above the sandstone cliff, and pebble tools are notoriously difficult to differentiate from naturally broken stones.

Parenti's primary aim, therefore . . . was to distinguish between human and natural agencies in terms of the site's contents in general, and of its lithic [stone] objects in particular. The stratigraphy comprised mostly sand as well as sandstone plaques that had fallen from the walls, with occasional rubble layers. It was a natural rubble "wall" in from the shelter which preserved the sediments within: in Piauí, only sites with such walls or those in protected locations contain Pleistocene layers. In all other shelters, the Pleistocene layers have been removed by flooding, because in Piauí that period was far more humid than the Holocene.

Within the Pedra Furada shelter, scattered through the stratigraphy, Parenti has identified over 150 "structures," that is, arrangements of sandstone plaques, of pebbles, or of both. His analysis indicates that they cannot be natural, as they have no correlation with the areas where they would have fallen. The stones have been selected and arranged, though some pebbles subsequently moved since they can easily roll (the site has a 10' slope from east to west). It is impossible for the pebbles to occur naturally within the shelter; they would have fallen down the two watercourses in the cliff-face and along the shelter drip-line outside the rubble wall; besides, some circular arrangements of pebbles occur immediately adjacent to the shelter's back wall, some 15 metres from and upslope of the drip-line.

Parenti's basic rules for recognizing human agency in the structures are probably valid, but even when he applied the most stringent criteria he was left with no less than 50 Pleistocene structures which would be attributed to human agency of archaeological sites anywhere in the world; some contain traces of heating, such as burned stones and fragments of charcoal, and have been interpreted as hearths.

Where the pebbles are concerned . . . even if the most stringent criteria of human agency are applied to the collection, Parenti has 595 Pleistocene pieces that he considers definite. Thousands more pebbles are ambiguous, and could be either natural or man-made. Finally, the site also has a coherent series of 54 radiocarbon dates from 5,000 to 50,000 years before present. Thermoluminescence dates will be forthcoming.

The thesis-defence itself lasted for four hours (the thesis itself is a four-volume monster, weighing 7 kg). The combined experience of the jury is a measure of the quality of the interrogation. The panel was presided over by Yves Coppens, the paleoanthropologist, and consisted of Niede Guidon herself; Claude Guerin, the paleontologist in charge of studying the faunal remains from Piauí's limestone sites; Jean-Philippe Rigaud, an expert on the Paleolithic rockshelters and stone-tool industries of southwest France; Jean Chavaillon, an Africanist and expert on archaic stone tools; and Daniele Lavallee, a specialist in Andean prehistory. All six were convinced by Parenti's data, even though some (notably Lavallee) admitted to having had strong doubts about Pedra Furada in the past, and some were familiar with—and equally unconvinced by—material from other controversial New World sites such as Calico, Pendejo and Old Crow. The thesis has effectively been proven through stringent—and public—peer review.

Regardless of the lack of early sites in North America, there is now solid archaeological evidence for a human presence in the New World tens of thousands of years ago. All other issues—such as when or how many times the [Bering] land-bridge may have been crossed, or the technological origins of the Clovis point, or why the Piauí stone tool industry is so archaic—become secondary to that. There will no doubt remain sceptics, especially in North America. But in December an international meeting is to take place in Piauí to which the foremost of them have been invited. Seeing may then be believing.

11 Olorgesailie

Glynn Ll. Isaac. *Olorgesailie: Archaeological Studies of a Middle Pleistocene Lake Basin in Kenya.* Chicago: University of Chicago Press, 1977. 84, 87, 92–93, 95–96.

This selection describes the lifestyle and living site of a group of people who lived in Kenya at least 60,000 and possibly as long as 400,000 years ago. On the basis of material artifacts and different layers of occupation, the author puts forward suggestions about the life and society of this group. In the absence of firm evidence, or where material artifacts have not survived, the author speculates on the basis of ethnography, that is, studies of peoples such as the San who follow a similar livelihood and economy in the contemporary era. In such groups men hunt and/or scavenge while women gather edible plant materials. Women provide up to ninety percent of the food for such groups.

The quantities of material at the sites cannot be used in group size estimates, since duration of occupation and frequency of reoccupation are unknown. However, it seems unreasonable to suppose that the 500 hand axes and cleavers, and an aggregate weight of worked stone amounting to considerably more than half a ton, was accumulated in the . . . area entirely by a human group that included only one or two adults.

• • •

At the present stage of research, regrettably little can be said about the economic function of the various artifact forms or about their role in the behavioral adaptation of the groups that made them. If one takes cognizance of ethnographic accounts of stone tool usage, then the range of artifacts at Olorgesailie is sufficient for the performance of any of the economic functions that one might reasonably attribute to Acheulean communities. With these tools, it would have been possible to dismember any carcass; to dress, pierce, and cut up hides; to cut down saplings and small trees; and to shape poles, staves, spears, clubs, and light wooden vessels. The potential of the tool kits is established by the fact that in Australia, stone equipment that is certainly no more elaborate than that found at Olorgesailie permits the performance of all these tasks. . . .

The large cutting tools commonly, but not invariably, show a combination of sharp edges, robust edges, and scraping edges, which might support the long-standing suggestion that they were multipurpose tools. The delicacy of many specimens precludes their use for heavy woodworking, and the universal ethnographic evidence for the use of pointed, resilient sticks for digging makes it seem unlikely but not impossible that these stone tools were used for digging. Their utility for skinning animals has been demonstrated by Leakey and others.

• • •

The assumption that the primeval state of mankind was that of a savage hunter has its origins in thought that lies outside anthropology. The folklore of the classic civilizations and the writings of various postmedieval philosophers have all developed this theme. Since bone is the most durable variety of food refuse, the notion of man as hunter was reinforced by many of the archeological discoveries of the nineteenth century and rapidly came to be regarded as an established fact. . . .

There is ample evidence that hunting and perhaps scavenging were persistent and widespread practices of [these] groups. At a small number of sites, the quantities of flesh implied by the bone refuse may be sufficient to justify the belief that meat was a predominant component of diet. However, in many areas . . . hunting opportunities may have been intermittent or seasonal. It is possible that other sites with abundant bone represent periodic hunting opportunities, rather than consistent success and a regular meat supply. Scavenging may have been as important as hunting.

At most Acheulean sites we know nothing of the plant components of diet and too little about population size and duration of occupation to estimate the importance of plants from an equation such as: calories from meat + vegetables = population × average daily requirement × number of days. . . . Though the prospects are remote, it is possible that future excavations will unearth sites where the evidence is complete enough for reasonable estimation of several of these factors. . . .

Data for Bushmen . . . [,] Hadza . . . and Pygmies* . . . show that, for all three groups, gathered vegetable foods form the staples of diet, with meat as an essential but smaller component. This dietary pattern appears general among non-agricultural peoples who live away from shorelines and outside the subarctic zone. Very likely it was also the feeding pattern of the Acheulean inhabitants of the Olorgesailie basin. The apparatus required for gathering and preparing plant food is so simple that artifacts afford few clues. . . . The !Kung Bushmen use two natural stones, one flattish and one round, for breaking up the mugongo nuts that form one dietary staple. Woodburn reports that the Hadza use similar unshaped equipment for pounding baobab and other seeds. Humanly introduced stones suitable for such tasks are abundant on the Olorgesailie sites, but their use in preparing vegetable foods is unproven.

Among the Bushmen and Hadza, hunting is the principal economic activity of the adult males, but it may take up less than 20% of their waking time, the remainder being spent in rest, recreation, or the leisurely pursuit of other tasks and crafts. It is also reported that the women who commonly gather vegetable food are usually able to obtain enough for their families in considerably less than half their waking hours. . . . The widespread notion that early Paleolithic life was filled with deprivation and the need for continuous questing after food is probably erroneous.

The fact that many Olorgesailie sites have yielded little bone may not mean that meat was not consumed at them . . . but it certainly suggests that very large

---

*The use of the terms "Bushmen" and "Pygmies" is outdated. Generally historians and other scholars now use the names people call themselves, such as Twa, Khoikhoi, or !Kung. Isaac uses the term "Bushmen" to mean hunter-gatherers, and "Pygmies" to refer to the peoples physically small in stature.

quantities of bone were never present and that dependence on meat for food was, therefore, not necessarily a feature of the life of all Acheulean groups. At Latamne and in the Acheulean layers at the Cave of Hearths, faunal remains have been found in similarly modest quantities. . . .

While the reconstruction of hunting practices on the bases of the . . . evidence is hypothetical, the site is interesting because it is one of a very small series of sites where any factual basis for reconstruction is available. At two other sites where bone refuse is relatively abundant, there is a high incidence of one species: elephants. . . . These cases may document game drives or the encirclement of herds. . . . Drives and herd encirclement would have involved the cooperation of social groups appreciably larger than nuclear family, and thus the practice has sociological as well as economic interest[;] . . . more generalized bags of game . . . may have been the result of more opportunistic hunting practices or of individual stalking of the quarry, or the bone remains could have accumulated by scavenging.

Even if men could not regularly kill pachyderms, such as hippopotamuses and elephants, the scavenging of their carcasses may have been an important source of meat. In view of the ineffectiveness of other scavengers in opening and dismembering these carcasses, man may have been able to occupy a partially vacant ecological niche.

• • •

Comparisons of the morphology of artifacts . . . indicates that . . . there were marked differences of a stylistic nature. . . .

If the worked material at each site were the product of one craftsman, then this variation would be no more than individual idiosyncrasy. However, the bulk of material at some sites is suggestive of recurrent stoneworking activity by a whole group or band. If this latter proposition is correct, then culture in the Olorgesailie lake basin exhibits a combination of micro-differences between groups, coupled with a broader conservative uniformity. This is precisely the cultural pattern . . . usual among sparse, nonagricultural populations[;] . . . principal social and economic units within such a population are commonly a series of fairly small exogamous bands. The identity of bands is generally maintained by continuity between successive generations of males. Most of the males in most of the bands are reared within the band, and the male groups are thus a series of partial cultural isolates. The females reared within any band are continually dispersed by marriage to men outside the band, and are replaced by wives drawn from other bands. The wives are often taken from appreciable distances, so that the groups of wives in a band commonly have varied cultural and linguistic origins. . . . Marked diversion in the specifics of local groups tradition, especially male traditions, may contrast with fundamental social and economic uniformity over wide areas.

The data from Olorgesailie are consistent with such a mechanism of social division and cultural transmission, but it cannot be said that the evidence is conclusive. Only recently has explicit attention been given to the notion that patterning in artifacts can reflect aspects of demography and the specific social mechanisms by which craft traditions were transmitted.

DISCUSSION QUESTIONS

1. In each case, what factors may have helped to preserve the site and its evidence? What types of evidence survive? What does not? How do archaeologists fill in the gaps?

2. What can you infer about the relationship of each group to their site and its environment? How and in what ways did they take advantage of the environment?

3. What can you tell about relations within each group? Between men and women? Between generations? Did class or labor stratification exist within each group?

4. How did you use evidence in each case to arrive at the answers to the question above? How do archaeologists analyze their findings? Do you agree with them?

5. What can the types of evidence found at these sites tell us as historians about people in the distant past? Could we find out about the same subjects through written records? Why or why not?

Chapter
3
River Valley Civilizations

*T*he success of the Neolithic revolution fostered great changes in human societies. Fixed agriculture meant that more people could be fed with less effort. While many other stable cultures existed without this resource, it was the foundation of the river valley civilizations of Mesopotamia, Egypt, northwestern India, and northern China. The fundamental difference between these cultures and others in the world was one of scale. The sheer size of their populations meant that the basic functions of society—establishing norms of behavior, regulating commerce, and providing for self-defense from aggressive neighbors—required more coordination and extensive bureaucratic control. These differences in scale also promoted differences in kind. With vastly successful agricultural production, river valley civilizations were more differentiated than those that had preceded them. In other words, people increasingly specialized in particular tasks as fewer of them were required to provide basic sustenance for the society.

One consequence of the growth of these societies—although not an inevitable one—was the introduction of written forms of communication. In the first selection, the remains of Shang divination records demonstrate the variety of issues that led rulers to seek guidance. These records, preserved as symbols etched in bone, offer not merely insights into Shang rulership, but are also the precursors to written Chinese language. The second selection is composed of excerpts from Indian Vedic hymns, prayers offered to the pantheon of gods worshipped by the Aryans. Like the Shang oracle bones, the Vedas are a ritualized form in which people sought divine or other-worldly inspiration for their day-to-day activities. The third selection, from Hammurabi's law codes, is among the most recognizable, and frequently cited, documents in world history. The law codes are meticulous in their detail, prescribing precise punishments for violations of the law. Through these codes, it is possible to see the complexity of Babylonian society and the degree to which one's life was shaped by status and gender. The "Tale of Sinuhe," the fourth selection in this chapter, describes the exile and return of an official of the Egyptian court.

12 Oracle Bone Divinations

Patricia Ebrey, ed. *Chinese Civilization and Society: A Sourcebook*. New York: The Free Press, 1993. 3–5.

In the late Shang era, rulers sought guidance from the spirit world by means of oracle bones. Cattle bones or turtle shells were heated while diviners asked what the rulers wanted to know. Stress cracks produced by the flames were interpreted, and both the requests and answers were recorded on the bones or shells. The exact meaning of all the divinations is not clear: in some cases the side of the bone would be inscribed with contradictory phrases. Others, however, are far easier to interpret. About 150,000 of these fragments have survived at Anyang in China. Note the wide variety of topics and advice received in the questions and answers of the oracle inscriptions that follow.

MOBILIZATIONS

This season, the king raises five thousand men to campaign against the Tufang; he will receive assistance in this case.

MILITARY CAMPAIGNS

It should be Zhi Guo whom the king joins to attack the Bafang, (for if he does) Di will (confer assistance) on us.

It should not be Zhi Guo whom the king joins to attack the Bafang (for if he does) Di may not (confer assistance) on us.

CHILDBIRTH

Lady Hao . . . will give birth and it will be good. The king read the cracks and said: "If it be on a ding day that she give birth, it will be good. If it be on a geng day that she give birth, it will be prolonged auspiciousness." After thirty-one days, on jiayin (day 51), she gave birth. It was not good. It was a girl.

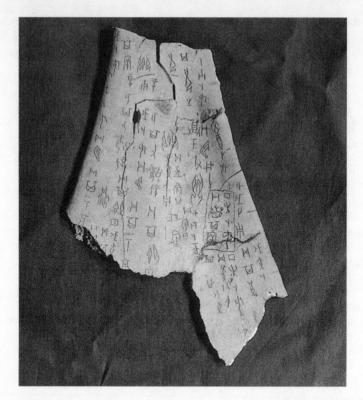

Figure 3.1 Chinese oracle bones.

Lady Hao will give birth and it may not be good.

After thirty-one days, on jiayin (day 51), she gave birth. It really was not good. It was a girl.

REQUESTS TO ANCESTRAL OR NATURAL POWERS

In praying for harvest to Yue, (a mountain spirit) we make a burnt offering of three small penned sheep (and) split open three cattle.

HUNTING EXPEDITIONS AND EXCURSIONS

On renzi (day 49) the king made cracks and divined: (We) hunt at Zhi; going and coming back there will be no harm. The king read the cracks and said: Prolonged auspiciousness. This was used. We caught forty-one foxes, eight mi-deer, one rhinoceros.

13 Indian Philosophy and Religion

"The Vedic Hymns." In *Sources of Indian Tradition*, ed. William de Bary. New York: Columbia University Press, 1958. 9–15, 20.

The Vedic hymns are the oldest surviving writings of the Vedic Aryans, who composed them long before they invaded India about 1500 BCE. Modified over time, the Vedic hymns stressed the importance of nature to their culture, particularly of the sun. Some scholars think that the conquest of India was led by a legendary leader named Indra, who subsequently became a god featured in some of the hymns. The hymns of the Rig Veda vary in content, from addresses to different gods to charms to guard against malady; the latter are thought to show the influence of the peoples the Aryans conquered upon Aryan religion. The text is seen by Hindus today as embodying some of the fundamental elements of their religion.

AGNI (THE GOD OF FIRE)

I extol Agni, the household priest, the divine minister of the sacrifice, the chief priest, the bestower of blessings. May that Agni, who is to be extolled by ancient and modern seers, conduct the gods here. Through Agni may one gain day by day wealth and welfare which is glorious and replete with heroic sons. O Agni, the sacrifice and ritual which you encompass on every side, that indeed goes to the gods. May Agni, the chief priest, who possesses the insight of a sage, who is truthful, widely renowned, and divine, come here with the gods. O Agni, O Angiras (messenger), whatever prosperity you bring to the pious is indeed in accordance with your true function. O Agni, illuminator of darkness, day by day we approach you with holy thought bringing homage to you. Presiding at ritual functions, the brightly shining custodian of the cosmic order (rita), thriving in your own realm. O Agni, be easy of access to us as a father to his son. Join us for our wellbeing.

VARUNA (THE COSMIC ADMINISTRATOR)

Unto the sovereign lord sing a sublime and solemn prayer . . . , one dear unto glorious Varuna, who has spread out the earth, as the butcher does the hide, by way of a carpet for the sun. Varuna has extended the air above the trees; he has put strength in horses, milk in cows, will-power in hearts, fire in waters, the sun in the heaven, and soma upon the mountain. Varuna poured out the leather-bag, opening downward, upon the heaven and the earth and the mid-region. Thereby does the lord of the whole creation moisten thoroughly the expanse of earth, as rain does the corn.

He moistens the broad earth and the heaven. When Varuna would have it milked (i.e., would shower rain) then indeed, do the mountains clothe themselves with clouds and the heroes, showing off their might, loosen those clothes (i.e., disperse the clouds). This great magic-work of renowned spiritual Varuna will I proclaim loudly; of Varuna, who standing in the mid-region, has measured the earth with the sun as with a measuring rod. No one, indeed, dare impugn this great magic-work of the wisest god, namely, that the many glistening streams, pouring forth, do not fill up one ocean with water.

DAWN

This light has come, of all the lights the fairest:
The brilliant brightness has been born effulgent [shining brightly]. Urged onward for god Savitar's uprising,
Night now has yielded up her place to morning.

Bringing a radiant calf she comes resplendent:
To her the Black One has given up her mansions.
Akin, immortal, following each other,
Morning and Night fare on, exchanging colors.

The sisters' pathway is the same, unending:
Taught by the gods alternately they tread it.
Fair-shaped, of form diverse, yet single-minded,
Morning and Night clash not, nor do they tarry.

Bright leader of glad sounds she shines effulgent:
Widely she has unclosed for us her portals.
Pervading all the world she shows us riches:
Dawn has awakened every living creature.

Men lying on the ground she wakes to action:
Some rise to seek enjoyment of great riches,
Some, seeing little to behold the distant:
Dawn has awakened every living creature.

One for dominion, and for fame another;
Another is aroused for winning greatness;
Another seeks the goal of varied nurture:
Dawn has awakened every living creature.

Daughter of Heaven, she has appeared before us,
A maiden shining in resplendent raiment [clothing].

Thou sovereign lady of all earthly treasure,
Auspicious Dawn, shine here today upon us.

INDRA (THE ATMOSPHERIC GOD)

Indra's heroic deeds, indeed, will I proclaim, the first ones which the wielder of
the vajra accomplished. He killed the dragon, released the waters and split open
the sides of the mountains. He killed the dragon lying spread out on the mountain; for him Tvashtar fashioned the roaring vajra. Like bellowing cows, the
waters, gliding, have gone down straightway to the ocean. Showing off his virile
power he chose soma; from the three kadrukas [wooden bowls] he drank of the
extracted soma. The bounteous god took up the missile, the vajra; he killed the
first-born among the dragons. When you, O Indra, killed the first-born among
the dragons and further overpowered the wily tricks of the tricksters, bringing
forth, at that very moment, the sun, the heaven, and the dawn—since then,
indeed, have you not come across another enemy. Indra killed Vritra, the
greater enemy, the shoulderless one, with his mighty and fatal weapon, the
vajra. Like branches of a tree lopped off with an axe, the dragon lies prostrate
upon the earth. For, like an incapable fighter, in an intoxicated state, he had
challenged the great hero (Indra), the mighty overwhelmer, the drinker of soma
to the dregs. He did not surmount the onslaught of his fatal weapon. Indra's
enemy, broken-nosed, was completely crushed. Footless and handless he gave
battle to Indra. He struck him with the vajra upon the back. The castrated bull,
seeking to become a compeer [a peer] of the virile bull, Vritra lay shattered in
many places.

Over him, who lay in that manner like a shattered bull flowed the waters for
the sake of man. At the feet of the very waters, which Vritra had (once) enclosed
with his might, the dragon (now) lay (prostrate). Vritra's mother had her vital energy ebbing out; Indra had hurled his fatal weapon at her. The mother lay above, the
son below; Danu lay down like a cow with her calf.

In the midst of the water-streams which never stood still nor had any resting
place, the body lay. The waters flow in all directions over Vritra's secret place;
Indra's enemy lay sunk in long darkness. With the Dasa as their lord and with the
dragon as their warder, the waters remained imprisoned, like cows held by the
Pani. Having killed Vritra, Indra threw open the cleft of waters which had been
closed. You became the hair of a horse's tail, O Indra, when he (Vritra) struck at
your sharp-pointed vajra—the one god (eka deva) though you were. You won the
cows, O brave one, you won soma; you released the seven rivers, so that the waters
should flow. Neither did lightning nor thunder, nor mist nor hailstorm, which he
had spread out, prove efficacious when Indra and the dragon fought. And the
bounteous god remained victorious for all time to come. Whom did you see, O
Indra, as the avenger of the dragon, that fear entered into your heart, after you had
killed the dragon, and frightened, you crossed nine and ninety rivers and the aeri-
al regions like the falcon? Indra, who wields the vajra in his hand, is the lord of

what moves and what remains rested, of what is peaceful and what is horned. He alone rules over the tribes as their king: he encloses them as does a rim the spokes.

A CHARM AGAINST JAUNDICE

Unto the sun let them both go up—your heartburn and your yellowness, with the color of the red bull do we envelop you.

With red colors do we envelop you for the sake of long life; so that this person may be free from harm and may become non-yellow.

Those cows that have Rohini (the Red One) as presiding divinity, as also cows which are red—their every form and every power—with them do we envelop you. Into the parrots do we put your yellowness and into the yellow green ropanaka birds. Similarly into the turmeric . . . do we deposit your yellowness.

EXORCISM OF SERPENTS

Let not the serpent, O gods, slay us with our children and with our men. The closed jaw shall not snap open, the open one shall not close. Homage to the divine folk. . . . Homage be to the black serpent, homage to the one with stripes across its body, homage to the brown constrictor, homage to the divine folk. I smite your teeth with tooth, I smite your two jaws with jaw; I smite your tongue with tongue; I smite your mouth, O Serpent, with mouth.

14 Mesopotamian Law

G. R. Driver and John C. Miles, eds. *The Babylonian Laws.* Oxford, England: The Clarendon Press, 1955. 7, 13–77.

The following are excerpts from the Code of Hammurabi, promulgated by the Babylonian ruler Hammurabi during his reign between 1800 and 1750 BCE. The laws of a society provide a wealth of information about crime and restitution, but they also show the differences among the status of people within that society. Insofar as the Code prescribes different punishments for men and women, free citizens and peasants or slaves, these laws show us how people were treated in the Babylonian world. Through these laws you will also get a sense of what Hammurabi felt were the most important features of his kingdom. As you read, ask yourself questions such as why certain crimes were punished severely and others not.

Reprinted from *The Babylonian Laws* edited by G.R. Driver and John C. Miles, vol. 2 (1955) by permission of Oxford University Press.

Figure 3.2 Stone tablet of Hammurabi with the sun god.

When the exalted Anum king of the Annunaki (and) Illil lord of heaven and earth, who allots the destinies of the land, allotted the divine lordship of the multitude of the people unto Marduk the first-born son of Ea, magnified him amongst the Igigi, called Babylon its exalted name (and) so made it pre-eminent in the (four) quarters of the world, and established for him an everlasting kingdom whose foundations are firmly laid like heaven and earth, at that time Anum and Illil for the prosperity of the people called me by name Hammurabi, the reverent God-fearing prince, to make justice to appear in the land, to destroy the evil and the wicked that the strong might not oppress the weak, to rise indeed like Shamash over the dark-haired folk to give light to the land. . . .

    If a man has accused a man and has charged him with manslaughter and then has not proved (it against) him, his accuser shall be put to death. . . .

If a man has come forward in a case to bear witness to a felony and then has not proved the statement that he has made, if that case (is) a capital one, that man shall be put to death. . . .

If a judge has tried a suit, given a decision, caused a sealed tablet to be executed, (and) thereafter varies his judgement, they shall convict that judge of varying (his) judgement and he shall pay twelve-fold the claim in that suit; then they shall remove him from his place on the bench of judges in the assembly, and he shall not (again) sit in judgement with the judges. . . .

If a man has stolen an ox or a sheep or an ass or swine or a boat, if (it is the property) of a god (or) if (it is the property) of a palace, he shall pay 30-fold; if (it is the property) of a villein [peasant], he shall replace (it) 10-fold. If the thief has not the means of payment, he shall be put to death. . . .

If a man kidnaps the infant (son) of a (free) man, he shall be put to death. . . .

If a man has let a slave of a palace or a slave-girl of a palace or the slave of a villein or the slave-girl of a villein escape by the great gate, he shall be put to death. . . .

If a man has harbored a lost slave or slave-girl of a palace or of a villein in his house and then has not brought (them) out at the proclamation of the herald, that owner of the house shall be put to death.

If a man has caught either a slave or a slave-girl fugitive in the open country and hales him to his owner, the owner of the slave shall give him 2 shekels of silver. . . .

If a man has broken into a house, they shall put him to death and hang him before the breach he has made. . . .

If a man has committed robbery and is caught, that man shall be put to death. If the robber is not caught, the man who has been robbed shall formally declare whatever he has lost before a god, and the city and the mayor in whose territory or district the robbery has been committed shall replace whatever he has lost for him. If (it is) the life (of the owner that is lost), the city or the mayor shall pay one maneh of silver to his kinfolk. . . .

If a fire has broken out in a man's house and a man who has gone to extinguish (it) has coveted an article of the owner of the house and takes the article of the owner of the house, that man shall be cast into that fire. . . .

If a man has taken up a field for cultivation and then has not raised corn° on the field, they shall convict him of not having done the (necessary) work on the field and he shall give corn corresponding to (the crops raised by) his neighbors to the owner of the field and shall plough the field, which he has left waste (and) harrow (it) and he shall render (it) to the owner of the field. . . .

If he has not cultivated the field but leaves (it) waste, he shall give corn corresponding to (the crops raised by) his neighbors to the owner of the field and shall

---

°In Britain, "corn" is a generic term for cereal grains such as wheat. American corn, or maize, did not exist in Europe, Asia, or Africa until after the voyages of Christopher Columbus at the end of the fifteenth century CE.

plough the field, which he has left waste (and) harrow (it), and he shall render (it) to the owner of the field. . . .

If a herdsman does not make an agreement with the owner of a field to let his sheep graze the green shoots and lets the sheep graze the green shoots and lets the sheep graze the field without (the consent of) the owner of the field, the owner of the field shall reap his field; the herdsmen, who has let his sheep graze the field without (the consent of) the owner of the field, over and above shall give 20 GUR of corn for every BUR (of land) to the owner of the field. . . .

If the merchant gives the silver to the agent for (mutual) advantage and he perceives a loss where he has gone, he shall repay the total amount of the silver to the merchant. If an enemy causes him to jettison anything that he is carrying whilst he is going on the journey, the agent may take an oath by the life of a god and he then goes free. . . .

If an ale-wife [tavern-keeper] does not accept the grain for the price of liquor (but) accepts silver by the heavy weight or (if) she reduces the value of beer (given) against the value of corn (received), they shall convict that ale-wife and cast her into the water.

If felons are banded together in an ale-wife's house and she does not seize those felons and she has not hauled (them) to the palace, that ale-wife shall be put to death.

If a priestess (or) a high-priestess, who is not dwelling in a cloister, opens an ale-house [tavern] or enters an ale-house for liquor, they shall burn that woman. . . .

If a man has caused a finger to be pointed at a high-priestess or a married lady and has then not proved (what he has said), they shall flog that man before the judges and shave half his head. . . .

If a man has taken a (woman to) wife and has not drawn up a contract for her, that woman is not a wife. . . .

If a married lady is caught lying with another man, they shall bind them and cast them into the water; if her husband wishes to let his wife live, then the king shall let his servant live. . . .

If a man has stopped the cries of a married lady, who has not known a man and is dwelling in her father's house, and has then lain in her bosom and they catch him, that man shall be put to death; that woman then goes free. If the husband of a married lady has accused her but she is not caught lying with another man, she shall take an oath by the life of a god and return to her house. If a finger has been pointed at the married lady with regard to another man and she is not caught lying with the other man, she shall leap into the holy river for her husband. . . .

If a man takes himself off and there is the (necessary) maintenance in his house, his wife (so long as) her (husband is delayed), shall keep (herself chaste; she shall not) enter (another man's house). If that woman has not kept herself chaste but enters another man's house, they shall convict that woman and cast her in the water. If the man has taken himself off and there is not the (necessary) maintenance in his house, his wife may enter another man's house; that woman shall suffer no punishment. If the man takes himself off and there is not the (necessary) maintenance in his house, (and) before his return his wife enters another man's house and then bears sons, (if) her husband afterwards returns and regains his city, that woman shall return to her first husband, the sons shall follow their (respective) fathers. . . .

If a man sets his face to divorce a lay-sister who has borne him sons or a priestess who has provided him with sons, they shall render her dowry to her and shall give her a half-portion of field plantation or chattels and she shall bring up her sons; after she has then brought up her sons, they shall give her a share like (that of) a single heir in anything that has been given (to her) for her sons, and a husband after her heart may marry her.

If a man wishes to divorce his first wife who has not borne him sons, he shall give her money to the value of her bridal gift and shall make good to her the dowry which she has brought from her father's house and (so) divorce her. If there is no bridal gift, he shall give her 1 maneh of silver for divorce-money. If (he is) a villein, he shall give her ⅓ maneh of silver. . . .

If a man after the death of his father lies in his mother's bosom, they shall burn both of them. . . .

If a man sets his face to disinherit his son (and) states to the judges "I will disinherit my son," the judges shall determine the facts of the case and, if he has not deserved the heavy penalty of disinheritance, the father may not disinherit his son.

If he deserves the heavy penalty of disinheritance at the hands of his father, a first time they shall pardon him, if he deserves the (same) heavy penalty a second time, his father may disinherit his son. . . .

If either a slave of a palace or a slave of a villein has married a lady and she bears sons, the owner of the slave shall make no claim to the sons of the lady for slavery. If a father has not bestowed a dowry on his daughter (who is) a priestess in a cloister. . . , after the father goes to (his) father [i.e., dies], she shall at the division take a share like (that of) one heir out of the property of the paternal estate and shall have the usufruct° (of it) so long as she lives. Her estate belongs to her brothers. . . .

If a man has taken an infant in adoption (to be called) by his name and brings him up, that adopted child shall not be (re)claimed. If the man has taken the infant in adoption (and), when he has taken it, it persists in searching for its father and its mother, that adopted child shall return to its father's house. . . .

If a craftsman has taken a son for bringing up (in his craft) and teaches him his handicraft, he shall not be (re)claimed.

If he does not teach him his handicraft, that adopted child may return to its father's house. . . .

If a son strikes his father, they shall cut off his fore-hand. . . .

If a man has put out the eye of a free man, they shall put out his eye. If he breaks the bone of a (free) man, they shall break his bone. If he puts out the eye of a villein or breaks the bone of a villein, he shall pay one maneh of silver. If he puts out the eye of a (free)man's slave or breaks the bone of a (free) man's slave, he shall

---

°Usufruct in this case means that the woman has the use of that property for the remainder of her life even though it belongs to her male relatives.

pay half his price. If a man knocks out the tooth of a villein, he shall pay ⅓ maneh of silver. If a man strikes the cheek of a (free) man who is superior (in rank) to him(self), he shall be beaten with sixty stripes with a whip of ox-hide in the assembly. If the man strikes the cheek of a free man equal to him(self in rank) he shall pay 1 maneh of silver.

If a villein strikes the cheek of a villein, he shall pay 10 shekels of silver. If the slave of a (free) man strikes the cheek of a free man, they shall cut off his ear. . . .

15 A Tale of Ancient Egypt

"The Tale of Si-nuhe," In *Ancient Near Eastern Texts Relating to the Old Testament*, 3rd edition with supplement, ed. James B. Pritchard. Princeton, N.J.: Princeton University Press, 1969. 18–22.

In the following story, an Egyptian official named Sinuhe goes into voluntary exile after the death of the king, Amenemhet I around 1960 BCE. While the reasons for his exile are never clear, Sinuhe travels into present-day Israel, Lebanon and Syria, where he gains fortune and is eventually invited to return to the Egyptian court by the new king, Senusert I. Sinuhe may have been a real person, or this tale may have been written about court officials who fell out of favor during the transition from one ruler to another. The earliest manuscripts that describe the tale of Sinuhe date from approximately 1800 BCE. The excerpts begin with Sinuhe's reaction to the death of Amenemhet and the ascension of Senusert.

I removed myself . . . to seek a hiding place. . . . I placed myself between two bushes, in order to cut myself off from the road and its travel.

I set out southward, but I did not plan to reach this Residence City,° for I thought that there would be civil disorder, and I did not expect to live after him. I crossed Lake Ma-aty near Sycamore, and I came to Snefru Island. I spent the day there on the edge of the fields. . . . When the time of the evening meal came, I drew near to Oxtown. I crossed over in a barge without a rudder, by aid of the west wind. . . . I came up to the Wall-of-the-Ruler, made to oppose the Asiatics† and to crush the Sand-Crossers. I took a crouching position in a bush, for fear lest the watchmen upon the wall . . . might see me.

One foreign country gave me to another. I set off for Byblos and approached Qedem, and spent a year and a half there. Ammi-enshi—he was ruler of Upper

---

°The city where the king resides.
†Throughout this text, the term Asiatics refers to the people who live literally to the west of Egypt inpresent-day Israel, Syria, Lebanon, etc.

Retenu—took me and said to me: "Thou wilt do well with me, and thou wilt hear the speech of Egypt." He said this, for he knew my character, he had heard of my wisdom, and the people of Egypt who were there with him had borne witness for me.

Then he said to me: "Why hast thou come hither? Has something happened in the Residence City?" Then I said to him: "The King of Upper and Lower Egypt . . . is departed to the horizon, and no one knows what might happen because of it." But I said equivocally: "I had come from an expedition to the land of Temeh, when report was made to me. My heart quailed; it carried me off on the way of flight. Yet no one had gossiped about me; no one had spat in my face; not a belittling word had been heard, nor had my name been heard in the mouth of the herald. I do not know what brought me to this country. It was as though it might be a god."

Then he said to me: "Well, what will that land be like without him, that beneficent god, the fear of whom pervaded foreign countries like the fear of Sekhmet in the year of pestilence?" I spoke to him that I might answer him: "Well, of course, his son has entered into the palace and has taken inheritance of his father. Moreover, he is a god without . . . peer. There is no other who surpasses him. . . ."

Then he said to me: "Well, really, Egypt is happy that it knows that he is flourishing. Now thou art here. Thou shalt stay with me. What I shall do for thee is good."

He set me at the head of his children. He married me to his eldest daughter. He let me choose for myself of his country, of the choicest of that which was with him on his frontier with another country. It was a good land, named Yaa. Figs were in it, and grapes. It had more wine than water. Plentiful was its honey, abundant its olives. Every kind of fruit was on its trees. Barley was there, and emmer.* There was no limit to any kind of cattle. . . . He made me ruler of a tribe of the choicest of his country. Bread was made for me as daily fare, wine as daily provision, cooked meat and roasted fowl, beside the wild beasts of the desert. . . .

I spent many years, and my children grew up to be strong men, each man as the restrainer of his own tribe. The messenger who went north or who went south to the Residence City stopped over with me. . . . I gave water to the thirsty. I put him who had strayed back on the road. I rescued him who had been robbed. When the Asiatics became so bold as to oppose the rulers of foreign countries, I counseled their movements. This ruler of Retenu had me spend many years as commander of his army. Every foreign country against which I went forth, when I had made my attack on it, was driven away from its pasturage and wells. I plundered its cattle, carried off its inhabitants, took away their food, and slew people in it by my strong arm, by my bow, by my movements, and by my successful plans. I found favor in his heart, he loved me, he recognized my valor, and he placed me at the head of his children, when he saw how my arms flourished.

• • •

Now when the majesty of the King of Upper and Lower Egypt . . . was told about this situation in which I was, then his majesty kept sending to me with presentations from the royal presence, that he might gladden the heart of this servant like the ruler of any foreign country. . . .

---

*A kind of wheat.

COPY OF THE DECREE WHICH WAS BROUGHT TO THIS SERVANT ABOUT BRINGING HIM BACK TO EGYPT. . . .

Thou hast traversed foreign countries, starting from Qedem to Retenu. One country gave thee to another, under the advice of thy own heart to thee. What hast thou done that anything should be done to thee? Thou has not cursed, that thy word should be punished. Thou has not spoken against the counsel of the nobles, that thy speeches should be opposed. This plan simply carried away thy heart. It was in no heart against thee. This thy heaven which is in the palace is firm and steadfast today. Her head is covered with the kingship of the land. Her children are in the court.*

MAYEST THOU LAY UP TREASURES WHICH THEY MAY GIVE THEE; MAYEST THOU LIVE ON THEIR BOUNTY. Do thou return to Egypt, that thou mayest see the home in which thou didst grow up and kiss the ground at the Great Double Door and join with the courtiers. For today, surely, thou hast begun to grow old; thou hast lost thy virility. Recall thou the day of burial, the passing to a revered state, when the evening is set aside for thee with ointments and wrappings for the hands of Tait [the goddess of weaving].

A funeral procession is made for thee on the day of interment, a mummy case of gold, with head of lapis lazuli, with the heaven above thee, as thou art placed upon a sledge, oxen dragging thee and singers in front of thee, when the dance of the muu is performed at the door of thy tomb, when the requirements of the offering table are summoned for thee and here is sacrifice beside thy offering stones, thy pillars being hewn of white stone in the midst of the tombs of the royal children. It should not be that thou shouldst die in a foreign country. Asiatics should not escort thee. Thou shouldst not be placed in a sheepskin when thy wall is made. This is too long to be roaming the earth. . . .

THIS DECREE REACHED ME AS I WAS STANDING IN THE MIDST OF MY TRIBE. It was read to me. I put myself upon my belly; I touched the ground; I scattered it upon my hair. I went about my encampments rejoicing and saying: "How can this be done for a servant whom his heart led astray to barbarous countries? But the indulgence which saved me from death is really good! . . . "

COPY OF THE ANSWER TO THIS DECREE. THE SERVANT OF THE PALACE SI-NUHE SAYS:. . . .

"This is the prayer of this servant to his Lord, the savior in the West. . . ."

"Now this flight which the servant made, it was not planned, it was not in my heart I had not worried about it. I do not know what severed me from my place. . . . I had not been afraid. No one had run after me. I had heard not a belittling word. My name had not been heard in the mouth of a herald. And yet—my body shuddered, my feet were trembling, my heart led me on, and the god who ordained this flight drew me away. . . . Whether I am at home or whether I am in this place, thou art he who covers this horizon, the sun disc rises at thy pleasure, the water in the River is drunk as thou wishest, and the air in the sky is breathed as thou biddest.

---

*Prior to his departure, Sinuhe had been in the service of Senusert's wife, now the queen of Egypt. These passages refer to her welfare.

This servant will hand over THE VIZIERSHIP WHICH THIS SERVANT HAS EXERCISED IN THIS PLACE."

Then they came for this servant. . . . I was permitted to spend a day in Yaa handing over my property to my children, my eldest son being responsible for my tribe. My tribe and all my property were in his charge: my serfs, all my cattle, my fruit, and every pleasant tree of mine.

Then this servant came southward. . . .

When day had broken, very early, they came and summoned me, ten men coming and ten men going to usher me to the palace. I put my brow to the ground between the sphinxes, while the royal children were waiting in recess to meet me. The courtiers who usher into the audience hall set me on the way to the private chambers. I found his majesty upon the Great Throne in a recess of fine gold. When I was stretched out upon my belly, I knew not myself in his presence, although this god greeted me pleasantly. I was like a man caught in the dark: my soul departed, my body was powerless, my heart was not in my body, that I might know life from death.

THEN HIS MAJESTY SAID TO ONE OF THE COURTIERS: "Lift him up. Let him speak to me." Then his majesty said: "Behold, thou art come. Thou hast trodden the foreign countries and made a flight. But now elderliness has attacked thee; thou hast reached old age. It is no small matter that thy corpse be properly buried; thou shouldst not be interred by bowmen [foreigners]. Do not, do not act thus any longer: for thou dost not speak when thy name is pronounced!" Yet I was afraid to respond, and I answered it with the answer of one afraid: "What is it that my lord says to me? I should answer it, but there is nothing that I can do: it is really in the hand of a god. It is a terror that is in my belly like that which produced the fated flight. BEHOLD, I AM BEFORE THEE. THINE IS LIFE, MAY THY MAJESTY DO AS HE PLEASES.

• • •

Then his majesty said: "He shall not fear. He has not title to be in dread. He shall be a courtier among the nobles. He shall be put in the ranks of the courtiers. . . .

So I went forth from the midst of the inner chambers, with the royal children giving me their hands. . . . Years were made to pass from my body. I was plucked, and my hair was combed. A load of dirt was given to the desert, and my clothes to the Sand-Crossers. I was clad in fine linen and anointed with prime oil. I slept on a bed. . . . I was given a house which had a garden, which had been in the possession of a courtier. Many craftsmen built it, and all its woodwork was newly restored. . . .

There was constructed for me a pyramid-tomb of stone in the midst of the pyramid-tombs. . . .

So I was under the favor of the king's presence until the day of mooring had come.

DISCUSSION QUESTIONS

1. The cultures you have read about in this section each developed a form of written language to preserve their ideas. What elements of their culture appear to be the most

prominent in the written record? What elements are not described in the written materials? What reasons might exist for the preservation of certain kinds of information in written form?

2. What clues to the livelihood of ordinary people are contained in the documents above? What information, if any, is available to you about how these societies provided food for themselves?

3. What relationship existed between leaders—political and/or religious—and their people? What relationship existed between those rulers and their gods?

4. Both the Shang divination bones and the Vedas offer clues about their respective societies. What issues or concerns were important in these cultures? Do these concerns seem similar to, or different from, those expressed in the "Tale of Sinuhe" and Hammurabi's law codes?

5. How did people understand their place in the different societies you have explored? How did the lived experience of daily life differ for people according to their status in society? gender? nationality, ethnicity, or race?

Two

THE CLASSICAL ERA AND BEYOND: 1000 BCE to 500 CE

On the foundations of the great river valley civilizations arose the "classical civilizations" of the Mediterranean, China, and India. These societies were "classical" in the sense that they were more complex than their predecessors, and therefore often believed to be the forerunners of modern societies in those same regions of the globe. Later societies found in the classical era traditions and values that they could emulate. The essence of this increased complexity within these extensive empires was the expansion of trade networks, greater cultural integration, and more centralized political control. In contrast to the river valley civilizations studied in Part I, the emerging societies of Han China, Greece and later Rome in the Mediterranean, and Mauryan India more closely resembled the empires of the modern world. However, the concept of a "classical age" in world history must be used with great caution.

To understand the changes occurring in the world, it is necessary to explore not only the "classical civilizations" but to look beyond them as well. In the Americas, complex societies arose that were completely isolated from Africa, Asia, and Europe. Yet the history of the Americas, and that of Sub-Saharan Africa, remains complicated by the tendency within Western scholarship to see the history of humanity in terms of a linear progression from hunter-gatherer groups to civilization. All societies are limited by the resources available to them. Just as the river valley civilizations emerged where there was water, fertile soil, and a mild climate, regions without these features in combination were less likely to develop the surplus agricultural production needed to support a complex civilization. Nevertheless, many American peoples cultivated maize (corn), a grain with a higher caloric output than any cultivated in Europe or Asia. Between 4000 BCE and 1000 CE the cultivation of maize spread, forming the basis of Iroquois society in North America, and for millions of people in the sphere of the Olmec empire (1200 to 500 BCE) in Mesoamerica. Thus, there were societies in the Americas that bore a strong resemblance to "classical" ones in Europe, Asia, and northern Africa.

Even with the Americas included in the concept of a classical age, the sedentary agriculturalists did not occupy much of the world's surface. Inhabiting the fringes of sedentary societies, or existing independently of them altogether, approximately 10 percent of the world's population lived in nomadic, or migratory, societies. Nomadic and sedentary peoples interacted in a number of complex ways characterized by cooperation as well as conflict. Pastoral nomads—migratory peoples who use domesticated animals such as camels—played important roles in shaping the destinies of Chinese and Roman empires. In addition, there were important historical processes—the spread of languages, cultures, and agricultural knowledge—that cut across the divide between sedentary and nomadic peoples. For these reasons, this section of the reader includes not only traditional documents drawn from the "classical civilizations," but documents and secondary material that explore the connections between sedentary peoples and migratory ones, as well as the diffusion of knowledge in regions throughout the globe.

Chapter
4

Nomads and City Dwellers

Between 1000 BCE and 500 CE, human societies displayed a wide variety of social organization and livelihoods. Historians have commonly divided societies into "civilizations" and "noncivilizations." Civilizations, according to conventional definitions, were sedentary. They demonstrated an agricultural surplus, specialization of tasks, written language, construction of monuments, hierarchy, and class stratification. This traditional view privileges societies that developed in geographical, environmental, and climatic conditions that favored this type of development, primarily, fertile river valleys and deltas.

In this section we explore a wide variety of societies that developed different organizations and livelihoods, partly on the basis of their environment. Some scholars distinguish between societies that adapt and organize themselves to fit their environment, and societies that settle in one place and transform it through permanent agriculture. This dichotomy obscures the role of the environment, topography, and climate of an area in allowing or precluding the possibility of the development of sedentary agriculture.

In addition to highlighting organization, the selections below show typical interaction between societies featuring different livelihoods. Western historians have usually viewed sedentary societies more favorably than nomadic cultures that often lived by raiding sedentary agricultural societies. One reason for this bias may be that Western societies are descendents of the latter.

In the following selections, we focus on the reasons, advantages, and implications of sedentary and nonsedentary ways of life. Thomas Barfield discusses the complex interaction between the Chinese empire and the Hsiung-nu confederacy on China's northern borders. Despite the Chinese view of their own unquestioned superiority, Barfield shows the considerable efforts of the Chinese administration to placate their northern neighbors. The biblical story of Jericho concerns a victory of nomads over city-dwellers, although no archaeological evidence for this tradition exists. Martin Hall describes the pastoral way of life of a southern African people, while Michael Coe discusses why the Maya practiced both sedentary and semisedentary agriculture. The final selection addresses the reasons why the hunter-gatherer culture of the Pacific Northwest was fully sedentary.

16   China and Northern Nomads

Thomas J. Barfield. "The Hsiung-nu Imperial Confederacy: Organization and Foreign Policy." *Journal of Asian Studies.* Vol. 41, No. 4 (November 1981). 45–63.

In this selection, Thomas Barfield examines the advantages of nomadic organization that allowed such societies to compete sucessfully with sedentary agriculturalists. The article discusses the Hsiung-nu, pastoral nomads who inhabited northern China from the third to the first century BCE and in the first centuries CE. Although conventional history tends to view culture as spread from centers of major civilizations, such as the river valley societies discussed in chapter three, Barfield argues that this theory is wrong. He argues that the broad economic and political changes that occurred within Hsiung-nu society were not copied from their imperial Chinese rivals.

This argument has a number of far-reaching implications for the understanding of nomadic states in Inner Asia. . . . The nomads did not "borrow" the state from their neighbors; rather, they were forced to develop their own peculiar form of state organization in order to deal effectively with their larger and more highly organized sedentary neighbors. These relations required a far higher level of organization than was necessary to handle livestock problems and political disputes within a nomadic society. It was no accident that . . . the most formally organized nomadic states emerged facing China, the world's largest and most complex traditional sedentary state. It was this relationship between China and the steppe [grasslands in northern China] that supported a state hierarchy among Inner Asian nomads. The nomadic state maintained itself by exploiting China's economy, and not by exploiting the production of scattered sheepherders who were effectively organized by the nomadic state to make this extortion possible. Therefore, it is not necessary to posit the development of class relations on the steppe to explain the existence of a state among nomads, nor was the nomadic state necessarily just the personal creation of a nomadic autocrat, doomed to disintegration at his death.

The Hsiung-nu empire is one of the best examples of a nomadic state supported by its relationship with China. Founded along China's northern frontier around 209 B.C. by the great conquests of Mo-tun, the Shan-yu (supra-tribal leader) of the Hsiung-nu tribe, it was contemporaneous with the establishment of the Han dynasty. The Hsiung-nu remained a political power on the Chinese frontier for more than 500 years; during the first 250 years, they completely dominated the steppe. . . . Researchers have shown that the Hsiung-nu economy was relatively complex, depending on trade, gifts or subsidies from China, and taxes from conquered areas, in addition to their own pastoral production. . . . The Hsiung-nu political organization was stable, and for the first 150 years its leadership passed peacefully, if not always without acrimony, through ten rulers. . . .

When the empire finally did fall into civil war in 57 B.C. the primary cause was a natural disaster that destroyed most of the Hsiung-nu livestock and helped produce an internal political crisis. . . .

• • •

The Hsiung-nu empire was brought into existence by conquest. It owed its continued survival and its ability to the role it played as intermediary between China and the tribes on the steppe. For this reason it was organized as an "imperial confederacy," autocratic and statelike in foreign affairs, but consultative and federally structured internally.

The Shan-yu and his court were the indigenous leaders of the Hsiung-nu core tribes, . . . thus . . . he could rely on consistent support from them. The indigenous leaders of the tribes incorporated into the empire by conquest or alliance were linked into the imperial administration under the control of one of the twenty-four imperial commanders, who acted as the Shan-yu's agents. Structurally, the weakest part of the system was the link between the leaders of the incorporated tribes and their imperial commanders. Although a leader of an incorporated tribe was part of the Hsiung-nu imperial hierarchy, he owed his power to the support of his own people and retained a great deal of autonomy at the local level. . . . Three possibilities were open to a dissatisfied tribal leader: to secede by moving to the west, to defect to China in the south, or to rebel.

• • •

In theory the Shan-yu could command complete obedience and impose any sanctions, but he was in fact constrained by the knowledge that the tribal kings were political actors in their own right and not his creations. For this reason the links between the tribes and the imperial government were more federal than autocratic.

• • •

These internal weaknesses forced the rulers of successful nomadic states to develop a more secure economic base. . . . The imperial government of the Hsiung-nu organized the nomadic tribes into a unified force that was used by the Shan-yu to extract goods and trade benefits from Han China. The Shan-yu retained the exclusive right to conduct foreign affairs and used this power to channel Chinese goods to the Hsiung-nu tribes. In time of war the Shan-yu organized raids that provided loot for both his followers and the Hsiung-nu state. In time of peace the Shan-yu acted as sole intermediary between China and the steppe, bringing trade and subsidies that could be redistributed throughout the state hierarchy. By drawing on resources from outside the steppe, the Hsiung-nu state gained a stability it could not otherwise have achieved.

In 201–200 B.C., the Hsiung-nu first came into conflict with the newly established Han dynasty in China. At that time the Hsiung-nu raided the frontier, and the ruler of T'ai province defected to them in rebellion against the central government. Fearful that his northern frontier might unravel, Emperor Kao-tsu (206–195) led the Han armies in person against the Hsiung-nu. The campaign ended in humiliating failure when Mo-tun surrounded Kao-tsu and his vanguard, a trap from which the emperor only narrowly escaped. Kao-tsu sent envoys to make peace with the Hsiung-nu, and he established the ho-ch'in policy as a framework for relations between the two states. . . . It had four major provisions: (1) The Chinese were to make annual payments of silk, wine, grain, and other foodstuffs to the Hsiung-nu; (2) the Han would give a princess in marriage to the Shan-yu; (3) the Hsiung-nu and the Han were to be ranked as coequal states; and (4) the Great Wall was to be the official boundary between the two states. . . .

From the perspective of the steppe, the Shan-yu was receiving tribute from China for which he merely promised to refrain from raiding the frontier. In fact the raids did not always stop. After a period of peace the frontier would suddenly be attacked, to be followed by a request for a new peace treaty with better terms for the Hsiung-nu, which included . . . a new demand for border markets.

[D]irect subsidies . . . could be used to entertain and reward the political elite of the empire. Once he achieved this goal, the Shan-yu then demanded that the Han court meet the needs of the regular nomads by permitting them to trade peacefully for Han products at border markets.

• • •

Legally these markets were restricted to the sale of goods that were of no military value to the Hsiung-nu, but they were also bases for smugglers who provided the nomads with restricted goods like iron.

• • •

In 133 B.C. Emperor Wu tried to solve China's Hsiung-nu problem once and for all by abandoning the Ho-ch'in policy in favor of an aggressive war policy.

• • •

Destroying the Hsiung-nu proved to be far more difficult than the Han court anticipated. In their many campaigns from 133 to 90 B.C., the Han won a number of tactical victories over the Hsiung-nu, forcing them to move their court to the northwest away from the Han frontier and to abandon many city states in Central Asia to Han control. However, these military campaigns were extremely expensive to the Han government in men, money, supplies, and horses. . . . In spite of Emperor Wu's best efforts, military action failed to break the power of the Shan-yu or the unity of the Hsiung-nu state.

• • •

Contrary to popular belief, the Hsiung-nu had no need or desire to conquer China, because their whole foreign policy was aimed at exploiting the Han state from a distance. Without the Chinese economy to exploit, there would have been no great Hsiung-nu state.

17 The Fall of Jericho

Joshua 6:1–26. *The Holy Bible*, Revised Standard Version. Grand Rapids, Mich.: Zondervan Bible Publishers, 1977.

Jericho is one of the oldest cities in the world with a continuous history dating back 8,000 years. The biblical account of the fall of the city of Jericho reveals the conflict that was often a part of interaction between nomadic peoples and city dwellers. After forty years of wandering in the desert, the twelve tribes of Israel, under the leadership of Joshua, successor to Moses, arrived in the land of Canaan. According to the Bible, they besieged, destroyed and looted the city of Jericho, preventing its reconstruction. Although, no evidence has been found in the archaeological record to support the biblical account of the fall of Jericho, this story provides valuable clues about the relationship between towns and nomadic peoples.

Now Jericho was shut up from within and from without because of the people of Israel: none went out, and none came in. And the Lord said to Joshua, "See, I have given into your hand Jericho, with its king and mighty men of valor. You shall march around the city, all the men of war going around the city once. Thus shall you do for six days. And seven priests shall bear seven trumpets of rams' horns before the ark; and on the seventh day you shall march around the city seven times, the priests blowing the trumpets. And when they make a long blast with the ram's horn, as soon as you hear the sound of the trumpet, then all the people shall shout with a great shout; and the wall of the city will fall down flat, and the people shall go up every man straight before him." So Joshua the son of Nun called the priests and said to them, "Take up the ark of the covenant, and let seven priests bear seven trumpets of rams' horns before the ark of the Lord." And he said to the people, "Go forward: march around the city, and let the armed men pass on before the ark of the Lord."

And as Joshua had commanded the people, the seven priests bearing the seven trumpets of rams' horns before the Lord went forward, blowing the trumpets, with the ark of the covenant of the Lord following them. And the armed men went before the priests who blew the trumpets, and the rear guard came after the ark, while the trumpets blew continually. But Joshua commanded the people, "You shall not shout or let your voice be heard, neither shall any word go out of your mouth until the day I bid you shout; then you shall shout." So he caused the ark of the Lord to compass the city, going about it once; and they came into the camp, and spent the night in the camp.

Then Joshua rose early in the morning, and the priests took up the ark of the Lord. And the seven priests bearing the seven trumpets of rams' horns before the ark of the Lord, while the trumpets blew continually. And the second day they marched around the city once, and returned into the camp. So they did for six days.

On the seventh day they rose early at the dawn of day, and marched around the city in the same manner seven times: it was only on that day that they marched around the city seven times. And at the seventh time, when the priests had blown the trumpets, Joshua said to the people, "Shout; for the Lord has given you the city. And the city and all that is within it shall be devoted to the Lord for destruction; only Rahab the harlot and all who are with her in her house shall live, because she hid the messengers that we sent. But you, keep yourselves from the things devoted to destruction, lest when you have devoted them you take any of the devoted things and make the camp of Israel a thing for destruction, and bring trouble upon it. But all silver and gold, and vessels of bronze and iron, are sacred to the Lord; they shall go into the treasury of the Lord." So the people shouted, and the trumpets were blown. As soon as the people heard the sound of the trumpet, the people raised a great shout, and the wall fell down flat, so that the people went up into the city, every man straight before him, and they took the city. Then they utterly destroyed all in the city, both men and women, young and old, oxen, sheep, and asses, with the edge of the sword.

And Joshua said to the two men who had spied out the land, "Go into the harlot's house, and bring out from it the woman, and all who belong to her, as you swore to her." So the young men who had been spies went in, and brought out Rahab, and her father and mother and brothers and all who belonged to her; and they brought all her kindred, and set them outside the camp of Israel. And they burned the city with fire, and all within it; only the silver and gold, and the vessels of bronze and of iron, they put into the treasury of the house of the Lord. But Rahab the harlot, and her father's household, and all who belonged to her, Joshua saved alive; and she dwelt in Israel to this day, because she hid the messengers whom Joshua sent to spy out Jericho.

Joshua laid an oath upon them at that time, saying, "Cursed before the Lord be the man that rises up and rebuilds this city, Jericho. At the cost of his first-born shall he lay its foundation, and at the cost of his youngest son shall he set up its gates."

18 The Khoikhoi in Southern Africa

Martin Hall. *Farmers, Kings, and Traders: The People of Southern Africa, 200–1860.* Chicago: University of Chicago Press, 1990. 58–60.

Nomadic pastoralism was practiced in southern Africa, where a people who called themselves the Khoikhoi herded livestock. In this excerpt, Martin Hall examines the relationship between nomadic pastoralists and their neighbors, some of whom were sedentary agriculturalists who also kept cattle, and others of whom were nomadic "gatherer-hunters." Hall asks a number of questions, including: How strict are the boundaries between these different methods of producing food resources? Were nomadic pastoralists always nomadic? As you will see, the absence of documentary sources for the centuries prior to the arrival of Europeans on the Cape coast does not hinder Hall who utilizes the rich archaeological research upon southern Africa to discuss the history of nomadic pastoralism from the second century CE to the nineteenth century.

Although the people who lived on the highveld and the grassland watersheds of the south-east depended heavily on their domestic livestock, they also grew crops: sorghum and, increasingly, maize, after its introduction by the Portuguese in the sixteenth or seventeenth centuries. Furthermore, although livestock were vital in the social and political networks that bound society together, it is probable that the harvest provided most of the food consumed. Consequently, although the high-veld farmers probably moved to outlying cattle posts to take advantage of seasonal grazing and . . . the people who lived on watersheds such as the Babanango plateau moved down into the valleys in the winter months, the perennial tasks of agriculture kept the population tied to one area for some time.

But in the western lands it was not possible to cultivate crop plants such as sorghum and maize, either because annual rainfall was too low and unpredictable or because the rains came in the winter months, preventing the propagation of the African cereal crops. These areas came to be used by nomadic pastoralists—descendants of the Tshu-khwe-speaking people. . . .

Although the bones of domestic sheep, as well as pottery, which many archaeologists consider to be a sure indicator of pastoralism, have now been found in many dated contexts in western and south-western Africa, the remains of actual settlements have been frustratingly difficult to find. The sheep whose bones have been found in rock shelter deposits could often have been the remains of hunters' kills, although the excavation of Boomplaas Cave, in the foothills of the southern Cape Swartberg, has shown accumulations of dung dated to about A.D. 250, suggesting that livestock were kept in the shelter when grazing in the nearby valley was optimal.

Andrew Smith has pointed out that the itinerant character of nomadic pastoralism, with shepherds moving frequently in search of pasture and rarely returning to the same place, would militate against the accumulation of substantial archaeological deposits. But in some areas there were specific resources which repeatedly attracted groups back to the same area, resulting in more substantial debris for the archaeologist to study.

One such area was the south-western coastland of St. Helena Bay. Here, from the second century A.D., herders camped many times. . . , collecting shellfish while their sheep and cattle grazed nearby. Another was far to the northeast, where herders built distinctive stone settlements on the lower reaches of the Riet River, a source of perennial water, between the sixteenth and nineteenth centuries. Other than these few settlements, the archaeological evidence for nomadic pastoralism is indirect: the changing settlement patterns of gatherer-hunters, perhaps reflecting their response to immigrant herders, and the efflorescence of rock painting in the mountains which, it has been suggested, may have been related to the social stress that gatherer-hunters underwent in adjusting to the changes that followed the introduction of food-producing [farming] into their world.

Fortunately, historical sources are richer than the archaeological evidence. Indeed, from the late fifteenth century, voyagers from Europe began to make landings on the western and southern Cape coasts, recording some details of their encounters with pastoralist communities, whom they called by the now-abusive name 'Hottentots', but who called themselves *Kwekwena* or *Khoikhoi*, according to dialect.

Although earlier writers described the Khoikhoi in the same terms that they would employ for the agro-pastoralist societies who lived in the east and southeast, observing towns, tribes and kings, Richard Elphick has pointed out that, in reality, political and social affiliations were more fluid than these terms imply. Thus the 'village' was mobile and unstable in composition, and was based on the kinship relations between its members rather than on any ownership of territory. Similarly, the larger groups were in a state of 'endemic flux', with 'tribes' splitting and reforming as affiliations changed.

Despite the distinctive way of life of these western nomadic pastoralists, it would be a mistake to see the Khoikhoi and their predecessors over almost two thousand years as completely separated from either the gatherer-hunters with whom they shared the western lands or the aero-pastoralists who made their living in the east. Recent comparative studies of nomadic pastoralists in many different parts of the world have shown that all such communities depend on at least occasional interaction with people practicing different economies in order to obtain essential commodities.

. . . [R]ather than a straightforward migration with the abrupt replacement of one way of life for another, the expanding frontier of food production represented a zone of interaction, in which gatherer-hunters were to develop a variety of economic interactions with pastoralists. . . . [Richard] Elphick and Carmel Schrire have also argued that there was additional economic flexibility, as herders were able to turn to gathering-hunting, and gatherer-hunters could obtain livestock, according to changing fortune. "Bushmen [gatherer-hunters] sometimes kept stock, and sometimes lost it, their subsistence depending on changing historical and environmental circumstances. They acted in a way that underscores the plasticity and opportunism of their socioeconomic behavior."

• • •

Whatever the nature of the relationship between herders and gatherer-hunters, there is evidence for long-distance connections between nomadic pastoralists and sedentary aero-pastoralists to the east. In this regard there are historical records of Khoikhoi trading cattle in return for dagga (a narcotic similar to hemp), iron and copper goods along trade routes that extended both eastwards and northwards, tracing back the routes of initial pastoralist dispersal. These contacts are reflected in the agricultural record as well, with a copper bead and bone that may have been cut with an iron blade found in the dung floors at Boomplaas Cave and fragments of copper artefacts from graves and enclosures once used by pastoralists on the Riet River. Such connections are common in other pastoralist societies, and were probably essential if herders were to obtain important commodities.

. . . . Rather than being separate, the highveld farmers and the nomadic pastoralists grazing their herds far to the west must seem as part of a single, interlocked system of food-producing—a 'division of labor' more than two distinct societies.

19 The Mayan Way of Life

Michael Coe. *The Maya.* New York: Thames and Hudson, 1987. 17–20, 46–47.

From at least 11,000 years ago, the Maya people have lived in what is now southern Mexico, Guatemala, and Honduras. Spanish explorers encountered their descendents in the sixteenth century, and Maya peoples still inhabit these areas today. Maya culture, social organization, and livelihood present a challenge to conventional definitions of city-dwellers and nomads. While they constructed permanent ceremonial centers, and possessed impressive astronomical and mathematical knowledge, the Maya were not completely sedentary. Maya farming combined raised, terraced fields with slash-and-burn agriculture in proportions that varied according to rainfall and soil quality of the areas they inhabited.

The lowland climate is hot, uncomfortably so toward the close of the dry season. In May come the rains, which last through October, but compared with other tropical regions of the world they are not especially abundant. In much of the Peten, for instance, only about 70–90 inches (178–229 cm) fall each year, and as one moves north to Yucatan there is a steady decrease from even this level. Nor is there total reliability in these rains, for in bad years there may be severe droughts. Really heavy precipitation is found in the far south of the Peten and Belize; in the Lacandon country of Chiapas; and in the Tabasco plains which are covered with great sheets of water during much of the summer and for that reason were largely shunned by the pre-Conquest Maya.

• • •

There is a rich fauna in the lowlands. Deer and peccary [wild pigs] abound, especially in Yucatan, which the Maya called "The Land of the Turkey and Deer." Spider monkeys and the diminutive but noisy howler monkeys are easy to hunt and well-favored in the native cuisine. Among the larger birds are the ocellated turkey, with it beautiful golden-green plumage, the currasow, and the guan. More dangerous beasts are the jaguar, largest of the world's spotted cats, which was pursued for its resplendent pelt, and the water-loving tapir, killed both for its meat and for an incredibly tough hide employed in making shields and armor for Maya warriors. Of more importance to the development of Maya civilization is the agricultural potential of the lowlands, which is by no means uniform.

While some of the soils of the Peten, for instance, are relatively deep and fertile, those of the Yucatan are the reverse. The sixteenth-century Franciscan bishop, Diego de Landa, our great authority on all aspects of Maya life, tells us that "Yucatan is the country with the least earth that I have seen, since all of it is one living rock and has wonderfully little earth." It is little wonder that the early Colonial chronicles speak much of famines in Yucatan before the arrival of the Spaniards, and it might be that the province relied less upon plant husbandry than upon its famed production of honey, salt, and slaves.

It is now almost universally recognized, albeit unwillingly, that many tropical soils which are permanently deprived of their forest cover quickly decline in fertility and become quite unworkable as a layer of brick-like laterite develops on the surface. Tropical rainfall and a fierce sun do their destructive work in a surprisingly brief span, and agricultural disaster results. On such soils about the only kind of farming possible is that practiced by the present-day lowland Maya—a shifting, slash-and-burn system under which the forest is permitted to regenerate at intervals. While seemingly simple, it requires great experience on the farmer's part. A patch of forest on well-drained land is chosen, and cut down in late autumn or early winter. The felled wood and brush are fired at the end of the dry season. . . . The maize seed is planted in holes poked through the ash with a . . . stick. Then the farmer must pray to the gods to bring the rain.

A milpa [temporary field] usually has a life of only 2 years, by which time decreasing yields no longer make it worthwhile to plant a third year. The Maya farmer must then shift to a new section of forest and begin again, leaving his old milpa fallow for periods which may be from 4 to 7 years in the Peten, and from 15 to 20 years in Yucatan. . . .

The long held notion that shifting cultivation was the only system of food production practiced by the ancient Maya has now been discarded . . . [since the finding of] raised fields[;] . . . these are narrow, rectangular plots elevated above the low-lying, seasonally inundated land bordering rivers.

• • •

And yet the claims that the Classic Maya were almost totally dependent upon the techniques of intensive maize agriculture are probably exaggerated through the understandable enthusiasm created by new finds. Much of the Maya lowland area is and was unsuitable for raised fields or for terracing, and it remains a certainty that most of the maize eaten by the pre-Conquest lowland Maya was grown in milpa plots by the still-used methods of shifting cultivation.

• • •

How are we to define the word "civilization"? How do the civilized differ from the barbaric? Archaeologists have usually dodged this question by offering lists of traits which they think to be important. Cities are one criterion. The late V.G. Childe thought that writing should be another, but the obviously advanced Inca of Peru were completely illiterate. Civilization, in fact, is different in degree rather than in kind from what precedes it, but has certainly been achieved by the time that state institutions, large-scale public works, temple buildings, and widespread, unified art styles have appeared. With few exceptions, the complex state apparatus demands some form of records, and writing has usually been the answer; so has the invention of a more-or-less accurate means of keeping time.

20 The Chinese Agricultural Calendar

The Book of Songs: The Ancient Chinese Classic of Poetry.
Translated by Arthur Waley. New York: Grove Press, 1987.
164–167, 244–246.

The following two excerpts are from *The Book of Songs,* a Chinese collections of poems, ballads, and orations that dates from the Zhou era, in the sixth century BCE. The passage is a song which describes the activities in a rural community during the year. The traditional calendar—referred to below in passages such as the "ninth" or "seventh" month—began in the spring. Yet the song also contains references to the Zhou calendar—as "in the days of the First" or "Second"—which began around the winter solstice. Thus, the first stanza traces events from late autumn through winter and early spring.

In the seventh month the Fire ebbs;
In the ninth month I hand out the coats.
In the days of the First, sharp frosts;
In the days of the Second, keen winds.
Without coats, without serge,
How should they finish the year?
In the days of the Third they plough;
In the days of the Fourth out I step
With my wife and children,
Bringing hampers to the southern acre
Where the field-hands come to take good cheer.

In the fourth month the milkwort is in spike,
In the fifth month the cicada cries.
In the eight month the harvest is gathered,
In the tenth month the boughs fall.
In the days of the first we hunt the raccoon,
And take those foxes and wild-cats
To make furs for our Lord.
In the days of the Second is the great Meet;
Practice for deeds of war.
The one year-old [boar] we keep;
The three year-old we offer to our Lord.

In the sixth month we eat wild plums and cherries,

In the seventh month we boil mallows and beans.
In the eighth month we dry the dates,
In the tenth month we take the rice
To make with it the spring wine,
So that we may be granted long life.
In the seventh month we eat melons,
In the eighth month we cut the gourds,
In the ninth month we take the seeding hemp,
We gather bitter herbs, we cut ailanto for firewood,
That our husbandmen may eat.

In the ninth month we make ready the stackyards,
In the tenth month we bring in the harvest,
Millet for wine, millet for cooking, the early and the late,
Paddy and hemp, beans and wheat.
Come, my husbandmen,
My harvesting is over,
Go up and begin your work in the house,
In the morning gather thatch-reeds,
In the evening twist rope;
Go quickly on to the roofs.
Soon you will be beginning to sow many grains.

In the days of the Second they cut the ice with tingling blows;
In the days of the Third they bring it into the cold shed.
In the days of the Fourth very early
They offer lambs and garlic.
In the ninth month are shrewd frosts;
In the tenth month they clear the stackgrounds.
With twin pitchers they hold the village feast,
Killing for it a young lamb.
Up they go into their lord's hall,
Raise the drinking-cup of the buffalo-horn:
'Hurray for our lord; may he live for ever and ever!'

21 Life in the Pacific Northwest

Herbert D.G. Maschner. "The Emergence of Cultural Complexity on the Northern Northwest Coast." *Antiquities.* Vol. 65 (1991). 924–931.

For over two thousand years, the Pacific Northwest coasts of Canada and the United States were the home of sedentary hunter-gatherer societies. Rather than moving periodically to exploit new areas and allow those left behind to recover, the proximity of salmon runs, flight paths of migratory birds, and the abundant plant and animal life of a temperate rain forest permitted settled life and presented the potential for greater population density. In the following selection, Herbert Maschner suggests that the need to ensure access to these resources gave rise to societies with defined class structures.

The northern Northwest Coast supported some of the most socially complex hunting and gathering societies on the Pacific Coast. The Tlingit, Haida and Tsimshian of this region share a rich ethnographic history that reveals hereditary social ranking, sedentary villages, intensive warfare, part-time craft specialization and dense population.

• • •

The northern Northwest Coast environment can be considered one of circumscribed abundance, for its dense resources were circumscribed both on the landscape and seasonally. . . . Five species of salmon, running from June through October, were present in millions in some mainland rivers and in hundreds of thousands in stream systems of the outer island. Herring spawned in hundreds of millions throughout the bays and fjords of the north coast, as did eulachon [a kind of fish] in the major rivers. Cod were extremely dense and were of primary importance in some regions. Halibut, the mainstay resource for the Haida, were a critical supplement for many Tlingit groups. . . . Sea mammals, particularly sea otter, harbour seal and sea lion, were important in all areas. Sitka black-tailed deer, black and brown bear and canids were the primary terrestrial species, with mountain goat and mountain sheep important on the mainland. This region is on the transcontinental flyway for the semi-annual migrations of waterfowl, and the intertidal zones are dense with numerous species of shellfish. In essence, the northern Northwest Coast environment may have been one of the richest landscapes ever encountered by hunters and gatherers.

• • •

An elaborate burial complex began in Prince Rupert Harbor [British Columbia, Canada] about 1000 BC. . . . Differential distributions of grave goods, which include copper, shell, and amber ornaments, may be indicative of status differences in some groups . . . analyses of various . . . skeletal remains show evidence of decapitation, depressed skull fractures and forearm parrying fractures, suggesting intense conflict and aggression.

House features . . . include superimposed hearth, floors of sand and gravel and an abundance of fire-cracked rock. Post moulds in the middens [garbage heaps] probably represent drying racks . . . fish weirs [a kind of fish trap] are found throughout southeast Alaska during the Middle phase (1500BC–AD500), as are large shell middens similar to the Prince Rupert Harbor sites.

• • •

[T]he development of large shell middens and the associated burial complex [occurred] after about 1000 BC. This probably represents the first development of small, seasonal or sometimes permanent villages. House remains are either small or ephemeral. Subsistence was probably based on a generalized strategy with seasonal storage of some species.

The last, and probably most significant, set of changes occurred after AD 500. The first of these changes is the formation of large sedentary villages . . . [;] the second addition is the construction of forts or defensive sites on bluffs or cliff edges. . . . The third change, the one probably responsible for the development of house depression villages and defensive sites, is the introduction of the bow and arrow to the Pacific coast of North America after AD 500. . . . Together these changes altered the entire organization of northern Northwest Coast society. Small villages congregated into large, sedentary communities with access to defensive locations. Permanent villages quickly depleted local shellfish beds, resulting in the patterns recognized in Prince Rupert Harbor as population stabilization. A greater emphasis was placed on the mass harvest of salmon, herring and other storable species.

. . .

I argue that the development of political complexity among the hunters and gatherers on the northern Northwest Coast is a function of several deeply integrated factors. The first is resource abundance and predictability. . . . It is absolutely necessary to assume that populations must reach a critical size and density in order for social ranking to develop. The second assumes that resources will be unevenly distributed in time and space, or environmentally circumscribed, causing groups to organize themselves around areas and periods of resource density. Areas of resource abundance on the north coast are differentially distributed on the landscape, with productive bays and fjords separated by large areas of relative paucity. . . . The third factor is social circumscription. At some point in time the landscape became sufficiently populated that conflicting factions in a specific bay or region could not fission and move to a different resource area, creating the opportunity for resource and political control. . . . The last requirement, based on human psychology, is founded in what [Marshall] Sahlins termed the "hierarchic strivings" present in higher primates. . . . I would argue that in all societies some individuals strive for status and political advantage, a striving that will lead to differential economic, political and reproductive success.

When all of these conditions are met, leaders will arise from the largest lineages or kin groups. On the Northwest Coast, these leaders were able to control access to quality resources locales; the rewards were high status, greater access to symbols of prestige and access to high-quality mates from other high-status families. Political complexity will arise in all situations when these conditions are met.

DISCUSSION QUESTIONS

1. What factors determine whether a society will be sedentary, semisedentary, or nomadic? Are intermediate or transitional ways of life, incorporating more than one of these patterns, possible? What effects does a nomadic or a sedentary way of life have on the political and social organization of a society?

2. What patterns of contact occur among societies with divergent organizations and ways of life? What factors seem important in determining the shape of relations (such as trading, diplomacy, raiding, war) between states?

3. From the readings, what seem to be the differences between societies defined as "states" and those defined as stateless, also sometimes called peoples or "tribes"? Do you think these distinctions are valid? Why or why not?

4. What is daily life like for ordinary people in agricultural societies compared to their counterparts in hunter/gatherer societies? What are the advantages and disadvantages of the lifestyle of each?

5. How would you define terms like "civilized" and "civilization"? How important are traits like a written language, cities, or the use of the wheel? Is it possible to define these terms in ways that incorporate people's beliefs about themselves, and their relationship to the world? Or, are the terms "civilized" and "civilization" too burdened by the way they have been used in the past to be of any use in the future?

Chapter 5

Empires in the Classical World

*T*he empires of the classical world grew on the foundations of river valley civilizations. They differed from those societies because they were larger and incorporated a wider variety of peoples and cultures than the river valley societies of an earlier period. Each empire you will study had remarkably complex relations with its neighbors: sometimes these relations were characterized by mutual cooperation and other times by conflict. These empires not only incorporated numerous cultures into their own but also had extensive trade and religious contacts with diverse peoples outside their spheres of political influence.

Often—although not always—empires expanded through conquest. In the first excerpt below, you will read *The Ramayana,* an epic that depicts the conquest of the Indian subcontinent from the northwest by the Aryans. The second selection is drawn from the *Iliad,* an epic poem by Homer about the war between Greece and Troy. The poem is part of an oral tradition meant to be read aloud, and thus demonstrates the importance of such works within Greek culture. In the third selection, the Roman historian Livy recounts the military campaigns of the Carthaginian ruler Hannibal, who fought a series of battles on the doorsteps of the Roman Empire. In the fifth and sixth excerpts, you will read documents on the growth and expansion of the Chinese empire, including the demise of the Xin dynasty due to an agrarian revolt, and relations on the Chinese frontier recorded in *The Chronicle of Fu Chien.*

In most accounts of imperial expansion, chroniclers memorialized the actions of emperors and military leaders. In each of these excerpts, you can see what qualities rulers were supposed to possess: you will also notice that these qualities vary in different societies. Another pattern in these accounts is the belief of imperial rulers that their own society represented all that was "civilized" in the world. Not surprisingly, peoples living on the fringe of established empires were often seen as "barbarians." For example, the Roman chronicler Livy refers to Hannibal's Gallic [French] allies as barbarians, but not to Hannibal himself because he came from the Carthaginian empire in North Africa.

What role do empires play in world history? Perhaps the greatest role was shaping the way we think about history itself. Until recently, the early history of the world was seen exclusively through archaeological artifacts and written records left by the empires of the Mediterranean (Greece and Rome especially). Over time, Asian scholars identified parallels between the Mediterranean experience and that of both Aryan India and the Chinese dynasties. Yet because of the reliance on written records, historians have overlooked empires that either lacked a written language, as in the case of the Huari-Tiahuanaco civilizations in the Americas, or whose records have not yet been deciphered, as in the case of the Kushitic empires of Meroe and Axum. However, even literate cultures maintained a place for oral traditions. The epics of Homer, though written down eventually, were meant to be performed. Empires, because of their size and power, played important roles in determining what people did, what they believed, and how they understood their world. Although this influence diminished as one moved further away from the center of the empire, empires nevertheless played an important part in human history.

22 The Aryan Conquests of India

R. K. Narayan. *The Ramayana*. New York: Viking Press, 1972. 107–113.

The Ramayana is an epic from India that dates from the fourth century BCE. It recounts the exile of Rama, the future ruler of the kingdom of Ayodhya, until his final battle with his archenemy, the demon Ravana. In the selection below, Rama intervenes in a fraternal quarrel, and mortally wounds Vali, the ruler of the monkey people. In the selection below, the dying Vali questions Rama about the morality of his act. Many scholars believe that the Ramayana describes part of the Aryan conquest of Lanka (led by Ravana in the epic), and neighboring Kishkindha (who are represented by Vali, his brother Sugreeva, and the monkey people). Geographically, the epic describes events in what is today southern India and the island nation of Sri Lanka.

Rama drew an arrow elegantly from his quiver, poised it on the bow-string, and let it go. It sped along and pierced Vali's chest like a needle passing through a fruit.

Overcome with astonishment, Vali paused for a moment to take stock of the situation. His grip around his brother's neck relaxed involuntarily. With one hand he had held on to the arrow's shaft and arrested its passage through his chest. Now he clung to it with his hands, his feet, and the coils of his tail, and broke and retarded its motion with such stubborn strength that even Yama, the god of death, stood back, nodding his head in admiration.

Vali had never thought, even as a possibility, that there was any power on earth or in the heavens which could subdue him with any weapon or stand up before him in a fight. All this was an accepted fact, but here he was like a miserable worm, not even able to understand what it was that had laid him low. Could it be the "Trisula" of Shiva or could it be the "Chakra" of Vishnu or Indra's "Vajrayudha"? He laughed ironically. At the same moment he felt an admiration for his unknown assailant. Who could it be? he speculated, forgetting his pain. He was invulnerable according to the promise of the gods, yet here was the reality, the arrow in his heart. He laughed bitterly at the cocksureness of these years; what could it be, who could it be? Why speculate? Let me find out. So saying he exercised all his remaining strength in pulling the arrow from his chest, to look at the mark on its handle. The might of Vali was applauded by the gods watching from high heavens, as he succeeded in drawing out the shaft. Blood gushed from the wound like a spring. At the sight of it, Sugreeva was grief-stricken and wept aloud. He forgot his animosity. With his ebbing strength, Vali held the arrow close to his eyes and spelt the name "Rama" engraved on it. Vali looked at the name on the arrow and almost was blinded with shock. The shock of the physical injury was not so agonizing as the spiritual shock of reading the name of Rama on the arrow. He looked at it and brooded over his own recklessness in castigating his wife for mentioning Rama's name. That poor creature showed better judgement than he.

"Rama, the Lord of culture, breeding, discrimination, and justice. How could you do this? You have destroyed the firm basis of your own virtues. Is it because of the separation from your wife [Sita] that you have lost all sense of fairness and act recklessly? If some demon like Ravana has acted treacherously, is that any justification for you to come here, slaughter the head of a monkey clan, entirely unconnected with the affair? Has your code of ethics taught you only this? What mistake have you seen in me, young man, that you should destroy me thus? Who will wear the badge of virtue in this world or others, when you have thrown it away so lightly? Is the foretaste of the *yuga* of *Kali*° to be had only by us, the creatures who crawl and are called monkeys? So, Kind One, are virtues intended to be practiced only on weaker creatures? When strong men commit crimes, they become heroic deeds? Oh, incomparable one, the treasure and kingdom given to you, you handed over to the younger brother. That you performed in the city; do you wish to repeat a similar act in these forests too by depriving an older brother of his life and kingdom? When two persons are opposed to each other, how can you in support of one, hide and attack the other? What you have done to me is not heroic or an act conducted within the laws of warfare. Surely, you do not consider me a burden on this weighty earth nor are you my enemy. Pray, tell me what drove you to this terrible decision? Ravana entrapped your wife and carried her off. To redeem her and to wreak your vengeance on him, you probably seek the support of Sugreeva, which is like courting a rabbit, when you can summon a lion to serve you. Pray what judgement is this? A word from you and I'd have plucked Ravana from his citadel and flung him at your feet.

°In the yuga of Kali, a period far in the future, the editor states that, "righteousness, virtue, and goodness completely disappear" and "Anger, distress, hunger, and fear prevail. . . ."

"You have done a thing which has ended my life. If someone has carried away your wife, instead of battling with him face to face, you stand aside, hide, and use all your accomplishment as an archer against an unarmed stranger. Has all your training as warrior been only for this end? Creatures like us test our worth and strength with our sinews and muscles and always fight barehanded, and never hold a weapon as you do."

Rama softly came out of his hiding, approached the dying Vali, and said with the utmost calmness, "When you disappeared into the subterranean world pursuing Mayavi, your brother waited in anxiety for a very long time, and then on a sudden resolve, started to follow your path into the tunnel since he feared that you might need help. But he was held back by the army chiefs and advisers in your court, who pressed him to rule as a trustee for the time being. But the moment you came back, you misunderstood everything and before he could even express his relief and joy on seeing you, you belaboured him mercilessly in the presence of others and attempted to take his life. When he still struggled to explain and sought your pardon for any mistake on his part, you rejected his appeal. And then after fully realizing that he had committed no wrong, you let your temper carry you on and on; you could afford, through your sense of power, to indulge your anger luxuriously, however unwarranted; and you assaulted and pursued him with the intention of killing him. After he fled, you left him alone, not because he had admitted his error and sought your pardon and asylum, and not even because it was wrong to pursue one whose back is turned in flight, not because he was your brother, but only because you dare not step on Matanga's Hill [where Sugreeva had fled]—merely self-preservation. And you bided your time. Even now you would have squeezed his life out but for my arrow. Beyond all this, you violated his wife's honor and made her your own. Guarding a woman's honor is the first duty laid on any intelligent being. But because you are conscious of your limitless strength, you act dishonorably and carry it off without any compunction as you feel no one can question you. You are well versed in the laws of conduct and morality and yet instead of affording protection to a helpless woman, life partner of a brother at that, you have molested her.

"Since Sugreeva sought my friendship and asked for help, I felt it my duty to help him by destroying you."

Vali replied, "You are judging us all wrongly, your basis is mistaken. You make too much of my acquiring my brother's wife. It's legitimate in our society. Although my brother was an enemy, I wanted to protect and help his wife while he was gone. I could not leave her to her fate."

"It is my primary duty to help the weak and destroy evil wherever I see it. Whether known or unknown, I help those that seek my help."

Vali replied, "Marriage and all its restraints on the relationship of men and women are of your human society and not known to us. Brahma has decreed for us absolute freedom in our sexual pursuits, habits, and life. In our society there is no such thing as wedlock. We are not a human society, we are monkeys and your laws and ethical codes are not applicable to us."

"I am not misled either by your explanation or appearance of being a monkey," Rama said. "I am aware that you are begotten by the chief of gods. You possess enough intelligence to know right from wrong and to argue your case even at this stage. You are fully aware of the eternal verities [truths]. You have erred and know it and how can you say now you are innocent? Could Gajendra, who prayed for Vishnu's help when a crocodile held him in its jaws, be classed as an ordinary elephant? Could Jatayu be called a common bird? An ordinary animal has no discrimination between right and wrong. But you display in your speech deep knowledge of life's values. Creatures in human shape may be called animals but if they display profundity cease to be animals and will have to be judged by the highest standards. There can be no escape from it. It was through your steadfast meditation and prayer to Shiva that you were endowed with strength superior to even the five elements. One who is capable of such achievement cannot but be judged by the highest standards of conduct."

"Very well," said Vali," I'll accept what you say; but how could you, protector of all creatures, aim your shaft from your hiding place, like some mean hunter tracking a wild beast, instead of facing me in a fight—if you felt that I deserved that honor?"

Lakshmana [Rama's brother and companion] gave the answer. "Rama had made a vow to support your brother Sugreeva when he came seeking refuge. This was a prior promise and had to be fulfilled, while if Rama had come before you face to face you might have made a similar appeal, which would have created confusion of purpose. That's the reason why he shot unseen by you."

Vali saw the inner purport of this explanation and said, "Now I understand your words differently from the way they sound. They are simple to hear but have inner strength and I feel assured that Rama has not committed an unrighteous act. Simpleminded ones like me can never realize eternal truths without constantly blundering and failing. Pray, forgive my errors and my rude speech. Instead of treating me as a mere monkey by birth, as I myself was content to think, you have elevated my status, and honoured me. After piercing my body with your arrow, and when I am about to die—you are touching my understanding with a supreme illumination, which I consider the greatest blessing ever conferred on me. In spite of my obstinacy you have helped me attain a profound understanding and opened my mind with your magic. While other gods confer boons after being asked, you confer them on the mere utterance of your name. Great sages have attempted, after aeons of austerities, to obtain a vision of God, but you have bestowed it on me unasked. I feel proud and happy at this moment. I have only one request. I hope my brother will prove worthy of your trust in him. But at any time if any weakness seizes him and you find him in the wrong, please do not send your arrow in his direction. Treat him kindly.

"Another thing. If your brothers, at any time, blame Sugreeva as one who had engineered the death of his brother, please explain to them that Sugreeva has only engineered my salvation."

23 War Between City-States

Homer. *The Iliad*. Translated by S. O. Andrew and M. J. Oakley. London: Everyman's Library, 1963. 90–95.

Little is known about the poet Homer, although some of the best known works of Greek literature, *The Iliad* and *The Odyssey*, are attributed to him.

He lived sometime between the seventh and the twelfth centuries BCE, likely in the city of Chios or Smyrna. According to tradition, he was blind. *The Iliad* and *The Odyssey* are epic poems: *The Iliad* recounts the war between Greece and Troy, while *The Odyssey* focuses on the homecoming of Odysseus, one of the war's heroes.

Although the poems are considered literature, they were actually oral traditions, memorized and performed orally, and probably written down well after the original date of their composition. Their great length has led some critics to suggest that Homer's poems were actually compilations of others' works. Although it is possible that both works were composed by one author, this hypothesis emphasizes the rich tradition of oral literature within Greece.

In the first excerpt below, the women of Troy, led by Hecuba, mother of the warrior Hector, ask the goddess Athena to grant their city victory in the war. In the second, Hector, before going off to fight on the Trojan side, bids farewell to his wife and child.

Then bright-plum's Hector spake . . .
"Lady mother . . .
Go thou to the shrine
Of Athena, driver of spoil; take offerings with thee,
Assembling the aged wives, and the robe thou accountest most graceful and large
of those in thy hall, and the dearest
To thine own self; on the knees of fair-hair'd Athena
Lay it, and vow thou wilt offer her there in her shrine
Twelve yearling kine that have toil'd not, if she will but pity
Troy town and the Trojan wives and their little children . . .

• • •

Then with wailing cries all [women] lifted their hands to Athena;
Then took the fair-cheeked Theano [Athena's priestess] the border'd robe
And upon the knees of the fair-hair'd Athena she laid it.
And with prayer besought the daughter of mighty Zeus;
"O Lady Athena, who keepest guard on our city,
Fairest of Goddesses, break now this Diomed's spear;
Made him headlong to fall in front of the Scaean gates
That we twelve yearling kine that never have toil'd
May sacrifice in they shrine, if thou wilt but pity
Troy town and the Trojan wives and their little children."

• • •

Away went bright-plum'd Hector, and came
With speed to his well-builded house; but there in his halls
He found not white-arm'd Andromache. She with her child
And a serving-woman clad in a beauteous robe,
Weeping and wailing had taken her stand on the wall,
So Hector, not finding his peerless wife within doors,
Went and stood on the threshold . . .
He came to the gate . . .
Andromache came to his side

And she clasp'd his hand in her own and spake to him thus:
"Dear heart, this valour of thine will be thy undoing.
No pity thou hast for thy little one her, nor for me, Poor wretch that I am, and
that soon thy widow shall be. . . .
Then Hector the great . . . spake to her thus:
"I were strangely asham'd
The Trojans to meet, and their wives in their trailing robes,
If here like a coward I skulked aloof from the fray.
My own heart will not let me; for aye have I learn'd
To be brave, and amid the foremost Trojans to fight,
In quest of my father's great glory and eke of mine own."

24 The Kingdom of Meroe

Basil Davidson. *Africa in History,* revised and expanded edition.
New York: Collier Books, 1966. 39–43.

The Egypt of the pharoahs was not the only empire situated along the Nile
River. In the south, another society called Kush thrived with its own distinct
culture. The rulers of Kush were for a time pharoahs of Egypt as well. In the
passage below, scholar Basil Davidson looks at the legacy of Meroe, a city-
state that became the center of Kush because of its access to iron ore in the
sixth century BCE. Unlike northern Egypt which had ties to the Mediterranean,
Meroe was linked by trade and culture to eastern Africa and the Indian Ocean.

The effects of iron-working upon Kushite civilization, basically a riverain farming
culture, can as yet be gauged only by inference. About a hundred years after their
retirement from Egypt, a new center of Kushite civilization emerged at one of
their southern cities, Meroe, lying about one hundred miles north of Khartoum,
although not for another two hundred years would [the city of] Napata lose its old
importance. Gradually, however, the weight of political and economic interest
shifted southward. Detectable reasons for this include the continuing desiccation
of the Napatan region and its consequent shortage of timber and pasture. Perhaps
Persian and other military pressure from the north, during the sixth century BC,
may have had something to do with the move. There is also the suggestive fact
that the region of Meroe, unlike that of Napata, has large deposits of good iron-
bearing ore; and this was a period in which the demand for iron was spreading
steadily. Within some three hundred years of the southward move, the metalwork-
ers of Meroe had in fact turned their city in to what appears, by the archaeological
evidence, to have been an important iron-founding center.

Whatever the precise reason for the southward move may have been, they
were accompanied by a growing anti-Egyptian reaction among the Kushites of the
towns. . . . Its gods and rituals were primarily those of Meroe, not Egypt. While

good Egyptian hieroglyphics continued to be used in temple inscriptions, the Kushites now began writing their own language in an alphabetic script which has yet to be understood. The fine painting of pottery reached a new excellence and the styles used were largely Kushite. Meroe became very much a civilization in its own right; and this civilization was one of considerable depth and range of culture.

The history of Meroitic Kush covers at least six centuries of energetic and often quite distinctive development in many fields, especially those of town and temple building, metal manufacture, and the elaboration of international trade with countries as remote as India and beyond. [I]mportant excavations [in] 1968–72, digging into residential quarters outside the walls of the royal buildings at Meroe, indicate a first major settlement there around 600 BC, which was considerably earlier than expected. This early date suggests rather clearly that Kushite culture had taken an early urban form, far towards the south, even during the imperial period of Napata or very soon afterwards; and this, in turn, was then confirmed by Hintze's excavations at Musawarat as-Safra, not far from Meroe, where the earliest buildings, there mainly religious in kind, also appear to date from the sixth century BC. What we are confronted with, in short, is a culture of great historical depth even before its major development at Meroe in the fourth century.

At any rate from the fourth century BC, there unfolded here a far-reaching process of inventive development whose influence on neighboring African lands is yet to be traced, but upon existing evidence was probably important. From Meroitic Kush the caravan trails went eastward to the ports of the Red Sea—to 'Aidhab, for example, still to be fully explored archaeologically—and links with the Indian Ocean trade; northward to Greek-ruled and then Roman-ruled Egypt and links with southern Europe; and south-eastward into the mountains of Ethiopia, and, at least after AD 100 or thereabouts, to the empire of Axum. There is much to suggest that other trails may have led westward towards the Niger.

Like some other geographically remote civilizations of antiquity, Kush was forgotten by a later world. There is a stray reference in the Book of Kings to the Pharaoh Taharqa (fifth of the Kushite dynasty), and another in the Acts of the Apostles to an envoy of the queen of the Ethiopians (that is, of the Kushites of Meroe) who was converted by one of Christ's apostles on the road that 'goeth down from Jerusalem to Gaza'. But misleading use of the Greek term 'Ethiopian', together with a general indifference to the historical claims of Africa, tends to sink the Kushites deep within a sea of scholarly indifference. Even when the nineteenth century brought a new interest in ancient civilizations, the early travellers and excavators were understandably dazzled by their brilliant discoveries in Egypt; and Kush was generally regarded, insofar as it was thought about at all, as no more interesting than a provincial poor relation.

The last seventy years, but above all the last twenty years, have wrought a change in this. Much remains to be understood about the Kushites of Meroe and their highly specific civilization, but enough is already clear to frame a picture of extraordinary diversity, creative skill and technological success. They combined a stubborn attachment to their own traditions with the speculative and syncretic approach to new ideas and fashions that may be characteristic of all trading cultures. Their temples and palaces owed a great deal to Egyptian examples, but nonetheless had styles and ornaments that were purely Meroitic. Much of their religion, like their alphabetical script and the best of their pottery, was all their own. Yet they had always welcomed innovation, and they continued to do so. As time went by, and the Ptolemaic Greek rulers of Egypt were displaced by the Romans, and trade across the Indian Ocean grew with greater skills in using the monsoon winds, the Kushites of Meroe and its sister-cities borrowed repeatedly from their neighbors and trading partners. One or two of their later buildings remind one of Syrian Palmyra. Not a few of their copper vessels seem to have been Chinese imports or at least to reflect Chinese styles. There is a Greek air about some of their art, while their four-armed lion-god Apedemak would look almost at home in an Indian temple. Yet the total effect remains powerfully distinctive and specific.

The high period of this civilization lay in the five centuries after the reign of Nastasen, whose period appears to have initiated or at any rate crystallized that profound cultural reaction against Egyptian ways and customs which led to many of the best achievements of Meroitic art and thought. Nastasen's exact dates are still contested, but he certainly ruled for about twenty years in the first half of the fourth century BC. It was not long afterwards, and perhaps under Arnekhamani (*c.* 235–18 BC) who built the Lion Temple at Musawarat al-Safra, that the priests and traders of Meroitic Kush appear to have begun to use their own cursive script, and pottery was painted with great beauty. By this time, too, Meroitic iron-using manufacture was getting into its stride, while Meroitic political and military power reached far to the south and west, eastward to the Red Sea, and northward beyond Napata to the region of the first and second cataracts. By 200 BC Meroitic Kush had become a large and powerful empire, endowed with the means of far-ranging trade and the benefits it continued to enjoy until the fourth century, when nomad incursions and an invasion from the Tigrean kingdom of Axum combined to bring the achievements of Meroitic Kush to an end.

25 The Second Punic War

Livy in Fourteen Volumes. Translated by B. O. Foster. Cambridge, Mass., and London: Harvard University Press and William Heinemann Ltd., 1982. 61, 67–69, 75–81, 93–97, 103–105, 111–115, 133–139.

The First and Second Punic Wars between Rome and Carthage marked the beginnings of an extended Roman Empire. Carthage was a trading empire, ruling the western Mediterranean Sea and with mercantile connections as far away as Britain and into the interior of Africa. As Rome grew, conflict ensued over Carthaginian influence in Sicily. Rome was victorious in the First Punic War (264–241 BCE), but over the following decades Carthage regained some of its lost wealth by conquering much of Iberia. In Spain, the new Carthaginian ruler, Hannibal, seized Saguntum, a city allied to Rome, as a prelude to an invasion of France.

From Saguntum, Hannibal's army and his allies crossed the Pyrenees Mountains, marched across present-day France, and then crossed the Alps into Italy. Between the years 218 and 203 BCE, Hannibal's army campaigned on the Italian peninsula, capturing towns but unable to capture fortified cities like Rome itself. The passages below cover some of the highlights between the fall of Saguntum and the successful crossing of the Alps. By any contemporary measure, Hannibal's accomplishments were extraordinary; although many know that Hannibal brought elephants from Africa for his campaigns, even in the cynical prose of the Roman historian Livy, the military accomplishments of the Carthaginian armies are astounding. Ironically, Carthage lost the Second Punic War as Roman forces seized territory in Spain and threatened to seize Carthage itself. The Carthaginians sued for peace in 203 BCE, and Hannibal returned to Carthage. At Zama in northern Africa in 202 BCE, Roman and Carthaginian armies fought a decisive battle that rendered Carthage powerless.

[The Roman consul] Publius Cornelius . . . after enrolling a new legion . . . , set out from the City [of Rome] with sixty ships of war, and coasting Etruria and the mountainous country of Liguria and the Salui, arrived at Massilia, and went into camp at the nearest mouth of the Rhone . . . hardly believing, even then, that Hannibal could have crossed the Pyrenees. But when he found that Hannibal was actually planning how to cross the Rhone, being uncertain where he should encounter him, and his soldiers not having as yet fully recovered from the tossing of the sea, he sent out a chosen band of three hundred cavalry . . . to make . . . a thorough reconnaissance, and have a look at the enemy from a safe distance.

Hannibal, having pacified the others [i.e., other Gauls] through fear or bribery, had now reached the territory of a powerful nation called the Volcae. They inhabit both banks of the Rhone, but doubting their ability to keep the Phoenician [Hannibal] from the western bank, they had brought nearly all their people over the Rhone, so as to have the river for a bulwark, and were holding the eastern bank with arms. The rest of the dwellers by the river, and such of Volcae themselves as had clung to their homes, were enticed by Hannibal's gifts to assemble large boats from every quarter and to fashion new ones; and indeed they themselves were eager to have the army set across as soon as possible and to relieve their district of the burden of so huge a horde of men. . . .

Everything was now in readiness for the crossing, which, however, was menaced by the enemy on the other side, who covered the whole bank with their horse and foot. In order to draw them off, Hannibal ordered Hanno, the son of Bomilcar, to set out in the first watch of the night with a part of the troops, chiefly Spaniards, and, making a march of one day up the stream, to take the first opportunity of crossing it, with the greatest secrecy, and fetch a compass with his column, so that, when the time came, he might assail the enemy in the rear. . . . They were tired by the night march and their strenuous exertions, but their commander allowed them but one day to rest, being intent on carrying out the stratagem at the proper time. Resuming their march on the following day they sent up a smoke-signal from an elevated place, to show that they had got over the river and were not far off. When

Hannibal saw this, he gave the order to cross, so as not to miss the favorable moment. The infantry had their skiffs all ready and equipped, while the cavalry had large boats, for the most part, on account of their horses. . . .

The Gauls [of Volcae] rushed to meet them on the bank, with all sorts of yells and their customary songs, clashing their shields together above their heads and brandishing darts in their right hands, despite the menace of so great a multitude of vessels coming against them and the loud roaring of the river and the confused hallooing of the boatmen and the sailors, as they strove to force their way athwart [across] the current or shouted encouragement to their fellows from the further bank. But the tribesmen were already somewhat daunted by the tumult which confronted them, when a still more appalling clamor arose in the rear, where Hanno had captured their camp. He was soon on the scene himself, and a twofold terror hemmed them in, as that mighty force of armed men came out upon the shore and the unlooked-for line of battle closed in from behind. When the Gauls had attempted charges in both directions and found themselves repulsed, they broke through where the way seemed least beset, and fled in confusion to their several villages. Hannibal brought over at leisure the rest of his forces, and giving himself no more concern over Gallic outbreaks, pitched his camp.

I believe that there were various plans for transporting the elephants [across the Rhone]; at all events the tradition varies as to how it was accomplished. Some say that the elephants were first assembled at the bank, and then the keeper of the fiercest of them provoked the beast and fled into the water; as he swam off, the elephant pursued him and drew the herd in his train; and though they were afraid of the deep water, yet as soon as each of them got out of his depth, the current swept him over to the other bank. It is, however, more generally believed that they were carried across on rafts. . . .

. . .

Publius Cornelius the consul, some three days after Hannibal had left the bank of the Rhone, marched in fighting order to the enemy's camp, intending to offer battle without delay. But finding the works deserted, and perceiving that he could not readily overtake the enemy, who had got so long a start of him, he returned to sea, where he had left his ships, thinking that he would thus be more safely and easily enabled to confront Hannibal as he descended from the Alps. . . .

Hannibal . . . reached the Alps without being molested by the Gauls who inhabited those regions. As their column began to mount the first slopes, mountaineers were discovered posted on the heights above, who, had they lain concealed in hidden valleys, might have sprung out suddenly and attacked them with great rout and slaughter. . . . He . . . employed Gauls, whose speech and customs did not differ greatly from those of the mountaineers, to mingle in their councils, and in this way learned that his enemies guarded the pass only by day, and at night dispersed, every man to his own home. As soon as it was light, he advanced up the hills, as though he hoped to rush the defile by an open attack in the daytime. Then having spent the day in feigning a purpose other than his real one, he entrenched a camp on the spot where he had halted. But no sooner did he perceive that the mountaineers had dispersed from the heights and relaxed their vigilance, than, leaving for show more fires than the numbers of those who remained in camp demanded . . . , he put himself at the head of some light-armed soldiers—all his bravest men—and, marching swiftly to the head of the defile, occupied those very heights which the enemy had held.

. . .

For two days they lay encamped on the summit. . . . The ground was everywhere covered deep with snow when at dawn they began to march, and as the column moved slowly on, dejection and despair were to be read in every countenance. Then Hannibal, who had gone on before the standards, made the army halt on a certain promontory which commanded an extensive prospect, and pointing out Italy to them, and just under the Alps the plains about the Po, he told them that they were now scaling the ramparts not only of Italy, but of Rome itself; the rest of the way would be level or downhill; and after one, or at most two battles, they would have in their hands and in their power the citadel and capital of Italy.

26 The Fall of the Xin (Ch'in) Dynasty

"Han shu, The History of the Former Han Dynasty." In *Sources of Chinese Tradition*, eds. Wm. Theodore de Bary et al. New York: Columbia University Press, 1960. 169–70.

While the Xin (Ch'in) Dynasty brought centralized rule to China between 221 and 207 BCE, the cost of that rule was despotic control of the people. After a series of revolts, many of them led by ordinary people like the agricultural laborer Ch'en She, the Xin Dynasty fell and was replaced by the Han Dynasty. The first Han Dynasty emperor, Liu Chu, was not from the nobility either, but managed to establish an empire that stretched for four hundred years between 202 BCE and 220 CE. The selection below, "The Rebellion of Ch'en She and Wu Kuang," is taken from *Han shu, the History of the Former Han Dynasty*, compiled in the first century CE.

THE REBELLION OF CH'EN SHE AND WU KUANG

When Ch'en She was young he was one day working in the fields with the other hired men. Suddenly he stopped his plowing and went and stood on a hillock, wearing a look of profound discontent. After a long while he announced: "If I become rich and famous, I will not forget the rest of you!"

The other farm hands laughed and answered: "You are nothing but a hired laborer. How could you ever become rich and famous?"

Ch'en She gave a great sigh. "Oh well," he said, "how could you little sparrows be expected to understand the ambitions of a swan!"

In the 7th month of the first year of the reign of the Second Emperor [209 BCE] the poor people of the village were sent to garrison Yü-yang, a force of nine hundred men. But when they got as far as the district of the Great Swamp in Ch'i, they encountered heavy rain and the road became impassable so that it was evident that they would not reach their destination on time. According to law, men who failed to arrive at the appointed time were executed. Ch'en She and Wu Kuang plotted together, saying, "If we try to run away we will die, and if we start a revolt we will likewise die. Since we die in either case, would it not be better to die fighting for a 'kingdom?'". . . . When the officer in command of the group was drunk, Wu Kuang made a point of openly announcing several times that he was going to run away. In this way, Wu Kuang hoped to arouse the commander's anger, to get him to punish him, and so stir up the men's ire and resentment. As Wu Kuang had expected, the commander began to beat him, when his sword slipped out of his scabbard. Wu Kuang sprang up, seized the sword, and killed the commander. Ch'en She rushed to his assistance and they proceeded to kill the other commanding officers as well. Then they called together all the men of the group and announced: "Because of the rain we encountered, we cannot reach our rendezvous on time. And anyone who misses a rendezvous has his head cut off! Even if you should somehow escape with your heads, six or seven out of every ten of you are bound to die in the course of garrison duty. Now, my brave fellows, if you are unwilling to die, we have nothing more to say. But if you would risk death, then let us risk it for the sake of fame and glory. Kings and nobles, generals and ministers— such men are made, not born!" The men all answered, "We are with you!"

27 Imperial Rule in Northern China

The Chronicle of Fu Chien: A Case of Exemplar History.
Translated by Michael C. Rogers. Berkeley, Calif.: University of California Press, 1968. 118–123.

This fourth-century chronicle recounts the life and exploits of Fu-Chien, a ruler in fourth-century northern China. Of Tibetan roots, he unified much of the area through conquest. Like all feudal rulers, he demanded tribute, or taxes, from the people to provide support for his government and military campaigns.

At that time the Hsiung-nu Worthy King of the Left,° Liu Wei-ch'en, sent an envoy to declare his submission to Chien and then requested land in the inner territory. Chien permitted this, but the General of the Yun-chung Protecting Army, Chia

---

°The Kings of the Left and Right are Hsiung-nu titles awarded during the Han dynasty, third to first century BCE. The titleholders are second only to the supreme leader of the Hsiung-nu and Shan-yu.

Yung, sent his Marshal Hsu Pin to lead cavalry and raid them, and Hsu Pin accordingly gave his troops free rein to forage and plunder. Chien was angry and said: I cannot forget great trust for the sake of small profit just when I am practicing Wei Chuang's stratagem for reconciling the western barbarians. Of old, the matter of the war between Chin and Wu began with women raising silkworms,° and then, by his kindness in watering melons,† Sung Ch'iu of Liang put a stop to the hostilities. . . . Stirring up the frontier and setting the hosts in motion is not advantageous to the state. The property and products which were captured shall be entirely restored." He deprived Chia Yung of his office and had him command the Protecting Army in the clothes of a commoner. He sent a commissioner to arrange a reconciliation and to show his faith and fealty. Liu Wei-ch'en thereupon entered and settled within the barriers, and his offerings of tribute followed in regular succession.

Tu-ku of the Wu-huan and Moiyu of the Hsien-pei, leading hosts of several myriads, also submitted to Chien. Chien at first wanted to settle them within the barriers. Fu Jung held that Hsiung-nu were a scourge whose rise dated from antiquity and that the reason the northern caitiffs [cowards] did not dare to turn their horses' heads to the south was that they dreaded the majesty [of the Chinese]. If now Fu Chien settled them in the inner territory, he would reveal its weaknesses; then they would surely spy out the military situation in the commanderies and prefectures and become an affliction to the northern frontiers. It would be better (he held) to move them outside the barriers, in order to maintain the fealty of the Desert Domain.°° Chien complied with this.

· · ·

Chien widely constructed houses of study and summoned scholars of the commanderies and kingdoms who were versed in one or more classics to fill them. The sons and grandsons of all from the dukes and ministers down were sent together to receive instruction. Those who had the learning to become Accomplished Scholars, whose talents could sustain responsibility for affairs, who acted from pure motives and were incorrupt and upright, who were filial and fraternal and were vigorous cultivators—upon all these he conferred standards of distinction. Thereupon people devoted themselves to urging and stimulating each other. . . . Robbery and brigandage came to a halt, and the route of petition for special favors was cut off. The fields were cultivated and reclamation practiced. The treasury was filled to capacity, and of the ceremonial paraphernalia [prescribed by] the canons and statutes there was nothing that was not completely provided. . . .

Chang Wang, the T'u-ko, having gathered a host of several thousands, called himself Great Shan-yu and invaded and plundered the commanderies and prefectures. Chien made his Secretary Teng Ch'iang General Establishing Fortitude and had him lead a host of seven thousand to chastise and pacify him. At that time merchants like Chao To, Ting Fei, and Tsou P'en all accumulated gold in their houses

---

°A reference to a sixth-century BCE war that began with a dispute among individuals and spread to governmental levels.

†This war ended when troops of one side watered the melon patches of the other side as a gesture of reconciliation.

°°The outermost frontiers of the Chinese state.

by the thousands of pieces. The plenitude [abundance] of their carriages and vestments mimicked the standards of the princes and marquises, and Chien's dukes competed in inducing them to become ministers° of their domains. The Squire-attendant of the Yellow Gate Ch'eng Hsien said to Chien, "Chao To and his like are all rude lackeys of traffickers, petty men of the market place, yet in carriages and houses, clothing and vestments, they usurp identity with the prices; they hold office on a par with gentlemen and become ranking ministers of the buffer states. They injure our mores and defeat our customs. When there is a defilement of the sacred culture, you should sternly clarify the canons and laws so that the clear and the muddy are manifestly distinct." Chien thereupon investigated. As for those who had induced To and his like to become ministers of their domains, he reduced their rank of nobility. Then he handed down regulations: those not commissioned knights or above could not ride in a carriage or on horseback within 100 li [one-third of a mile] of the capital walls, and as for gold, silver, brocades, and embroideries, artisans and merchants and their menials, lackeys, wives, and daughters could not wear them; violators would be executed in the market-place. . . .

The Hsiung-nu under the Worthy King of the Right Ts'ao Ku and the Worthy King of the Left Liu Wei-ch'en raised their troops in rebellion [against Fu Chien]. Leading a host of two myriads, [Ts'ao Ku] attacked the commanderies and prefectures to the south of Chien's city of Hsing-ch'eng. He camped at Ma-lan Mountain. The Bald-headed Caitiff Wu-yen and others also rebelled against Chien and communicated with Liu Wei-ch'en and Ts'ao Ku. Chien led elite shock troops of the inner and outer forces to chastise them. He put General of the Van Yang An and General Stabilizing the Army Mao Sheng in command of the forward spearhead. Ku sent his younger brother Huo to fight a defensive battle at T'ung-Kuan Stream, and Yang An severely defeated him, beheading Huo and more than 4,000 of his ranks. Ku was frightened and surrendered. Chien displaced to Ch'ang-an more than 6,000 households of Ku's chiefs and braves and then advancing, attacked Wu-yen and beheaded him. Teng Ch'iang made a punitive expedition against Wei-ch'en and captured him at Muken Mountain. Chien, setting out from Ts'ung-ma City, went to Shuo-fang inspecting and soothing the eastern and northern barbarians. He made Wei-ch'en Duke of Hsia-yang and had him take control of his host. Ts'ao Ku subsequently died, and Fu Chien partitioned his encampments: the more than 20,000 encampments to the east of Erh'ch'eng he gave as fief to his younger son Ts'ao Yin as Marquis of Li-ch'uan. For this reason Yin and Hsi were called "the eastern and western Ts'ao's."

In the two provinces of Ch'in and Yung the earth quaked and was rent, and springs of water gushed forth; gold elephants grew fur. In Ch'ang-an a great wind, thunder, and lightning destroyed houses and killed people. Chien, frightened, increased his cultivation of virtuous government.

°Of agriculture and of security forces.

28 Andean Civilization and Empire

Stuart J. Fiedel. *Prehistory of the Americas.* Cambridge, England: Cambridge University Press, 1987. 329–332.

The archaeological remains of two Andean cities, Tiahuanaco and Huari, show that at least one major empire existed in the South American mountains between 400 BCE and 700 CE. By looking at the spread of pottery from these cities, as well as similarities in architecture in the surrounding communities, scholars conclude that both Tiahuanaco and Huari conquered their neighbors in an effort to control vital agricultural resources. More specifically, the motive for conquest appears to have been "vertical integration," the need for the mountain-dweller imperial powers to control all the resources from the coast to the mountain plains. Dwellers at high altitudes produced potatoes, quinoa (a type of wheat), and livestock, while lowland agriculture produced chili peppers, fruit, and other produce. Imperial conquest ensured access to these resources. Scholars think that Huari may have begun as a colony of Tiahuanaco, and subsequently became independent.

The ruins of Tiahuanaco stand 12,600 feet above sea level . . . [:] the central core of monumental structures, occupying an area of 125 acres, was surrounded by an extensive residential zone. . . . Tiahuanaco was not a vacant ceremonial center but a true city, with a population estimated at anywhere from 20,000 to 40,000 people. Most of the potatoes and other crops on which the city's inhabitants subsisted were grown in artificially drained fields. Some 200,000 acres of lake-side marshes were reclaimed for agriculture, by means of a system of ditches and ridges. . . . The lake also yielded fish, which helped meet the protein needs of the city's residents.

• • •

The image of the "Staff God" [a deity depicted with a staff] was one of the decorative motifs painted on Tiahuanaco pottery. Other motifs were pumas, human figurines and religious symbols . . . a characteristic Tiahuanaco vessel form was the drinking goblet, or *kero.* The same designs, which evidently had the official approval of the state, also were applied to textiles, wood carvings and metal ornaments.

The outstanding achievement of Tiahuanaco civilization was in the realm of stone architecture. The stone masons' skill is most evident in the temple platform of Puma-Punku, which was composed of huge stone blocks, perfectly fitted using no mortar. Some of the blocks weighed as much as 100 tons. . . .

Tiahuanaco had been occupied as early as 400 BCE and [as] the city grew . . . Tiahuanaco's artwork and ideology diffused widely through the Central Andes after CE 375. . . . This stylistic diffusion . . . is generally believed to be a manifestation of the imperial expansion, by conquest, of the Tiahuanaco state.

On the southern shore of Lake Titicaca [in present-day Bolivia], two secondary centers, Luqurmata and Pajchiri, were established by the Tiahuanaco state;

they probably housed administrators who oversaw the land reclamation projects in that area. Smaller sites, with terraced mounds, constituted a third level of settlement, and still smaller habitation mounds, presumably occupied by the peasants, formed the fourth level of the settlement hierarchy. . . .

Tiahuanaco's region of control extended southward into . . . northern Chile, where economic colonies were established on the coast and in interior oases.° These colonies were linked to Tiahuanaco and to one another by llama caravans. Textiles, gold keros and wooden snuff trays, decorated in the purest Tiahuanaco style, were deposited in graves in Chile; these pieces may have been imported from the capital city . . . to be used by colonial officials. Economic colonies were also set up on the edge of the eastern jungles. These lowland sites provided the highland centers with such items as coca, maize, peppers, tropical fruits, medicinal plants and dried fish. The history of Andean highland-based empires, from Tiahuanaco to the Incas, can be interpreted as essentially an effort by mountain-dwellers to ensure a steady supply of low-altitude products, that is, to achieve vertical control.

While the archaeological evidence clearly demonstrates Tiahuanaco's imperial expansion to the south, west and east, the . . . situation to the north of the Titicaca basin is more difficult to interpret. The picture is complicated by the presence of a major center, . . . Huari, . . . evidently quite a large city, covering 750 acres at its peak, around 700 CE. Its central core, containing at least one temple, was encircled by a massive wall; around the core sprawled a residential zone which contained thousands of multi-family dwellings. Some of the houses had more than one story, and their walls were built of mud and roughly split stones, surfaced with mud stucco or gypsum plaster. Huari's growth seems to have been unplanned, for there is no evidence of an overall grid pattern. At a late stage in the city's development, huge compounds or enclosures were built, containing residences and open land. . . .

[The c]ultural influence from Tiahuanaco becomes evident . . . around 500 CE. At Conchopata, a site near Huari which seems to have been a religious shrine, large beaker-shaped urns were found which bore painted polychrome depictions of the Tiahuanaco "Staff God." These vessels appear to have been locally made; some of the designs were indigenous, and Conchopata-style pottery has not been found at Tiahuanaco itself. It seems most likely that Tiahuanaco priests introduced the cult and symbols of the "Staff God" to the people of Conchopata. The Conchopata style, and the cult in which the urns were used, soon spread to Huari and other sites in the area. New ceramic styles . . . resulted from this influence. The introduction of these wares into the Nazca valley, the northern sierra, and the central and northern coast, is probably a reflection of Huari's conquest of these regions, which may have occurred around 700 CE. . . . Huari conquerors were responsible for the construction of new architectural units in the coastal valleys—large, rectangular adobe-walled compounds. . . . In each case a road ran through the middle of the compound. These traces of roads, along with a site that resembles later Inca . . . way stations, suggest that a network of roads may have connected Huari provincial centers. The compounds are assumed to have served some imperial administrative function, whether as garrisons, store houses, or governors' palaces.

°The coast of northern Chile contains the Atacama Desert.

The relationship of the Huari and Tiahuanaco states is unclear. Were these cities the centers of separate northern and southern-oriented empires, or dual capitals of a single empire? Some archaeologists recognize a break in ceramic style distributions which may mark the boundary between the northern and southern states; on the other hand, the regular plan of the compounds is more reminiscent of Tiahuanaco's architecture than of the . . . buildings of Huari. Moreover recent excavations at Huari have revealed traces of Tiahuanaco-like dressed stone architecture underlying the level with mud and split stone walls. This raises the possibility that Huari may have begun as a colony of Tiahuanaco.

DISCUSSION QUESTIONS

1. How are rulers and military leaders portrayed in the passages you have read? What qualities do they share? What differences exist in their qualities?

2. How are people outside of empires characterized in the documents you have read? How are rival empires depicted? How are conquered peoples portrayed?

3. Are the chronicles you have read simply records of events, or did their authors intend them to have particular messages about morality, proper behavior of rulers, or anything else?

4. How might empires, and imperial conquests, have affected ordinary people in the places you have read about?

5. If you were asked to explain the differences and similarities between the life of people outside of empires with that of peoples living within empires that you have studied here, what would you say?

Chapter
6

Religions and Cultures

Religion is an element present in virtually all human societies, past and present. From the vantage point of our contemporary Western and heavily secularized society, it is easy to underestimate the importance of religion in human history. However, if the ways in which religion influences politics, education, and other arenas are considered, both in the contemporary United States as well as in other countries, it becomes evident that religion has been and is still an important component of human identity.

Religion was also crucial to societies in the past. Myths are often oral traditions of nonliterate societies, and are considered by some scholars to be a less developed form of religion or history. However, such views are biased in that they privilege the written sources of literate societies over the oral traditions of nonliterate cultures. This issue is discussed further in the introduction to Chapter Five. As you read, what similarities and differences do you see between religious texts and myths? Is the distinction valid?

As in Chapter Five, we use religious documents as historical evidence. The documents below belong to a number of different religious traditions and date from 10,000 BCE to 500 CE. Each one reveals how its society regarded itself, its members, its neighbors, its gods, and its environment. Selections from the traditions of Buddhism, Confucianism, Hinduism, Judeo-Christian tradition, and the Mayan Popol Vuh highlight the nature of these religions and the societies which practiced them. Buddhism places little importance on human agency, but the Bible and the Popul Vuh stress human actors and actions. This suggests different views on the relationship between people and their deities. In including various texts in the readings, implicit questions are posed concerning the ways in which religious texts are similar to and different from nonreligious texts, and how both can be subjected to historical analysis.

29 Duties of Mayan Lords

Popol Vuh: The Definitive Edition of the Mayan Book of the Dawn of Life and the Glories of Gods and Kings. Translated by Dennis Tedlock. New York: Simon and Schuster, 1986. 218–222.

In the sixteenth century, Spanish missionaries attempted to destroy all evidence of the Maya religion. One of the few Maya texts to survive is the Popul Vuh. It was written by anonymous authors of three noble lineages of the Quiché, a Maya group, in Guatemala during the sixteenth century, following the Spanish conquest of the area. Its origin, however, is far older, and it was transmitted orally for many generations. The text recounts the origin of the Quiché people, their gods, and their early history. In the following passage, the religious responsibilities of the nobility are discussed. These duties were crucial, for the Maya believed that earlier beings who had not paid sufficient homage to the gods were transformed into monkeys.

And now we shall name the names of the houses of the gods, although the houses have the same names as the gods:

Great Monument of Tohil is the name of the building that housed Tohil of the Cauecs. Auilix, next, is the name of the building that housed Auilix of the Greathouses. Hacauitz is the name, then of the building that housed the god of the Lord Quiches. Corntassel, whose house of sacrifice can still be seen, is the name of another great monument.

These were the locations of the stones whose days were kept by the Quiche lords. Their days were also kept by all the tribes. When the tribes burned offerings, they came before Tohil first.

After that, they greeted the Keeper of the Mat and Keeper of the Reception House Mat next, then they handed over their quetzal feathers and their tribute to the lords, these same lords.

And so they nurtured and provided for the Keeper of the Mat and Keeper of the Reception House Mat, who had been victorious over their citadels.

They were great lords, they were people of genius. Plumed Serpent and Cotuha were lords of genius, and Quicab and Cauizimah were lords of genius. They knew whether war would occur; everything they saw was clear to them. Whether there would be death, or whether there would be famine, or whether quarrels would occur, they knew it for certain, since there was a place to see it, there was a book. Council Book was their name for it.

But it wasn't only in this way that they were lords. They were great in their own being and observed great fasts. As a way of cherishing their buildings and cherishing their lordship, they fasted for long periods, they did penance before their gods.

And here is their way of fasting:

For nine score days they would fast, and for nine they would do penance and burn offerings.

Thirteen score was another of their fasts, and for thirteen they would do penance and burn offerings before Tohil and their other gods. They would only eat zapotes, matasanos, jocotes; there was nothing made of corn for their meals.

Even if they did penance for seventeen score, then for seventeen they fasted, they did not eat. They achieved truly great abstinence.

This was a sign that they had the being of true lords. And there weren't any women with them when they slept; they kept themselves apart when they fasted. They just stayed in the houses of the gods, each day. All they did was keep the days, burn offerings, and do penance. They were there whether it was dark or dawn; they just cried their hearts and their guts out when they asked for light and life for their vassals and their domain. They lifted their faces to the sky, and here is their prayer before their gods, when they made their requests.

And this is the cry of their hearts, here it is:

"Wait! On this blessed day,
thou Hurricane, thou Heart of the Sky-Earth,
thou giver of ripeness and freshness,
and thou giver of daughters and sons,
spread thy stain, still thy drops
of green and yellow;
give life and beginning
to those I bear and beget,
that they might multiply and grow,
nurturing and providing for thee,
calling to thee along the roads and paths,
on rivers, in canyons,
beneath the trees and bushes;
give them their daughters and sons.

"May there be no blame, obstacle, want or misery;
let no deceiver come behind or before them,
may they neither be snared nor wounded,
nor seduced, nor burned,
nor diverted below the road nor above it;
may they neither fall over backward nor stumble;
keep them on the Green Road, the Green Path.

"May there be no blame or barrier for them
through any secrets or sorcery of thine;
may thy nurturers and providers be good
before thy mouth and thy face,
thou, Heart of Sky; thou, Heart of Earth;
thou, Bundle of Flames;
and thou, Tohil, Auilix, Hacauitz,
under the sky, on the earth,
the four sides, the four corners;
may there be only light, only continuity within,
before thy mouth and thy face, thou god."

So it was with the lords when they fasted during nine score, thirteen score, or seventeen score days; their days of fasting were many. They cried their hearts out over their vassals and over all their wives and children. Each and every lord did service, as a way of cherishing the light of life and of cherishing lordship.

Such were the lordships of the Keeper of the Mat, Keeper of the Reception House Mat, Minister, and Crier to the People. They went into fasting two by two, taking turns at carrying the tribes and all the Quiche people on their shoulders.

• • •

It wasn't merely that they became lords; it wasn't just that they gathered in gifts from nurturers and providers who merely made food and drink for them. Nor did they wantonly falsify or steal their lordship, their splendor, their majesty. And it wasn't merely that they crushed the canyons and citadels of the tribes, whether small or great, but that the tribes paid a great price:

There came turquoise, there came metal.

And there came green and red featherwork, the tribute of all the tribes. It came to the lords of genius Plumed Serpent and Cotuha, and to Quicab and Cauizimah as well, to the Keeper of the Mat, Keeper of the Reception House Mat, Minister, and Crier to the People.

What they did was no small feat, and the tribes they conquered were not few in number. The tribute of Quiche came from many tribal divisions.

And the lords had undergone pain and withstood it; their rise to splendor had not been sudden. Actually it was Plumed Serpent who was the root of the greatness of the lordship.

Such was the beginning of the rise and growth of Quiche.

30 Religious Thought in India

"The Upanishads." In *Sources of Indian Tradition*, William Theodore de Bary, ed. New York: Columbia University Press, 1958. 33–36.

The Upanishads are a body of religious texts in the Hindu tradition thought to have been produced by religious holy men who lived a life of seclusion in Indian woodlands around 600 BCE. Scholars consider them to be a reinterpretation of earlier Vedic texts, examples of which you read in Chapter Three. They grapple with the difficult issue of understanding the nature of human existence. The following selection uses the dialogue between a father and his son, newly returned from school, to discuss the nature of knowledge and of human existence.

THE ESSENTIAL REALITY UNDERLYING THE WORLD

There, verily was Shvetaketu, the son of Uddalaka Aruni. To him his father said: "O Shvetaketu, live the disciplined life of a student of sacred knowledge. No one, indeed, my dear, belonging to our family, is unlearned in the Veda and remains a brahman only by family connections as it were." He, then having approached a teacher at the age of twelve and having studied all the Vedas, returned at the age of twenty-four, conceited, thinking himself to be learned, stiff. To him his father said: "O Shvetaketu, since, my dear, you are now conceited, think yourself to be learned, and have become stiff, did you also ask for that instruction whereby what has been unheard becomes heard, what has been unthought of becomes thought of, what has been uncomprehended becomes comprehended?" "How indeed, Sir, is that instruction?" asked Shvetaketu. "Just as, my dear, through the comprehension of one lump of clay all that is made of clay would become comprehended—for the modification is occasioned only on account of a convention of speech, it is only a name; while clash as such alone is the reality. Just as, my dear, through the comprehension of one ingot of iron all that is made of iron as such become comprehended—for the modification is occasioned only on account of a convention of speech, it is only a name; while iron as such alone is the reality. . . . So, my dear, is that instruction?" "Now, verily those veritable teachers did not know this; for, if they had known it, why would they not have told me?" said Shvetaketu. "However, may the venerable sir tell it to me." "So be it, my dear," said he.

"In the beginning, my dear, this world was just being, one only without a second. Some people, no doubt, say: 'In the beginning, verily, this world was just nonbeing, one only, without a second; from that nonbeing, being was produced.' But how, indeed, my dear, could it be so?" said he. "How could being be produced from nonbeing? On the contrary, my dear, in the beginning this world was being alone, one only, without a second. Being thought to itself: 'May I be many, may I procreate.' It produced fire. That fire thought to itself: 'May I be many, may I procreate.' It produced water. Therefore, whenever a person grieves or perspires, then it is from fire alone that water is produced. That water thought to itself: 'May I be many; may I procreate.' It produced food. Therefore, whenever it rains, then there is abundant food; it is from water alone that food for eating is produced. . . . That divinity thought to itself: 'Well, having entered into these three divinities [fire, water, and food] by means of this living Self, let me develop names and forms. Let me make each one of them tripartite.' That divinity, accordingly, having entered into those three divinities by means of this living Self, developed names and forms. . . . It made each one of them tripartite. . . ."

"Bring hither a fig from there." "Here it is, sir." "Break it." "It is broken, sir." "What do you see there?" "These extremely fine seeds, sir." "Of these, please break one." "It is broken, sir." "What do you see there?" "Nothing at all, sir." Then he said to Shvetaketu: "Verily, my dear, that subtle essence which you do not perceive—from that very essence, indeed, my dear, does this great fig tree thus arise. Believe me, my dear, that which is the subtle essence—this whole world has that essence for it Self; that is the Real; that is the Self; that [subtle essence] art thou, Shvetaketu." "Still further may the venerable sir instruct me." "So be it, my dear," said he.

"Having put this salt in the water, come to me in the morning." He did so. Then the father said to him: "That salt which you put in the water last evening—please bring it hither." Even having looked for it, he did not find it, for it was completely dissolved. "Please take a sip of water from this end," said the father. "How is it?" "Salt." "Take a sip from the middle," said he. "How is it?" "Salt." "Take a sip from that end," said he. "How is it? "Salt." "Throw it away and come to me." Shvetaketu did so thinking to himself: "That salt, though unperceived, still persists in the water." Then Aruni said to him: "Verily, my dear, you do not perceive Being in this world; but it is, indeed, here only: That which is the subtle essence—this whole world has that essence for its Self. That is the Real. That is the Self. That art thou, Shvetaketu." "Still further may the venerable sir instruct me. " "So be it, my dear," said he.

"Just as, my dear, having led away a person from Gandhara [the western boundary of Indian culture] with the eyes bandaged, one might then abandon him in a place where there are no human beings; and as that person would there drift about toward the east or the north or the south: 'I have been led away here with my eyes bandaged, I have been abandoned here with my eyes bandaged'; then as, having released his bandage, one might tell him: 'In that direction lies Gandhara, go in that direction.' Thereupon he, becoming wise and sensible, would, by asking his way from village to village, certainly reach Gandhara. Even so does one who has a teacher here know: 'I shall remain here [in this phenomenal world] only as long as I shall not be released from the bonds of nescience [state of human existence]. Then I shall reach my home.'"

31 The Origins of Buddhism

Robert Allen Mitchell. *The Buddha: His Life Retold.* New York: Paragon House, 1989. 18–19, 23–27, 43–46, 54.

In this segment, you will examine the origins of Buddhism through the life of the Buddha himself. These excerpts are taken from a modern rendition of the life of Prince Siddhartha Gautama, who lived ca. 563–483 BCE. The opening passages recount the awakening of Siddhartha to his destiny as the Buddha. At his birth, it was foretold that if he led a sheltered life, he would grow to be a powerful monarch. If he ventured forth, he would become the Buddha and renounce his future as a leader of his people in India. The second section of excerpts describe Buddha's realizations that led to "supreme enlightenment." The final section describes the Four Noble Truths that are at the center of the Buddhist faith.

THE FOUR SIGNS

Then eight brahmins (Rama, Dhadya, Laksana, Manti, Kaundinya, Bhodya, Svayama, and Sudatta) who were well versed in the art of prophesying fortunes from a consideration of bodily marks and characteristics stepped forward and examined the Bodhisattva [the prince] carefully. Seven of the eight each raised two fingers and gave a double interpretation, saying:

"If a man possessing such marvelous marks and characteristics continue in the household life, he becomes a universal monarch; but if he retire from the world, he becomes a Buddha, a Supremely Awakened One."

The youngest of the eight brahmins, a mere youth whose family name was Kaundinya, raised only one finger and gave but a single interpretation.

"I see nothing to make him stay in the household life," said Kaundinya. "He will undoubtedly become a Buddha and save the world from ignorance and pain."

"Now, King Suddhodana became increasingly disturbed by predictions of Buddhahood for his son. The Sakyas were a race of warriors; and Suddhodana, as their chieftain, was determined that Prince Siddhartha should one day become a ruler of men, even a king of all earth. The very thought that his own son might enter religious life, calling nothing his own and begging his daily bread, filled the proud sovereign with dismay.

"What makes you so sure that there is nothing here to detain my son from embarking upon the life of a religious mendicant?" demanded Suddhodana of the young brahmin.

"Several characteristics, O king; thirty-two in all, and four in particular," replied Kaundinya. "Do you see the tiny circlet of white hairs on his forehead between the eyebrows? And the protuberance of the top of his head? And his black body hairs curling to the right? And the fine golden color of his skin? Without any doubt at all, the Four Signs will induce the prince to renounce the worldly life."

"The Four Signs?" asked the king with dread in his voice. "Pray, brahmin, name the four!"

"An old man, a sick man, a dead man, and a monk."

Suddhodana rose to his feet, eyes flashing anger.

"From this time forth," he commanded, "let no such persons approach the prince! It will never do for my son to become a Buddha! Prince Siddhartha is destined to exercise sovereign rule and authority over all great continents with their thousands of attendant isles!"

• • •

When the Bodhisattva was twenty-nine years old, [his wife] Princess Yasodhara was far gone with child. And on the morning of a beautiful day when winter had been vanquished by summer, Yasodhara addressed the prince, saying, "Go, beloved husband, to the park of the summer palace and enjoy the trees and flowering plants which are now coming into bloom. I shall remain here in Kapilavastu, for the time of my delivery draws near."

Prince Siddhartha accordingly summoned Chandaka, his charioteer, and proceeded to the park in an elegant chariot drawn by four white horses of royal breed.

As the Bodhisattva passed through a village of gardeners not far from Kapilavastu, a decrepit old man, bent of body, leaning on a staff, toothless and gray-haired, stumbled out into the road.

The horses neighed with fright as Chandaka tightened the reins to avoid running down the tottering old man.

"Chandaka!" cried the prince in astonishment. "What kind of man is that? Never before have I seen a man in such a deplorable condition!"

"It is an old man, master," replied Chandaka, "a man who has seen many years come and go."

"But his face—see how wrinkled it is! Was he born in that unfortunate state?"

"No, master, he was once young and blooming as you are now."

"Are there many more such old persons in the world?"

"Yes, master. It is the course of nature that all who are born must grow old and feeble if they do not die young."

"I, also, Chandaka?"

Chandaka lowered his head out of deference to the Bodhisattva. "You also, master."

The ardor of youth fled at once from the prince. "Shame on birth, since to everyone born old age must come! Return to the palace, Chandaka!"

And so the prince returned to his father's palace in Kapilavastu.

King Suddhodana, astonished by his son's hasty return, summoned the charioteer. "What happened on the way? Why has my son returned so quickly?"

"He has seen an old man, O king," answered Chandaka, "and because he has seen old age he desires to seek out the nature of Birth and Death."

"Do you want to kill me, man, that you say such things? We must not let the prince enter the religious life. We must not allow the prophecies of the brahmin soothsayers to come true."

The next day the Bodisattva again desired to go to the park; and the king, learning of this, stationed guards all along the road. But despite these preparations, Siddhartha's eyes fell upon a sick man, suffering and very ill, fallen in his own excrements by the roadside.

"Chandaka!" cried the Bodhisattva. "Stop the chariot at once!"

When Chandaka failed to stop, Siddhartha took the reins from the charioteer's hands. And after the chariot had been turned around, the prince drew to the side of the road where the sick man was.

"What, Chandaka, has that man done that his eyes are not like the others' eyes? nor his voice like the voice of other men?"

"He is what is called sick, master."

"Sick? Are all people liable to sickness?"

"Yes, master."

"Then, I, too, could become like this, I, the glory of the Sakyas! Let us return to the palace: enough of going to the park!"

Notwithstanding his discovery of human misery, the Bodisattva set out for the third time on the following morning.

The trip was uneventful until the chariot had reached the outskirts of the gardeners' village. There a corpse was being carried to a funeral pyre by weeping relatives.

Prince Siddhartha looked upon the scene with impatience, not knowing what to make of it. But perspiration broke out on Chandaka's forehead as he silently prayed to the gods to withhold the sight of death from the prince.

The gods, however, were of a different mind. Like an invisible hand, a sudden gust of wind swooped down upon the bier and ripped away the pall in fluttering tatters.

Prince Siddhartha's mouth opened in horror when his gaze fell upon the dead body. Could *that* once have been human? Could *that* even have been alive?

"And to think," gasped the prince, "that that vile body was once a thing of delight to its owner, a source of fleeting pleasures! Is the man dead, Chandaka, hopelessly and irretrievably dead?"

"His relatives and friends will not see him any more," replied Chandaka, "nor will he see them."

"It has become clear to me, Chandaka, that death is universal. I, too, am subject to death, not beyond the sphere of death. Now what if I, being subject to old age, sickness, and death, were to investigate the nature of birth, likewise the nature of old age, sickness, and death? What if I, having seen the wretchedness of mundane existence, were to seek out the Unborn, the Undying, the supreme peace of Nirvana?". . . .

Early in the morning of the fourth day, the Bodhisattva set out again for the pleasure park of the summer palace. And as the chariot approached the park, the prince caught sight of a religious recluse walking by the side of the road.

"Who, Chandaka, is that man clad in a simple yellow robe, his head shaved, his face radiant with peace and joy?"

"That man," replied the charioteer, "is a monk, one who has gone forth from the household life and lives on food he has begged. He is one who is thorough in the religious life, thorough in the peaceful life, thorough in good actions, thorough in meritorious conduct, thorough in harmlessness, thorough in kindness to all living beings."

"A monk!" exclaimed the Bodhisattva. "Never before have I seen such happiness and inner peace shining forth from the face of a man! Is it possible, friend Chandaka, that I, too, might find rapture and peace of mind by leaving the world, by becoming such as he and living on food I have begged?"

"We are approaching the summer palace, master."

"Friend, I beg you to tell me! Why, pray, do men leave the world?"

"For the sake of subduing and calming themselves," replied Chandaka, "and for attaining Nirvana."

NIRVANA! "Happiness" or "Extinction" as one looks at the world! On hearing the word *Nirvana,* the Great Being was delighted; and taking pleasure in the thought of abandoning the world, he bade Chandaka to drive into the park."

• • •

THE SUPREME ENLIGHTENMENT

Night had fallen, and the full moon peeped over the trees of the forest as if from a desire to behold the Great Being. And while the Bodhi tree sprinkled coral-red sprigs of bloom upon his robes as though doing homage to him, the Bodhisattva attained and abode in the Four Absorptions of the fine-material sphere:

1. Detached from sensual desires and unwholesome thoughts, he entered the First Absorption, which is accompanied by reasoning and discursive thought, born of detachment, and filled with rapture and happiness.
2. After the fading away of reasoning and discursive thought, and by the gaining of inward tranquility and one-pointedness of mind, he entered into a state free from reasoning and discursive thought, the Second Absorption, which is born of concentration and filled with rapture and happiness.
3. After the fading out of rapture, he abode in equanimity—clearly conscious, mindful, and experiencing that feeling of which the Arya[n]s say, "happy

lives the man of equanimity and attentive mind,"—and thus entered the Third Absorption.

4. After the rejection of pleasure and pain, and through the cessation of previous joy and grief, he entered into a state beyond pleasure and pain, the Fourth Absorption, which is purified by equanimity and attentiveness.

a. Then beginning in the first watch of the night, with mind purified and concentrated, the Great Being directed his mind to the remembrance of his former existences up to hundreds of thousands of births, up to many cycles of dissolution and evolution of the universe.
"There I was of such and such a name, family, station of life, and livelihood," Gautama realized. "Such pleasure and pain did I experience; and passing away from there I was reborn elsewhere. Thus do I remember all of my former existences with their special modes and details."

b. Then in the middle watch of the night the Great Being directed his mind to the passing away and rebirth of beings. With superhuman vision he saw them dying and being reborn, low and high, in happy or wretched existences according to their karma.
"Those beings who lead evil lives in deed, word, or thought," he realized, "who hold to false views and acquire unfavorable karma thereby, are reborn in a state of misery and suffering in hell. But those beings who lead good lives in deed, word, or thought, who hold to right views and acquire favorable karma thereby, are reborn in a state of joy and bliss in heaven."

c. Then in the last watch of the night the Great Being directed his mind to the complete destruction of the "Poisons," thereby acquiring a Wisdom in conformity with the reality of the Four Aryan Truths, namely, Suffering, its Cause, its Cessation, and the Path which leads to its cessation.

And as he thus knew and thus perceived, his mind was completely emancipated from the Poison of lust (sensual desire), from the Poison of existence-infatuation (the desire for continued separate existence or for annihilation at death), from the Poison of false view (delusion and superstition), and from the Poison of ignorance (of the Four Aryan Truths).

And as the Great Being reflected on the Four Aryan Truths, his Fully Awakened Mind fathomed the Twelve Causes in the chain of Dependent Origination.

"This being present as a cause, that arises. This not being present as a cause, that does not arise."

In the past life (he realized):
1. There is ignorance.
2. Ignorance conditions the predisposing mental formations.
In the present life:
3. The predisposing mental formations condition discriminative consciousness.
4. Discriminative consciousness conditions mind-and-body.
5. Mind-and-body conditions the six senses.
6. The six senses condition contact.
7. Contact conditions feeling.

    8. Feeling conditions craving.
    9. Craving conditions attachment.
    10. Attachment conditions the process of becoming.
In the future life:
    11. The process of becoming conditions rebirth.
    12. Rebirth conditions decay and death, likewise sorrow, lamentation, pain, grief, and despair.

"Thus does the entire mass of suffering arise. But on the complete fading out and cessation of ignorance, this entire mass of suffering comes to an end."

THE FOUR NOBLE TRUTHS

    1. What, monks, is the Aryan Truth about Suffering? Birth is suffering, old age is suffering, sickness is suffering, death is suffering, likewise sorrow, lamentation, pain, grief, and despair. Contact with the unpleasant is suffering, separation from the pleasant is suffering, unsatisfied desire is suffering. . . .

    2. What, monks, is the Aryan Truth about the Cause of Suffering? Verily, suffering originates in that rebirth-causing craving which is accompanied by sensual pleasure and which seeks satisfaction now here, now there—craving for sensual pleasures, craving to be born again, craving to be annihilated.

    3. What, monks, is the Aryan Truth about the Cessation of Suffering? Verily, it is passionlessness, the complete destruction of this craving for sensual pleasures, for becoming, and for annihilation; the forsaking and relinquishing of this craving, the harboring no longer of this craving.

    4. What, monks, is the Aryan Truth about the Path that leads to the Cessation of Suffering? Verily, it is this Aryan Eightfold Path of Right View, Right Thought, Right Speech, Right Action, Right Livelihood, Right Effort, Right Attentiveness, and Right Concentration.

32 Confucian Thought

William Theodore de Bary. *Sources of Chinese Tradition.* New York: Columbia University Press, 1960. 22, 25, 27–35.

Confucian belief remains a powerful intellectual tradition in China today centuries after Confucius lived (551–479 BCE). Later disciples of his teaching compiled the *Analects,* a collection of 497 verses about Confucius and his teachings. In the words of one Chinese scholar, "Confucius chose to direct attention away from the supernatural and toward the vital problems of human society and the ordering of the state." So while outwardly Confucian thought is secular, it has features in common with many of the explicitly religious texts you have read, including a deep sense of piety and an eye toward the daily relations of humankind.

CONFUCIUS THE MAN

1. In his leisure hours, Confucius was easy in his manner and cheerful in his expression.
2. Confucius was gentle yet firm, dignified but not harsh, respectful yet well at ease.

CONFUCIUS THE TEACHER

22. Confucius said: "By nature men are pretty much alike; it is learning and practice that set them apart."
23. Confucius said: "In education there are no class distinctions."
24. Confucius said: "The young are to be respected. How do we know that the next generation will not measure up to the present one? But if a man has reached forty or fifty and nothing has been heard of him, then I grant that he is not worthy of respect."
25. Confucius said: "When it comes to acquiring perfect virtue, a man should not defer even to his own teacher."

THE TEACHINGS OF CONFUCIUS

40. Tzu Kung asked: "Is there any one word that can serve as a principle for the conduct of life?" Confucius said: "Perhaps the word 'reciprocity': Do not do to others what you would not want others to do to you."
41. Confucius said: "Perfect indeed is the virtue which is according to the Mean. For long people have seldom had the capacity for it."
42. Confucius said: "It is man that can make the Way great, not the Way that can make the man great."
43. Chung-kung asked about humanity. Confucius said: "Behave when away from home as though you were in the presence of an important guest. Deal with the common people as though you were officiating at an important sacrifice. Do not do to others what you would not want others to do to you. Then there will be no dissatisfaction either in the state or at the home."
44. Confucius said: "The humane man, desiring to be established himself, seeks to establish others; desiring himself to succeed, he helps others to succeed. To judge others by what one knows of oneself is the method of achieving humanity."

HUMANITY

45. Fan Ch'ih asked about humanity. Confucius said: "Love men."
46. Tzu Chang asked Confucius about humanity. Confucius said: "To be able to practice five virtues everywhere in the world constitutes humanity." Tzu

Chang begged to know what these were. Confucius said: "Courtesy, magnanimity, good faith, diligence, and kindness. He who is courteous is not humiliated, he who is magnanimous wins the multitude, he who is of good faith is trusted by the people, he who is diligent attains his objective, and he who is kind can get service from the people."

47. Confucius said: "Without humanity a man cannot long endure adversity, nor can he long enjoy prosperity. The humane rest in humanity; the wise find it beneficial."

48. Confucius said: "Only the humane man can love men and can hate men."

49. Someone inquired: "What do you think of 'requiting injury with kindness'?" Confucius said: "How will you then requite kindness? Requite injury with justice, and kindness with kindness."

FILIAL PIETY

56. Tzu Yu asked about filial piety. Confucius said: "Nowadays a filial son is just a man who keeps his parents in food. But even dogs or horses are given food. If there is no feeling of reverence, wherein lies the difference?"

57. Tzu Hsia asked about filial piety. Confucius said: "The manner is the real difficult thing. When anything has to be done the young people undertake it; when there is wine and food the elders are served—is this all there is to filial piety?"

58. Confucius said: "In serving his parents, a son may gently remonstrate with them. If he sees that they are not inclined to follow his suggestion, he should resume his reverential attitude but not abandon his purpose. If he is belabored, he will not complain."

59. The Duke of She observed to Confucius: "Among us there was an upright man called Kung who was so upright that when his father appropriated a sheep, he bore witness against him." Confucius said: "The upright men among us are not like that. A father will screen his son and a son his father—yet uprightness is to be found in that."

RELIGIOUS SENTIMENT

67. Tzu Lu asked about the worship of ghosts and spirits. Confucius said: "We don't know yet how to serve men, how can we know about serving the spirits?" "What about death," was the next question. Confucius said: "We don't know yet about life, how can we know about death?"

68. Fan Ch'ih asked about wisdom. Confucius said: "Devote yourself to the proper demands of the people, respect the ghosts and spirits but keep them at a distance—this may be called wisdom."

72. Confucius said: "He who sins against Heaven has none to whom he can pray."

THE GENTLEMAN

78. Confucius said: "When nature exceeds art you have the rustic. When art exceeds nature you have the clerk. It is only when art and nature are harmoniously blended that you have the gentleman."
80. Confucius said: "The gentleman occupies himself with the Way and not his livelihood. One may attend to farming, and yet may sometimes go hungry. One may attend to learning and yet may be rewarded with emolument. What the gentleman is anxious about is the Way and not poverty."
81. Ssu-ma Niu asked about the gentleman. Confucius said: "The gentleman has neither anxiety nor fear. Ssu-ma Niu rejoined: "Neither anxiety nor fear—is that what is meant by being a gentleman?" Confucius said: "When he looks into himself and finds no cause for self-reproach, what has he to be anxious about; what has he to fear?"

GOVERNMENT BY PERSONAL VIRTUE

95. Confucius said: "If a ruler himself is upright, all will go well without orders. But if he himself is not upright, even though he gives orders they will not be obeyed."
96. Tzu Lu asked about the character of the gentleman [man of the ruling class]. Confucius said: "He cultivates himself in reverential attention." Tzu Lu asked: "Is that all there is to it?" Confucius said: "He cultivates himself so as to be able to bring comfort to other people." Tzu Lu asked again: "Is that all there is to it?" Confucius said: "He cultivates himself so as to bring comfort to the whole populace. . . ."
97. Confucius said: "Lead the people by laws and regulate them by penalties, and the people will try to keep out of jail, but will have no sense of shame. Lead the people by virtue and restrain them by the rules of decorum, and the people will have a sense of shame, and moreover will become good."
98. Chi K'ang Tzu asked Confucius about government, saying: "Suppose I were to kill the lawless for the good of the law-abiding, how would that do?" Confucius answered: "Sir, why should it be necessary to employ capital punishment in your government? Just as you genuinely desire the good, the people will be good. The virtue of the gentleman may be compared to the wind and that of the commoner to the weeds. The weeds under the force of the wind cannot but bend."

33 Judeo-Christian Thought

Exodus 20; Job 1–3, 38, 42; Ecclesiastes 1, 3. *The New English Bible*. Oxford and Cambridge, England: Oxford and Cambridge University Presses, 1970.

Both Judaism and Christianity regard the first books of the Old Testament as fundamental texts. The first excerpts in this passage are taken from Exodus. After delivering the Jews from slavery in Egypt, God announces through Moses the fundamental laws of his rule. The second set of excerpts comes from the Book of Job, believed to have been written around the sixth century BCE. In the passages below, Job's faith in God is tested by the loss of everything that he holds dear. The final set of passages is taken from Ecclesiastes (a Greek translation of *Koheleth*, meaning "preacher") written in the third century BCE; in them, the author offers a skeptical view that one's life is ruled by chance but concludes that the one must be in "awe" of God.

EXODUS 20

God spoke, and these were his words:

I am the LORD your God who brought you out of Egypt, out of the land of slavery.

You shall have no other god to set against me.

You shall not make a carved image for yourself nor the likeness of anything in the heavens above, or on the earth below, or in the waters under the earth.

You shall not bow down to them or worship them; for I, the LORD your God, am a jealous god. I punish the children for the sins of the fathers to the third and fourth generations of those who hate me. But I keep faith with thousands, with those who love me and keep my commandments.

You shall not make wrong use of the name of the LORD your God; the LORD will not leave unpunished the man who misuses his name.

Remember to keep the sabbath day holy. You have six days to labour and do all your work. But the seventh day is a sabbath of the LORD your God; that day you shall not do any work, you, your son or your daughter, your slave or your slave-girl, your cattle or the alien within your gates; for in six days the LORD made heaven and earth, the sea, and all that is in them, and on the seventh day he rested. Therefore the LORD blessed the sabbath day and declared it holy.

Honour thy father and your mother, that you may live long in the land which the LORD your God is giving you.

You shall not commit murder.

You shall not commit adultery.

You shall not steal.

You shall not give false evidence against your neighbour.

You shall not covet your neighbour's house; you shall not covet your neighbour's wife, his slave, his slave-girl, his ox, his ass, or anything that belongs to him.

JOB 1–3, 38, 42

There lived in the land of Uz a man of blameless and upright life named Job, who feared God and set his face against wrongdoing. He had seven sons and three daughters; and he owned seven thousand sheep and three thousand camels, five hundred yoke of oxen and five hundred asses, with a large number of slaves. Thus Job was the greatest man in all the East. . . .

The day came when the members of the court of heaven took their places in the presence of the LORD, and Satan was there among them. The LORD asked him where he had been. "Ranging over the earth," he said, "from end to end." Then the LORD asked Satan, "Have you considered my servant Job? You will find no one like him on earth, a man of blameless and upright life, who fears GOD and sets his face against wrongdoing." Satan answered the LORD, "Has not Job good reason to be God-fearing? Have you not hedged him round on every side with your protection, him and his family and all his possessions? Whatever he does you have blessed, and his herds have increased beyond measure. But stretch out your hand and touch all that he has, and then he will curse you to your face." Then the LORD said to Satan, "So be it. All that he has is in your hands; only Job himself you must not touch." And Satan left the LORD's presence.

When the day came that Job's sons and daughters were eating and drinking in the eldest brother's house, a messenger came to Job and said, "The oxen were ploughing and the asses were grazing near them, when the Sabeans swooped down and carried them off, after putting the herdsmen to the sword; and I am the only one to escape and tell the tale." While he was still speaking, another messenger arrived and said, "God's fire flashed from heaven. It struck the sheep and the shepherds and burnt them up; and I am the only one to escape and tell the tale." While he was still speaking, another arrived and said, "The Chaldaeans, three bands of them, have made a raid on the camels and carried them off, after putting the drivers to the sword; and I am the only one to escape and tell the tale." While this man was speaking, yet another arrived and said, "Your sons and daughters were eating and drinking in the eldest brother's house, when suddenly a whirlwind swept across the desert and struck the four corners of the house, and it fell on the young people and killed them; and I am the only one to escape and tell the tale." At this Job stood up and rent his cloak; then he shaved his head and fell prostrate on the ground saying:

Naked I came from the womb,
Naked I shall return whence I came.
The LORD gives the LORD takes away;
blessed be the name of the LORD.

Throughout all this Job did not sin; he did not charge God with unreason.

Once again the day came when the members of the court of heaven took their places in the presence of the LORD. . . . Then the LORD asked Satan, "Have you considered my servant Job? You will find no one like him on earth, a man of blame-less and upright life, who fears God and sets his face against wrongdoing. You incit-ed me to ruin him without a cause, but his integrity is still unshaken." Satan answered the LORD, "Skin for skin! There is nothing the man will grudge to save himself. But stretch out your hand and touch his bone and flesh, and see if he will not curse you to your face." Then the LORD said to Satan, "So be it. He is in your hands; but spare his life." And Satan left the LORD's presence, and he smote Job with running sores from head to foot, so that he took a piece of broken pot to scratch himself as he sat among the ashes. . . .

After this Job broke his silence and cursed the day of his birth:

"Perish the day when I was born, and the night which said, 'A man is con-ceived'! May that day turn to darkness; may God above not look for it, nor light of dawn shine on it. May blackness sully it, and murk and gloom, cloud smother that day, swift darkness eclipse its sun. Blind darkness swallow up that night; count it not among the days of the year, reckon it not in the cycle of the months. That night, may it be barren for ever, no cry of joy be heard in it.

Cursed be it by those whose magic blinds even the monster of the deep, who are ready to tame Leviathan himself with spells. May no star shine out in its twi-light; may it wait for a dawn that never comes, nor ever see the eyelids of the morn-ing, because it did not shut the doors of the womb that bore me and keep trouble away from my sight. Why was I not still-born, why did I not die when I came out of the womb? Why was I ever laid on my mother's knees or put to suck at her breasts? Why was I not hidden like an untimely birth, like an infant that has not lived to see the light? For then I should be lying in the quiet grave, asleep in death, at rest, with kings and ministers who built themselves palaces, with princes rich in gold who filled their houses with silver. There the wicked man chafes no more, there the tired labourer rests; the captive too finds peace there and hears no taskmaster's voice; high and low are there, even the slave, free from his master. Why should the sufferer be born to see the light? Why is life given to men who find it so bitter? They wait for death but it does not come, they seek it more eagerly than hidden treasure. They are glad when they reach the tomb, and when they come to the grave they exult. Why should a man be born to wander blindly, hedged in by God on every side? My sighing is all my food, and groans pour from me in a torrent. Every terror that haunted me has caught up with me, and all that I feared has come on me. There is no peace of mind nor quiet for me; I chafe in torment and have no rest."

· · ·

Then the LORD answered Job out of the tempest:

Who is this whose ignorant words cloud my design in darkness? Brace yourself and stand up like a man; I will ask questions, and you shall answer. Where were you when I laid the earth's foundations? Tell me, if you know and understand. . . . Have you visited the storehouse of the snow or seen the arsenal where hail is stored, which I have kept ready for the day of calamity, for war and the hour of battle? By what paths is the heat spread abroad or the east wind carried far and wide over the earth? Who has cut channels for the downpour and cleared a passage for the thun-derstorm, for rain to fall on land where no man lives and on the deserted wilderness, clothing lands waste and derelict with green and making grass grow on thirsty ground? Has the rain a father? Who sired the drops of dew? Whose womb gave birth to the ice, and who was the mother of the frost from heaven, which lays a stony cover over the waters and freezes the expanse of the ocean?. . . .

Then Job answered the LORD:

I know that thou canst do all things and that no purpose is beyond thee. But I have spoken of great things which I have not understood, things too wonderful for me to know. I knew of thee only by report, but now I see thee with my own eyes. Therefore I melt away; I repent in dust and ashes.

ECCLESIASTES 1, 3

The words of the speaker, the son of David, king in Jerusalem. Emptiness, emptiness, says the Speaker, emptiness, all is empty. What does man gain from all his labour and his toil here under the sun? Generations come and generations go, while the earth endures forever.

The sunrises and the sun goes down; back it returns to its place and rises there again. The wind blows south, the wind blows north, round and round it goes and returns full circle.

• • •

For everything its season, and for every activity under heaven its time:
a time to be born and a time to die;
a time to plant and a time to uproot;
a time to kill and a time to heal;
a time to pull down and a time for building up;
a time to weep and a time to laugh;
a time for mourning and a time for dancing;
a time to scatter stones and a time to gather them;
a time to embrace and a time to refrain from embracing;
a time to seek and a time to lose;
a time to keep and a time to throw away;
a time to tear and a time to mend;
a time for silence and a time for speech;
a time for love and a time for hate;
a time for war and a time for peace.

What profit does one who works get from all his labour? I have seen the business that God has given men to keep them busy. He has made everything to suit its time; moreover he has given men a sense of time past and future, but no comprehension of God's work from beginning to end. I know that there is nothing good for man except to be happy and live the best life he can while he is alive. Moreover, that a man should eat and drink and enjoy himself, in return for all his labours, is a gift of God. I know that whatever God does lasts for ever; to add to it or subtract from it is impossible. And he has done it all in such a way that men must feel awe in his presence. Whatever is has been already, and God summons each event back in turn.

DISCUSSION QUESTIONS

1. How do religions reflect ideal behavior and attitudes in their societies? Do they seem optimistic or fatalistic? Why?

2. What are the common elements of rituals? What purposes do they serve?

3. How are gods portrayed? How would you describe the relationship between gods and people? What might this tell you about the societies you are studying?

4. How is the relationship among people, animals, and the environment portrayed in each selection?

5. Compare the experiences and attitudes of Siddhartha, Job, and Shevataketu.

6. Compare the *Analects* of Confucius with the Four Noble Truths and the Path to Self-Enlightenment of Buddha.

Chapter
7

The Spread of Peoples and Cultures

What are the most important events in world history? Scholars throughout history have answered this question by discussing the great empires and particular moments in the past such as the fall of the Roman empire, the conquests of Alexander the Great, or more recent events such as the Second World War. While certainly important, these dramatic events are not the only ones to affect human history. The migration of peoples, the diffusion of agricultural techniques, and the spread of languages are equally important phenomena. Slow and tenuous as these processes may be, they have linked together more of the world's populations than any empire. In these events, the agents of change are not military or religious leaders, but ordinary people living out their own lives, adapting new ideas while maintaining older traditions, in order to better their own situation.

The first selection explains the similarities between different Indo-European languages, and argues that language was brought from one region to another not by conquerors—as earlier historians believed—but at the same time as new agricultural techniques spread from West Asia to Europe. The second selection discusses a similar phenomenon in African history, the spread of Bantu-speaking peoples throughout the sub-Saharan region. The authors also create a picture of the original Bantu-speakers by looking at the words in their vocabulary. Here, too, the process by which peoples and culture spread is one of voluntary migration. The third selection, a brief passage from a Luba creation story, provides an oral history account that parallels the archaeological and linguistic evidence of the Bantu migrations. The fourth reading uses similar linguistic evidence to discuss the migrations of Polynesian ancestors through Melanesia. Like the Bantu migrations, the process here was piecemeal, with the important difference that the Polynesian migrations took place as peoples moved from one island to another. The fifth selection examines the origins of the Taino, a people Christopher

Columbus encountered in the Caribbean but who largely disappeared as a result of epidemic disease in the sixteenth century. This analysis is perhaps the most difficult of all, because there is little tradition or linguistic evidence to support archaeological research. The sixth and final selection is an excerpt from the Roman historian Tacitus' history of the Germans. It describes the time when fixed agriculture and iron tools had just begun to affect German life during the first century CE.

34 The Spread of Indo-European Languages

Colin Renfrew *Archaeology and Language.* London: Jonathon Cape, 1987. 10–11, 14–15, 146–151.

There are remarkable similarities between many present and ancient European and west Asian languages. Scholars have longed believed that these languages derived from a common ancestor, called Indo-European. Archaeologists and linguists have tried to identify where and when this original language was spoken. In this article, Colin Renfrew suggests that Indo-European might have been spread through the advance of agricultural production westward from present-day Turkey some 7500 years ago. The similarity of languages in Europe and Western Asia is not simply a linguistic curiosity, but a valuable clue to the connections between peoples and cultures in the past.

The idea of languages being related to one another was not a new one. It had long been realized that many of the languages of contemporary Europe—for instance, Italian, French, Spanish and Portuguese—were related, both in vocabulary and in grammatical structure. Indeed in this case the explanation was not far to seek. The "common source" in this case was Latin.

. . .

That several languages of Europe should be derived from Latin is not very surprising. We can fairly readily accept that other European languages . . . might be related to these and to the Germanic languages also, as well as to Ancient Greek, but that these should be all closely related to many of the languages of India and Iran is something which our knowledge of the history of Europe and Western Asia would simply not lead us to predict. For between Europe and Iran and India lies a great tract of land where very different languages are spoken. So how and why should these . . . languages . . . be related?

. . .

Until the turn of the century . . . the question of the origins of the Indo-European language itself must have been spoken in prehistoric times. With the development of prehistoric archaeology it was, however, inevitable that the material evidence surviving from the prehistoric period should be scrutinized for any light it might shed on the question.

$\cdots$

If we look at the distribution of the Indo-European languages of Europe when we first see them in the centuries shortly before or after the beginning of the Christian era . . . virtually the whole of Europe seems to have been Indo-European speaking.

$\cdots$

What historical reality lies behind the common ancestral origin of all these languages? . . .

We . . . come upon one major process which undoubtedly radically affected the whole of Europe. This was the adoption of farming.

It is widely accepted today that most of the major plant domesticates and probably some of the animals also, which formed the basis for the early farming cultures of Europe, were ultimately imports into the area. . . . It seems safe to say that the first farmers of Europe were settled in Greece . . . before 6000 BC. . . .

I suggest that the spread of farming in Europe took place by a process much like [a] wave of advance. . . . This implies that the bulk of the population in each new area which comes to practise a farming economy is not of local ancestry. In the main this is not an indigenous, acculturated population, but one where the children, in most cases, were born perhaps twenty or thirty miles away from the birthplaces of their parents. There is absolutely no need to suggest any organized migrations: no individual in this model needs to have moved more than forty to sixty kilometres in his or her entire life. Yet gradually, because of the great increase in population which the development of farming allows in an area, the result would have been to fill Europe not only with a new, farming economy, but to a large extent with a new population.

$\cdots$

If that was the case, we would expect that the language of those first farmers in Greece around 6500 BC would be carried across the whole of Europe. Of course it would change in the process. In areas close to Greece, the language of the first farmers would be rather similar to that of their farming ancestors. But with the passing of the years, if the two regions were now isolated, divergences would emerge and dialects would form. Over a period of millennia, these would separate into distinct although cognate languages. This is very much the process which, as we have seen, happened to Latin at the end of the Roman Empire, where a number of the different provinces diverged linguistically with the formation of their own Romance languages. Further to the north-west, and many centuries later, the language of the first farmers as they arrived might already be rather different from their ancestors in Greece, and even more so from their distant cousins in Greece at the same point in time. There is no difficulty then, in imagining the development of a whole series of different languages, and ultimately of language families in the different parts of Europe.

So far, however, we have completely ignored the pre-existing, hunter-gatherer . . . population. On one view we might disregard them, suggesting that they exploited a rather different ecological niche from that used by the first farmers. . . . If they kept themselves to themselves, so to speak, they would soon come to represent a small linguistic minority representing perhaps no more than 1 per cent of the population in most areas. Gradually they might have been linguistically assimilated, although contributing words and perhaps grammatical features to the language of each area. In cases where the . . . population was much denser—perhaps in Brittany or on the shores of Portugal . . . their contribution might have been larger, and where the local . . . population actually took up farming itself, it too would undergo much the same increase in population density. In such a case its language would have a greater probability of surviving. On this model, that could be the explanation for the occasional pockets of non-Indo-European languages which survived into historic times, such as Etruscan or Basque.

35 Bantu Language and Migrations

Philip Curtin et al. *African History*. Boston and Toronto: Little, Brown and Company, 1978. 25–30.

In the previous selection, you read about the diffusion of Indo-European languages westward from—Colin Renfrew argued—Anatolia through Europe. The diffusion of languages was by no means a uniquely Eurasian phenomenon. In the passage below, you will learn how Bantu-speakers spread eastward and southward from present-day Nigeria beginning (at the latest) in the first centuries BCE. By studying words common to the Bantu languages, the authors reconstruct a picture of the original Bantu society and discuss how their language spread throughout the subcontinent. You will notice, however, that the reasons for the Bantu migrations are not known. Although an earlier generation of scholars argued that the Bantu possessed iron tools and weapons, and hence were able to clear the forests and subdue hunter-gatherer peoples, the authors of this excerpt find that particular interpretation implausible.

The Kongo on the Atlantic Ocean call a person *muntu*, with a plural *bantu*. On the Indian Ocean the Swahili say *mtu* (singular) *watu* (pl.). In the equatorial forest the Mongo say *bongo* (sg.), *banto* (pl.), while the Duala in Cameroons say *moto* (sg.), *bato* (pl.), and the Xhosa of the Eastern Cape say *umntu* (sg.), *bantu* (pl.). The similarity in all these words is clear. Linguists recognized this similarity very early and called this group of languages *Bantu* after the term the ancestral language used to designate "people." The ancestral language is called Proto-Bantu.

Bantu languages are spoken in Africa south of a line running roughly from the Bight of Biafra to the Indian Ocean near the Kenya-Somali border. The group includes more than four hundred languages, all as closely related to each other as are the Germanic languages. The Bantu-speakers occupy a huge area, for the only

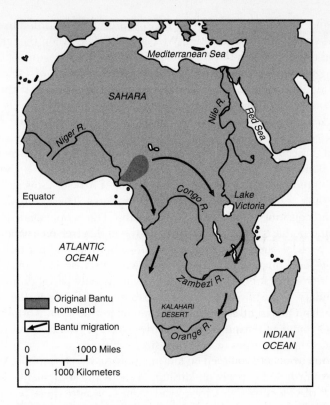

Figure 7.1 Map of Bantu Migrations.

non-Bantu languages in the subcontinent are the Khoisan tongues, which are now restricted to parts of South and Southwestern Africa.

This linguistic discovery raises a major question. How did the Bantu languages spread? From where, and when? Were any movements of people associated with the spread of languages? The answer to these questions is still taxing the ingenuity of historians today. . . .

Comparable and well-known cases indicate that languages have been spread either by the migration of large numbers of people who imposed their language on the minority they overran, or by migration of a small number of people who imposed their language because they either conquered the area or were considered by both the local people and themselves as vastly superior in civilization. Most of the Germanic languages spread in the first way; the Romance languages (for example French) diffused in the second fashion.

But how did so many come to speak the Bantu languages? . . . It is becoming clear that the migration of Bantu-speakers began somewhere in Nigeria and brought them first to Cameroon and Gabon. Gradually they spread eastward north of the forest and southward to the forest's edge near the lower Congo to Zaire and Lower Kasai. . . .

In order to know when the Bantu spread, one has to rely on other sources. The only certain date is that of the eighth century A.D., when a Bantu language was in use in Zanzibar and the coast opposite; Bantu words were recorded by Arab geographers and travelers of that century. We can only guess when the language may have arrived there, or when the Bantu expansion may have begun.

But linguists can tell us other things about the speakers of early Bantu languages through their reconstruction of Proto-Bantu vocabulary. If the languages from which later Bantu languages are derived from included words like *canoe, fishhook, goat, leader, witch,* or *religious specialist,* it is fair to assume that the culture of the people who spoke that language also included those features. . . . From this Central African protovocabulary the following picture can be reconstructed. The Proto-Bantu were fishermen. They used canoes, nets, lines, and fishhooks. They also hunted big and small game and cultivated African yams and palm trees as well as some cereals, probably millets or sorghums. The grains were crushed into flour and consumed as porridge after cooking. The people made pottery, used barkcloth, and perhaps already wove fibers of the raphia tree on a wide loom. They bred goats, perhaps sheep, and had some cattle. But they did not take cattle with them during their migrations. They did not work iron, so tools must have been fashioned of wood or stone. Data about weaving is only partly derived from the protovocabulary. It rests partly on the distribution of looms in the nineteenth-century A.D., and the fact that cloth was woven on a wide loom is attested by some Nok cultures that date from the first centuries B.C. The fishermen were sedentary and lived in compact villages of unknown size.

Social organization was based on kinship; polygyny was common. Village organization was not based entirely on kinship. Perhaps the settlement was governed by a council of elders, perhaps by a headsman. Certainly there is a term which meant "leader," and it was linked to territorial power. In eastern Bantu the same term later came to mean "diviner." The ancestral Bantu-speakers feared witches and blamed them for most evil. They employed religious specialists who were often both medicine men and diviners at the same time. It is probable, but less clear, that they believed in nature spirits as well as in the power of ancestors. . . .

The exceptionally large Proto-Bantu vocabulary gives even more detail about some other aspects of culture. The Proto-Bantu kept dogs, for instance, but no fowl, pigs, ducks, or pigeons. . . . All of the preceding linguistic data have been a launching pad for historians and anthropologists. Some have maintained that it was because the Bantu knew how to smelt iron that they could enter deep into the forest, cut the trees, and also overcome Stone Age enemies. Their superiority in technology allowed them to dominate all peoples they met and thus their language diffused. But the forest can be burned more efficiently than it can be cut, and there is no clear evidence that any word for iron or the technology associated with it is Proto-Bantu. Others have thought that the Proto-Bantu adopted the cultivation of plantains, bananas, and the Asiatic yam, allowing them to live comfortably in the forest. But again the evidence from the protovocabulary does not bear this out. . . .

Why the Bantu-speakers could impose their language on other people has raised further speculation. Here, the answers are more like a hypothesis bolstered by analogy to known processes elsewhere than a deduction from known evidence. One possible explanation, for example, comes from analogy to the alien settlement of the Americas: European and African newcomers from the much more diverse disease environment of Afro-Eurasia brought diseases with them to which they themselves had acquired immunities, but against which the Amerindians in their comparative isolation had no defenses. For the Americas, the result was a population decline of 50 to 100 percent in the first century after Columbus [i.e., after 1492 CE]. Something similar might have happened to the relatively isolated peoples of the African forest zone and the southern savanna, just as the Khoikhoi of the far south were to suffer once more from the impact of sea-borne smallpox in the eighteenth century.

Because Bantu-speaking people settled in compact villages in the midst of scattered non-Bantu speakers, hypothetically the village would act as a center for a region and in time set standards of value. This and intermarriage would lead to a gradual predominance of Bantu speech, even if the absolute number of Bantu-speaking migrants had been smaller at first than that of the native-born inhabitants. . . .

Still, no available hypothesis can yet explain the full complexity of reality over such a long time so far in the past. Ecological readaptations to forest, then savanna again, must have been extremely complex and varied. In theory, something could be made of archaeological materials, but artifacts that have survived tell nothing about the language of those who made or used them. . . . In India, correlations between archaeological "cultures" and the Aryan invasion are certain only because myths and epics have survived about this invasion and their clues correlate completely with the archaeological evidence. . . .

Most, if not all, scholars agree that the last areas into which the Bantu languages moved were eastern Africa and a little of southern and southwestern Africa. . . . In southern Africa the large influence from languages spoken before the Bantu arrived suggests that Bantu speech did not have as much time to assimilate all of these borrowings as it had in Central Africa, where one can scarcely detect traces of the aboriginal languages. . . . A close examination of the grammar and vocabulary of each of the Bantu languages will add much to the possibility of finding traces of aboriginal languages, and will certainly add to our knowledge of how the Bantu-speakers accommodated themselves to the aboriginal inhabitants.

36 Bantu Oral Tradition

Luc de Heusch. *The Drunken King, or the Origin of the State.*
Bloomington, Ind.: Indiana University Press, 1982. 15–16.

In the case of the Aryan invasion of the Indian subcontinent, there is both strong archaeological evidence as well as the recorded epic of the *Ramayana* to describe how Aryan customs and language spread. In your previous reading, the authors suggest that this is precisely what is lacking in the case of the Bantu migrations—corroborating evidence in the form of oral tradition. Yet the following excerpt is from the oral traditions of the Luba people in Nigeria, and describes a powerful leader—Mbidi Kiluwe—who brings "proper customs" to a neighboring people. Could this tale be distant evidence of the Bantu migrations? Consider, as you read the passages, that one difference between the Bantu and their southern neighbors, such as the Khoisan peoples of southern Africa, was that the skin color of the Bantu people is darker.

Later a fisherman called Muleya Monga lived near Lake Boya. He had three children by one of his wives, who was called Mwamba or Ndai. Of the children, one was a boy called Nkongolo ("Rainbow") because of his pale skin. There were also two girls, Mabela and Bulanda. By his second wife, Kaseya, Muleya Monga had another daughter, called Sungu.

One day, Nkongolo was struck by the sight of a column of ants carrying off termites. He had the idea of organizing a merciless army. He gathered some followers about him and soon showed himself to be so tyrannical that he was driven out of the country. Some time later, however, he returned to Lake Boya and, with the help of the diviner Mijibu, reasserted his domination over the Kalanga people. These people were of lighter color than the Luba. Nkongolo was a brutal and ruthless chief. Being suspicious of the power of women, he decided to avoid marrying outside of his own family. So he took his half sister Sungu as his wife.

At the same time, the hunter Ilunga Kiluwe reigned in Bupemba (presumably Buhemba, a country to the east). He had two sons, Mbidi Kiluwe and Ndala, and a daughter called Mwanana of whom he was very fond. When he became old, Ilunga Kiluwe wanted his daughter to succeed him, while his subjects wanted Mbidi Kiluwe. Mwanana had a pet lion. This animal escaped while Mbidi Kiluwe was playing with it. Enraged, Mwanana threatened to have her brother put to death unless he recaptured the lion. Mbidi Kiluwe was obliged to pursue the animal. He took with him ten of his wives, fifty slaves, and his youngest son, Mwema Mwimbi. He lost the lion's trail at the Lualaba River. He went on until he came to the river Lovoi, where he found a country rich in game. He began hunting, killing men and animals without discrimination. When he came to the confluence with the Kiankodi River, his wives and slaves refused to go any further. Mbidi Kiluwe continued on his way with his son Mwema, who carried the bows and arrows.

Meanwhile, at Lake Boya, the diviner Mijibu warned Nkongolo that "power is coming." He advised his master, on pain of losing his life, to give generous welcome to the chief who was approaching. Mbidi Kiluwe and his son followed the Kiankodi River upstream to its source in the highlands. Then they followed the course of the Luvidyo River downstream to the Munza lake. There they met two beautiful young women, Nkongolo's sisters Mabela and Bulanda, who were trying to drag from the water a net full of fish that was too heavy for them. Mbidi Kiluwe drew it out with ease and took his leave of the two young women, who had fallen in love with the hunter. They were greatly impressed with his beauty, his strength, and his dark color. They begged their brother to spare the life of the handsome stranger, for because of the prophecy of Mijibu, Nkongolo either killed or enslaved all foreigners. Mbidi Kiluwe remained on the alert. When he saw some of Nkongolo's soldiers approaching, he hid in a tree. The two young women tried in vain to find the hunter's trail. While they were resting by a stream, they saw in the water the reflection of Mbidi, who was watching them from his hideout in the branches in a tree above them. They begged him to come down and accompany them to the home of Nkongolo. Mbidi agreed, and instructed his son Mwema to fetch his wives and slaves. . . .

Mijibu told him to rejoice because the hunter was introducing the proper customs of divine kingship.

37 The Polynesian Migrations

Irving Rouse. *Migrations in Prehistory: Inferring Population Movement from Cultural Remains.* New Haven, Conn.: Yale University Press, 1986. 437–442.

This selection discusses how and when people first arrived in Polynesia, the generic name given to island groups in the Pacific. The reading combines linguistic and archaeological research with the oral traditions of contemporary peoples living in the area. Based on these three elements, along with knowledge of weather patterns and prevailing ocean currents, scholars can suggest when, from where, and by whom different islands were settled.

[T]he ancestors of the Polynesians moved through Melanesia from west to east, entering it via the smaller islands off New Guinea and leaving it through Fiji. From there, they passed into Tonga and Samoa on the east side of the Polynesian triangle. . . . Present evidence indicates that they then crossed the triangle to the Marquesas Islands on its east side, whence they radiated to Easter Island in its southeast corner, to Hawaii at its apex, to Tahiti in its center, and finally to New Zealand in its southwest corner. Their entry into Polynesia is dated around 1300 BC, their settlement of Marquesas about 300 AD, and their arrival in New Zealand ca. 900 AD. . . .

Polynesia was virgin territory, without previous languages, cultures, and races that would have blended differently with those of the migrants. Such a one-to-one relationship between language, culture and race does not occur in less isolated parts of the world.

• • •

The Polynesians have preserved oral traditions about the manner in which they settled the islands. These traditions can be used to test parts of the linguistic and archeological conclusions. For example, the Maori, who live in New Zealand, tell us that their ancestors first settled there in the tenth century AD. This date agrees nicely with the linguistic and archeological estimates.

According to the Maori, there were two subsequent migrations into New Zealand, one in the twelfth century and the other in the fourteenth century, the former by members of a single family and the latter by a fleet of canoes. Neither of these events could have caused a repeopling of New Zealand; they are examples of immigration rather than population movement. . . .

But can we be sure that both events actually took place? Subsequent individuals may have claimed to be descended from the leaders of fictitious migrations in order to justify chiefly status. This possibility could be eliminated archaeologically by searching for sites containing the cultural complex diagnostic of twelfth- and fourteenth-century Tahiti, whence the migrants are said to have come. In the absence of such evidence, the two traditions of immigration must be considered untested hypotheses.

Peoples do not move at a steady pace. . . . [T]he ancestors of the Polynesians paused for more than one thousand years in Tonga and Samoa before penetrating the heart of the Polynesian triangle. . . .

The halt at the Tongan-Samoan frontier must have been due, at least in part, to the need to develop new equipment and techniques with which to travel the far longer distances between islands in the heart of the Polynesian triangle. Discovery of a sailing canoe at an early site on Huanine Island, near Tahiti, has provided us with knowledge of the equipment. This canoe had an estimated length of sixty-five feet, was double hulled, and, to judge from historic examples, contained a cabin.

As for techniques, Polynesianists have conducted a series of experimental voyages in native-type canoes, seeking to determine how the peopling of the islands took place. They have been particularly concerned with the migrants' solution to the problem of sailing into the prevailing trade winds, which blow from the northeast above the equator and from the southeast below the equator . . . [:] the migrants could have waited for intervals in which westerlies temporarily replaced the trade winds and made it possible to sail from Melanesia to Polynesia. . . .

These canoes had been more highly developed in the western Pacific than in the New World and . . . as a result . . . migrations were more likely to have proceeded against the prevailing winds.

The authorities have also debated whether the ancestors of the Polynesians made intentional voyages of colonization or accidentally drifted to new islands. A computer-assisted study of the possibilities indicates that intentional voyages are more likely to have been the case. Westerners, who are used to the emptiness of the Atlantic Ocean, find it difficult to conceive that anyone would intentionally seek islands in an unknown sea. However, the migrants into Polynesia came from seas that were full of islands, hence they must have had greater confidence in their ability to find new land.

When the migrants first advanced into the central part of the Polynesian triangle, they encountered the same moist, tropical conditions from which they had come. When they continued on into the corners of the triangle, however, they had to adapt to different conditions—subtropical in the case of Easter Island and Hawaii, which they settled next, and temperate in the case of New Zealand, at the end of their journey. This is a good example of the process of adaptive radiation.

In the central part of the triangle, for instance, they relied both upon taro,° grown in paddies like those used elsewhere for rice, and on yams, grown in dry fields cleared by the slash and burn technique. They were forced by the relatively dry, cool conditions in the corners of the triangles to place more emphasis on yams, and on the sweet potato when this became available in South America.

°Taro is an edible root similar to a potato.

38 Taino Migrations in the Caribbean

Irving Rouse. *Migrations in Prehistory: Inferring Population Movement from Cultural Remains.* New Haven, Conn.: Yale University Press, 1986. 151–155.

In the following passage, an archaeologist attempts to explain the settlement of the Caribbean by peoples who were decimated soon after the Spanish conquest of the archipelago at the turn of the sixteenth century. Their absence precludes drawing conclusions from modern ethnographic studies. Instead, Irving Rouse bases his arguments on material and linguistic evidence to determine where these peoples came from. For the purposes of the article, prehistoric refers to the period before European contact with the Americas, and historic for the period thereafter.

We now realize that peoples mentioned in historical documents, such as the Tainos, cannot be traced back into prehistory—we must work instead with population groups defined by the two kinds of evidence about prehistory currently available, linguistic and archeological. We use the linguistic evidence to formulate and trace speech communities in terms of their languages and the archeological evidence to formulate and trace peoples in terms of their cultures.

• • •

The current results of linguistic and archeological research . . . indicate that the island Carib and Taino Indians developed in situ as the result of a single population movement from South America around the time of Christ. The linguists have shown that the proto-Northern speech community entered the West Indies about that time and eventually pushed the previous inhabitants back into the western end of Cuba, where Columbus encountered them. The newcomers diverged into two new speech communities, Island Carib in the Lesser Antilles and Taino in the Greater Antilles and the Bahamas.

• • •

This is not to say that the West Indies became isolated from the adjacent mainland after the colonization of the islands by Ceramic Age peoples. There must have been frequent intercommunication, resulting in the spread of loan words from continental speech communities to the emerging Island Carib and Taino communities. There must also have been weak interaction, resulting in transculturation and immigration from island to island. But neither linguistic nor archeological research has revealed convincing evidence of a period of strong interaction, resulting in acculturation or population movement.

The spread of the South American ball game into the West Indies . . . is a possible example of transculturation. . . . The Island Carib invasion of the Windward Islands and Guadeloupe may be an example of immigration. Fortunately for us, this movement took place late enough in prehistoric time to be remembered in the traditional history of the area and to be reflected in the linguistic structure of the historic Indians.

• • •

From a geographical point of view, the ancestors of the Tainos could have entered the West Indies via either the east coast of Venezuela, Trinidad, or the Guianas. The historic evidence favors Trinidad and the Guianas; Arawakan speakers were concentrated there during the Historic Age. Nevertheless, archeologists, and, to a lesser extent, linguists have focused upon Trinidad and the east coast of Venezuela in tracing the ancestors of the Tainos back to the mainland. Having failed in this endeavor, they are now turning their attention to the Guianas.

• • •

Why did we originally overlook the possibility of movement out of the Guianas? In part, we were victims of historical accident. [A particular style of] pottery was first found on the continental islands and we traced it back from there into the Orinoco Valley and onto the east coast of Venezuela. This led us to hypothesize that the ancestors of the Tainos had come from some combination of the three places, and we began to search for them there, not realizing that it is a mistake to limit oneself to the areas indicated by the available evidence. One should always take into consideration all potential migration routes and design one's research accordingly.

We were also misled by the present situation in the Caribbean area. The Guianas are now peripheral to the Caribbean Basin, and we assumed that this was also true during the Ceramic Age. . . . We were wrong. We should have expanded our range of multiple working hypotheses to include the possibility of movement into the Antilles via that region.

A third event that has brought the Guianas to our attention is the rise of interest among archeologists in residential and subsistence patterns, that is, the places where people have chosen to live and the manner in which they have exploited the food resources available in each place. Studies of these subjects indicate that, as the ancestors of the Tainos entered the West Indies, they headed for the major streams, settled along their banks some distance from their mouths, and exploited the resources in the surrounding forests, paying relatively little attention to seafood. The only places in northeastern South America where they could have acquired these preferences are in the Orinoco valley and on the Guiana coastal plain.

39 Germans on the Roman Frontier

The Agricola and Germany of Tacitus, and the Dialogue on Oratory. Translated by Alfred John Church and William Jackson Brodribb. New York: Macmillan Company, 1906. 87–107.

Living on the fringes of the Roman empire, the inhabitants of Germania [that part of Germany north of the Rhine River] instilled in their Roman neighbors a healthy respect for their fighting abilities. The following description of the Germans was written by the Roman historian Tacitus in the first century CE. Tacitus' perceptions of the Germans reflect both his criticisms of the Roman empire by way of comparison with a different society, and his comments on the lifestyle of a people he clearly views as inferior to his own.

The Germans themselves I should regard as aboriginal, and not mixed at all with other races through immigration or intercourse. For, in former times, it was not by land but on shipboard that those who sought to emigrate would arrive; and the boundless and, so to speak, hostile ocean beyond us, is seldom entered by a sail from our world. And, beside the perils of rough and unknown seas, who would leave Asia, or Africa, or Italy for Germany, with its wild country, its inclement skies, its sullen manners and aspect, unless indeed it were his home? In their ancient songs, their only way of remembering or recording the past, they celebrate an earth-born god, Tuisco, and his son Mannus, as the origin of their race, as their founders. . . . Some with the freedom of conjecture permitted by antiquity, assert that the god had several descendants, and the nation several appellations. . . . The name Germany, on the other hand, they say, is modern and newly introduced, from the fact that the tribes which first crossed the Rhine and drove out the Gauls, and are now called Tungrians, were then called Germans. Thus what was the name of a tribe, and not of a race, gradually prevailed, till all called themselves by this self-invented name of Germans, which the conquerors had first employed to inspire terror.

• • •

The tribes of Germany are free from all taint of intermarriages with foreign nations, and they appear as a distinct, unmixed race, like none but themselves. Hence, too, the same physical peculiarities throughout so vast a population. All have fierce blue eyes, red hair, huge frames, fit only for a sudden exertion. They are less able to bear laborious work. Heat and thirst they cannot in the least endure; to cold and hunger their climate and their soil inure them.

• • •

They choose their kings by birth, their generals by merit. These kings have not unlimited or arbitrary power, and the generals do more by example than by authority. . . . But to reprimand, to imprison, even to flog, is permitted to the priests alone, and that not as a punishment, or at the general's bidding, but, as it were, by the mandate of the god whom they believe to inspire the warrior. . . . And what most stimulates their courage is, that their squadrons or battalions, instead of being formed by chance or by a fortuitous gathering, are composed of families and clans. Close by them too, are those dearest to them, so that they hear the shrieks of women, the cries of infants. . . .

Tradition says that armies already wavering and giving way have been rallied by women who, with earnest entreaties and bosoms laid bare, have vividly represented the horrors of captivity, which the Germans fear with such extreme dread on behalf of their women. . . . They even believe that the sex has a certain sanctity and prescience, and they do not despise their counsels, or make light of their answers. . . .

Mercury is the deity whom they chiefly worship, and on certain days they deem it right to sacrifice to him even with human victims. . . .

Augury and divination by lot no people practice more diligently. The use of lots is simple. A little bough is lopped off a fruit-bearing tree, and cut into small pieces; these are distinguished by certain marks, and thrown carelessly and at random over a white garment. In public questions the priest of the particular state, in private the father of the family invokes the gods, and, with his eyes towards heaven, takes up each piece three times, and finds in them a meaning according to the mark previously impressed on them. . . . It is peculiar to this people to seek omens and monitions from horses. Kept at the public expense, in these same woods and groves, are white horses, pure from the taint of earthly labor; these are yoked to a sacred car, and accompanied by the priest and the king, or chief of the tribe, who note their neighings and snortings.

• • •

When they go into battle, it is a disgrace for the chief to be surpassed in valor, a disgrace for his followers not to equal the valor of the chief. And it is an infamy and a reproach for life to have survived the chief, and returned from the field. To defend, to protect him, to ascribe one's own brave deeds to his renown, is the height of loyalty. The chief fights for victory; his vassals fight for their chief. . . . Feasts and entertainments, which though inelegant, are plentifully furnished, are their only pay. The means of this bounty come from war and rapine. Nor are they as easily persuaded to plough the earth and to wait for the year's produce as to challenge an enemy and earn the honor of wounds. Nay, they actually think it tame and stupid to acquire by the sweat of toil what they might win by their blood.

Whenever they are not fighting, they pass much of their time in the chase, and still more in idleness giving themselves up to sleep and to feasting, the bravest and the most warlike doing nothing, and surrendering the management of the household of the home, and of the land, to the women, the old men and all the weakest members of the family. . . . It is the custom of the states to bestow by voluntary and individual contribution on the chiefs a present of cattle or of grain, which, while accepted as a compliment, supplies their wants. They are particularly delighted by gifts from neighboring tribes . . . such as choice steeds, heavy armor, trappings, and neckchains. We have now taught them to accept money also.

It is well known that the nations of Germany have no cities, and that they do not even tolerate closely contiguous dwellings. They live scattered and apart, just as a spring, a meadow, or a wood has attracted them. Their villages they do not arrange in our fashion, . . . but every person surrounds his dwelling with an open space, either as a precaution against the disasters of fire, or because they do not know how to build. No use is made by them of stone or tile; they employ timber for all purposes, rude masses without ornament or attractiveness. . . .

They all wrap themselves in a cloak which is fastened with a clasp, or, if this is not forthcoming, with a thorn, leaving the rest of their persons bare. . . . They also wear the skins of wild beasts. . . .

Their marriage code, however, is strict, and indeed no part of their manners is more praiseworthy. Almost alone among barbarians they are content with one wife, except a very few among them. . . . Lest the woman should think herself to stand apart from aspirations after noble deeds and from the perils of war, she is reminded by the ceremony which inaugurates marriage that she is her husband's partner in toil and danger, destined to suffer and to dare with him alike both in peace and in war. . . .

Very rare for so numerous a population is adultery, the punishment for which is prompt, and in the husband's power. Having cut off the hair of the adulteress and stripped her naked, he expels her from the house in the presence of her kinfolk, and then flogs her through the whole village. The loss of chastity meets with no indulgence; neither beauty, youth nor wealth will procure the culprit a husband. No one in Germany laughs at vice, nor do they call it the fashion to corrupt and to be corrupted. . . . To limit the number of their children or to destroy any of their subsequent offspring is accounted infamous, and good habits are here more effectual than good laws elsewhere.

• • •

It is a duty among them to adopt the feuds as well as the friendships of a father or a kinsman. These feuds are not implacable; even homicide is expiated by the payment of a certain number of cattle and of sheep, and the satisfaction is accepted by the entire family, greatly to the advantage of the state, since feuds are dangerous in proportion to a people's freedom.

• • •

[S]laves are not employed after our manner with distinct domestic duties assigned to them, but each one has the management of a house and home of his own. The master requires from the slave a certain quantity of grain, of cattle, and of clothing, as he would from a tenant, and this is the limit of subjection. All other household functions are discharged by the wife and children. To strike a slave or to punish him with bonds or with hard labor is a rare occurrence. They often kill them, not in enforcing strict discipline, but on the impulse of passion, as they would an enemy, only it is done with impunity. The freedmen do not rank much above slaves, and are seldom of any weight in the family, never in the state, with the exception of those tribes which are ruled by kings. There indeed they rise above the freeborn and the noble; elsewhere the inferiority of the freedman marks the freedom of the state.

Of lending money on interest and increasing it by compound interest they know nothing,—a more effectual safeguard than if it were prohibited.

Land proportioned to the number of inhabitants is occupied by the whole community in turn, and afterwards divided among them according to rank. A wide expanse of plains makes the partition easy. They till fresh fields every year, and they have still more land than enough; . . . corn [wheat] is the only produce required from the earth; hence even the year itself is not divided by them into as many seasons as with us. Winter, spring, and summer have both a meaning and a name; the name and blessings of autumn are alike unknown.

DISCUSSION QUESTIONS

1. How are languages spread? What are the relationships between the spread of particular languages and the spread of culture and technical knowledge?

2. How does the Bantu oral legend support the linguistic evidence for the Bantu migrations? Do you find oral memory a convincing source in this case?

3. How is language used to trace the movement of a particular people? What might a future scholar learn by studying English? For example, think of the following words: night (German), algebra (Arabic), and canoe (Taino [Arawak]). What other word origins do you know?

4. How and why do peoples migrate? How do the migrations of the Taino, the Polynesians, and the Bantu-speakers compare?

5. What did the Roman historian think of the Germans on the northern frontier of the empire? How would you describe German society?

PART
Three

CONVERGENCE AND COMPLEXITY: 500 CE to 1450 CE

*T*here are a number of divergent views of the history of the world between 500 and 1000 CE. Scholars have traditionally seen this period as a "dark age" that involved simplification and loss of human knowledge after the fall of the so-called classical empires. However, this representation is Eurocentric, and does not apply to regions outside of Europe in this era. In addition, in light of recent scholarship, this view no longer appears to be accurate even for Europe.

A major trend that occurred throughout the major regions of the world at this time was an expansion and intensification of contacts among societies through commerce, travel, religion, and war. Of these, the major spheres of interaction between societies during this period were trade and religion. While warfare sometimes played a part in these contacts, it was less influential than the peaceful contacts of commerce, exchange, and pilgrimage. In these exchanges, common elements of language, behavior, and social rules for interaction existed that helped individuals of different societies relate to each other.

This section examines a number of aspects common to these societies in this period. Themes involving both relations between societies, such as the spread of religions and long-distance trade, and themes within societies, are examined. Polities in this period became increasingly diverse, specialized, and complex. Sedentary societies were characterized by agricultural surpluses and specialization of occupations. Internally, authorities became increasingly concerned with the regulation of the behavior of their subjects. Such regulation could be accomplished through law, religious teachings, social pressure, or court etiquette. In addition, some governments took on increasing responsibility for the physical welfare of their subjects. Literature concerning the appearance of the Black Death across Europe and Asia illustrates reactions to a catastrophe against which both individuals and societies seemed fragile and helpless; however, attempts to curb famine and drought in states such as the Mongol empire, and policies of assistance and relief in the face of disaster, are also evident in this period.

This section ends in Chapter 13 with an examination of the world in 1450. This date represents the end of this era because the processes of global integration accelerated at this time. These processes are the subject of Part 4 and are carried over into the second volume of this reader. Chapter 13 examines the world on the eve of global integration, revealing the variety of societies that existed, the daily lives of ordinary people within them, and the extent of interaction between different societies.

Chapter
8

Societies Linked by Trade and Exchange

*I*n this period societies in different areas came into increasing contact with each other. As trading networks both within and between different areas expanded, societies in Europe, Asia, and Africa, as well as societies within the Americas were brought into contact through the commercial exchange of trade goods.

The topic of trade actually encompasses trade goods, merchants and merchant networks, means of transportation and communication, cartels and monopolies, and different methods of business transactions. The following selections examine some of these trades and the people involved in them. The document dealing with Padua and Lombardy (Italian centers of trade) suggests the relationship among peaceful trade, looting, and conflict, and reveals the role of negotiation and governmental intervention in business transactions. In addition, a contract for the sale of a slave is also included. The sale of human beings was common to most of the world before the nineteenth century. Whereas today, only one's labor is sold for salaries on the initiative of individuals themselves, in the past persons sold as slaves belonged to those who bought them as property.

Other readings reveal the extent to which the world was tied together during this period. The documents from several medieval Italian city-states demonstrate the variety of trading contacts and commodities that existed. The reading from Norway discusses the ideal activities and behavior for a merchant engaging in trade across cultures. The documents from the Cairo Geniza shows the actual activities of real merchants conducting long-distance trade. Chao Ju-kua describes Chinese trading links, which extended through Asia and into Europe and Africa. While the Americas did not have contact with other continents, long-distance networks of trade and redistribution also existed there. Garcilaso de la Vega discusses the state-organized redistribution of goods produced over several ecological zones spread throughout the Inca empire.

40 Medieval Mediterranean Trade

Robert S. Lopez and Irving W. Raymond, eds. *Medieval Trade in the Mediterranean World.* New York: Columbia University Press, 1955. 57–58, 116, 127.

The Italian city-states beginning in the tenth century were centers for both European and international trade, with linkages into Eastern Europe and Asia. Some scholars suggest that business practices were diffused from Arab merchants to their Italian partners, and from there through the rest of Europe. The passages that follow discuss trading fairs, practices, negotiation, and types of merchandise. Human beings, usually captured from other societies, were included as merchandise to be sold as property. Slavery, or some form of coerced labor, was common to much of the world at this time.

PAVIA, 1010–1020 CE

... merchants entering the kingdom [of Lombardy, an Italian kingdom] were [obliged] to pay the *decima* [ten percent tax] on all merchandise at the customs houses and at the roads appertaining to the king [public highways]. . . . All persons coming from beyond the mountains are obligated to pay the *decima* on horses, male and female slaves, woolen, linen, and hemp cloth, tin, and swords. . . . But everything that [pilgrims] bound for Rome to Saint Peter's take with them for expenses is to be passed without payment of the *decima.* No one ought to exact the *decima* from the pilgrims themselves bound for Rome or to hinder them in any way. . . .°

. . . the Angles and Saxons† . . . have come and were [obliged] to come with their merchandise and wares. . . . [W]hen they saw their trunks and sacks being emptied at the gates, they grew angry and started rows with the employees of the treasury. The[y] were wont to hurl abusive words and in addition very often inflicted wounds. . . . But in order to cut short such great evils and to remove danger, the king of the Angles and Saxons and the king of the Lombards agreed together as follows: The nation of the Angles and Saxons is no longer to be subject to the *decima.* And in return . . . the king of the Angles and Saxons . . . [is] bound and . . . obligated to send to the palace in Pavia and to the king's treasury, every third year, fifty pounds of refined silver, two large, handsome greyhounds, hairy or furred, in chains, with collars covered with gilded plates sealed or enameled with the arms of the king, two excellent embossed shields, two excellent lances, and two excellent swords wrought and tested. And to the master of the treasury they are obligated to

---

°The same custom is found in Muslim empires for pilgrims bound for Mecca.
†From England.

give two large coats of miniver [a white fur] and two pounds of refined silver. And they are to receive a safe conduct from the master of the treasury that they may not suffer any annoyance as they come and go. . . .

• • •

At that time the emperor [of the Byzantine Empire, Michael VIII Palaeologus] decided to humble the Genoese, who were full of impudence. In fact, the Venetians and their community formerly surpassed them in wealth, in arms, and in all [kinds of] materials because they made greater use of the [narrow] waters than did the Genoese and because they sailed across the high sea [Black Sea] with long ships [galleys rowed by people], and they succeeded in gaining more profit than did the Genoese in transporting and carrying wares. But once the Genoese became masters of the Black Sea by grant of the emperor and with all liberty and franchise, they braved that [sea], and sailing in the midst of winter in ships of reduced length [sailboats, using wind power], they not only barred the Romans from the lanes and the wares of the sea but also eclipsed the Venetians in wealth and material [goods]. . . . [T]hey came to look down not only upon those of their own kin but also upon the Romans themselves. Now the emperor personally had granted to a certain Genoese nobleman, called Manuele Zaccaria, the mountains to the east . . . which contained alum metal. [These] the latter exploited after having settled down there with his own people. And having collected a good deal [of profit] from these works, he wanted to obtain still more from the benevolence and good disposition of the sovereign toward him. Thus he thought it fitting that the Genoese be not allowed to transport across the Black Sea the alum-bearing metal from the mountainous districts [which was of better quality than his]—for they use a large quantity of it in dyeing the woolen textiles in different colors . . . and the emperor, assenting, made a law.*

• • •

A GENOESE SLAVE CONTRACT DATED 1248 CE

I, Giunta, son of the late Bonaccorso of [F]lorence, sell, give, and deliver to you, Raimondo Barbiere, a certain slave of mine, called Maimona, formerly of Malta† for the price &5 s.10, which I acknowledge that I have received for her from you . . . And I call myself fully paid and quit from you, waiving the exception that the money has not been counted and received. I acknowledge that I have given you power and physical dominion [over the slave], promising you that I shall not interfere nor take away the aforesaid slave in any way, but rather I shall protect [her] for you and keep her out [of the power] of any person [under penalty] of 720 Genoese which I promise you, making the stipulation, the promise remaining as settled. . . . And I, said Maimona, acknowledge that I am a slave, and I wish to be delivered and

---

*Genoese breaking this law were caught and blinded, under Byzantine law.
†This slave was white. The word *slave,* derived from the Latin *sclavus,* comes from Slav, an Eastern European people whose members were often enslaved in Western Europe and West Asia.

sold to you, Raimondo. And I acknowledge that I am more than ten [years old]. Witnesses called: Oberto de Cerreo, notary, and Antonio of Piacenza, notary. Done in Genoa behind the Church of Saint Laurent, 1248, on May 11. . . .

41 Advice to a Norwegian Merchant

"Advice to a Norwegian Merchant." In *The King's Mirror*. New York: Twayne Publishers, Inc., 1971. 79–86.

In the following passage, a father living in thirteenth-century Norway advises his son, who wants to be a merchant, on how to be successful at his chosen trade. Aside from revealing information on father-son relationships, his monologue expresses contemporary views on merchants in his society. In addition, it deals with different aspects of the commerce. Shipping, mathematics, law, language, and religious practices are all within the realm of knowledge needed by merchants. In addition, the reading discusses how an ideal merchant should behave. His strong emphasis on the importance of respecting foreign cultures and business practices is an essential part of ideal behavior.

FATHER: I have no fault to find with that calling [merchant], for often the best of men are chosen for it. But much depends on whether the man is more like those who are true merchants, or those who take the merchant's name but are mere frauds and foisters, buying and selling wrongfully.

SON: I desire to have you inform me as to the practices of such men as seem to be capable in that business.

FATHER: The man who is to be a trader will have to brave many perils, sometimes at sea and sometimes in heathen lands, but nearly always among alien peoples; and it must be his constant purpose to act discreetly wherever he happens to be. . . .

. . . [W]herever you are, be polite and agreeable; then you will secure the friendship of all good men. Make it a habit to rise early in the morning, and go first and immediately to church wherever it seems most convenient to hear the canonical hours . . . join in the worship, repeating such psalms and prayers as you have learned. When the services are over, go out to look after your business affairs. If you are unacquainted with the traffic of the town, observe carefully how those who are reputed the best and most prominent merchants conduct their business. You must also be careful to examine the wares that you buy before the purchase is finally made to make sure that they are sound and flawless. And whenever you make a purchase, call in a few trusty men to serve as witnesses as to how the bargain was made.

You should keep occupied with your business till breakfast or, if necessity demands it, till midday; . . . serve enjoyable meals if you can afford it. After the meal you may . . . stroll about . . . to see what other good merchants are employed with, or whether any new wares have come to the borough which you ought to buy. On returning to your lodgings examine your wares, lest they suffer damage after coming into your hands. If they are found to be injured . . . do not conceal the flaws from the purchaser: show him what the defects are and make such a bargain as you can; then you cannot be called a deceiver. Also put a good price on your wares, though not too high, and yet very near what you see can be obtained; then you cannot be called a foister.

Finally . . . whenever you have an hour to spare . . . make a study of all the laws, but while you remain a merchant there is no law that you will need to know more thoroughly than the Bjarkey code [laws regulating commerce]. If you are acquainted with the law, you will not be annoyed by quibbles when you have suits to bring against men of your own class, but will be able to plead according to law in every case.

. . . I regard no man perfect in knowledge unless he has thoroughly learned and mastered the customs of the place where he is sojourning. And . . . you must learn all the languages, first of all Latin and French, for these . . . are most widely used; and yet do not neglect your native tongue. . . .

And further, there are certain things which you must beware of and shun like the devil himself: these are drinking, chess, harlots, quarrelling, and throwing dice for stakes. For upon such foundations the greatest calamities are built; and unless they strive to avoid these things, few only are able to live long without blame or sin.

Observe carefully . . . the course of the heavenly bodies, . . . and . . . learn also how to mark the movements of the ocean . . . for that is knowledge which all must possess who wish to trade abroad. Learn arithmetic thoroughly, for merchants have great need of that.

If you come to a place where the king . . . has his officials, seek to win their friendship; and if they demand any necessary fees on the ruler's behalf, be prompt to render all such payments, lest by holding too tightly to little things you lose the greater. Also beware lest the king's belongings find their way into your purse; for . . . it is easier to be cautious beforehand than to crave pardon afterwards. If you can dispose of your wares at suitable prices, do not hold them long; for it is the wont of merchants to buy constantly and to sell rapidly.

If you are preparing to carry on trade beyond the seas and you sail your own ship, have it thoroughly coated with tar in the autumn. . . . Always buy shares in good vessels or in none at all. Keep your ship attractive, for then capable men will join you and it will be well manned . . . do your travelling while the season is best . . . and never remain out at sea in late autumn. . . .

. . . When you come to a market town where you expect to tarry, seek lodgings from the innkeeper who is reputed the most discreet and the most popular among both kingsmen and boroughmen. Always buy good clothes and eat good fare if your means permit; and never keep unruly or quarrelsome men as attendants or messmates. . . .

If your wealth takes on rapid growth, divide it and invest it in a partnership trade in fields where you do not yourself travel; but be cautious in selecting partners. Always let Almighty God, the holy Virgin Mary, and the saint whom you have most frequently called upon to intercede for you be counted among your partners. . . .

If you have much capital invested in trade, divide it into three parts: put one-third into partnerships . . . place the other two parts in various business ventures; for if your capital is invested in different places, it is not likely that you will suffer losses in all your wealth at one time . . . but if you find that the profits of trade bring a decided increase to your funds, draw out two-thirds and invest them in good farm

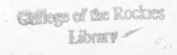
College of the Rockies
Library

land, for such property is generally thought the most secure. . . . Discontinue your own journeys at sea or as a trader in foreign fields, as soon as your means have attained sufficient growth and you have studied foreign customs as much as you like. Keep all that you see in careful memory . . . remember evil practices as a warning, and the good customs adopt.

42 The Inca State and Tribute

Garcilaso de la Vega. *Royal Commentaries of the Incas and General History of Peru.* Austin, Texas: University of Texas Press, 1966. 248–261.

As we saw in Chapter Five, Andean empires and trade centered on the control and redistribution of resources from two different ecological zones: the mountains and the coastal lowlands. This held true for the Inca empire, founded in the thirteenth century, and it shaped the form that trade took in this society. The author of this passage, Garcilaso de la Vega, an Inca noble who lived through the sixteenth-century Spanish conquest, later joined Spanish expeditions to Florida, and died in Spain. Here de la Vega talks about the organization of production and redistribution in the Inca empire, the equivalent of trade. The Inca state required production of goods as tribute from its subjects, stored them in government warehouses for redistribution or for times of scarcity. This policy necessitated stronger state intervention in the realm of trade than in other societies, but ensured that the majority of the population possessed their basic needs.

The principal tribute was the tilling and fertilizing of the lands assigned to the Sun and the Inca, the harvesting of whatever crops it produced and their storage in bins and the royal granaries that existed in each village for collecting the harvest.

• • •

In the whole of the province called Colla, for a distance of over 150 leagues, the climate is very cold and maize does not grow. A great deal of quinoa, [a high-protein wheat] . . . is grown, as well as other plants and vegetables, which give root crops, including what they call papa [potato]. This is round and damp, and because of its dampness it easily rots. . . .

In addition to the main tribute which took the form of sowing the soil, cultivating, and harvesting the crops of the Sun and of the Inca, they paid also a second tribute which consisted of clothes, footwear, and weapons for use in time of war and for the poor, that is those who could not work through age or infirmity. . . . Throughout the mountainous region clothing was made from wool which the Inca supplied from the innumerable flocks belonging to him and to the Sun. On the . . . seacoast . . . they made cotton cloth from cotton grown on the land of the Sun and of the Inca. All the Indians supplied was their labor. They made three kinds of woolen cloth. The coarsest . . . was for the common people. Another finer sort was

... worn by the nobility. . . . Other very fine clothes . . . were made for those of royal blood. . . . The fine cloth was woven in provinces where the natives were most ingenious and expert in its manufacture, and the coarser sort was made elsewhere where the natives were less skilled. All the wool for this cloth was spun by the women, who also wove the coarse cloth. . . . The finer sort was woven by men, for the work was done standing. Both kinds were made by the vassals, and not by the Incas, who did not even make their own clothing. . . .

Shoes were made in the provinces where hemp was most abundant, for they were produced from the leaves of the plant called maguey. Weapons were also furnished by districts that had the most abundant supply of the necessary materials. In some they made bows and arrows, in other lances and darts, elsewhere clubs and axes, and in others slings and ropes for transport, or shields and targets. . . .

• • •

Another sort of tribute was given by the infirm we have called poor: this was that every so many days they were obliged to deliver some hollow reeds full of lice. . . . It is said that the Incas demanded this tribute so that no one except those who were exempt from tribute, should avoid paying something. . . .

• • •

We must now explain how the tribute was kept and on what it was used. Throughout the whole kingdom there were three sorts of storehouses to hold the harvest and tribute. Every village . . . had two storehouses: one was used to hold the supplies kept for the use of the people in lean years, and the other was used for the crops of the Sun and of the Inca. . . .

For a distance of fifty leagues round the city of Cuzco the crops of the Sun and of the Inca were brought in for the use of the court. . . .

The crops of the other villages . . . were collected in the royal storehouses that existed and thence transferred to the stores on the royal roads where garrisons, arms, clothes and footwear were kept for the armies that marched along to the four quarters of the world. . . .

Just as there was an orderly system for supplying abundant clothing for the armies, so also wool was distributed every two years to all the subjects . . . so they could have clothes for themselves, their wives and children. . . .

• • •

The custom that no one begs for alms was still preserved in my own times. Until 1560, when I left Peru, I never saw in all my journeying there an Indian man or woman who asked for alms, except an old woman in Cuzco called Isabel: she begged, but it was rather as a pretext to go gossiping from door to door as gypsies do than from need. . . . As there was no coined money in my country in those days, she was given maize as alms.

43 Jewish Traders in West Asia

S.D. Goitein. *Letters of Medieval Jewish Traders.* Princeton, N.J.: Princeton University Press, 1973. 45–49, 187–90, 280–283.

Conducting trade in the eleventh-century Mediterranean Sea and Indian Ocean was a profitable but risky venture. Goods—like silk and spices—were traded throughout the region in a vast trading network that reached as far away as China and England, but without common currencies or investment banks. Few records of the day-to-day transactions of merchants and traders have survived but a treasure trove of documents survived the centuries preserved in the Cairo Geniza.* To preserve written documents in which the name of God appeared, Jewish traders deposited their records in a chamber (called a *geniza*) attached to a local synagogue. What makes the Cairo Geniza unique is the number of secular documents (some 1200) describing the activities of Jewish merchants in the region. The documents are in the Arabic language yet written in Hebrew characters. In the first selection, a trader in Palestine writes the merchant who financed his trading expedition to explain that disaster struck the shipment of silk while at sea around 1066 CE. The trader—Ya'qub [Jacob] b. Salman al-Hariri—sold Egyptian flax in exchange for silk from Lebanon and Cyprus, as well as cotton from Syria. The letter also mentions figs and raisins that originated in southwest Asia. In the second letter, a trader writes to an Indian merchant about the shipment of Asian spices and iron that was damaged in a shipwreck near the straits between the Arabian peninsula and northeastern Africa in 1139 CE. This particular letter was preserved by the merchant until he departed India after seventeen years to return to his native Tunisia. The final excerpt is a portion of a trader's accounts for business he did on the north African coast. The records detail the sales the trader made and the expenses he incurred between September 1045 and September 1046.

A LETTER FROM PALESTINE TO TUNISIA (CA. 1066 CE)

I trust in God. Praised be the Lord who resurrects the dead.

My master and lord, may God prolong your life, make your wellbeing and happiness permanent, and keep away from you all evil in his mercy. I am writing from Ramle on the 8th of Teveth (approximately: January), feeling well in body, but being worried in mind. . . .

I set sail for Jaffa, the port of Ramle. But a wind arose against us from the land. It became a storm, chasing and driving us out to the high sea, where we remained

---

*Actually, the Cairo Geniza was located in Fustat, two and one-half miles south of the contemporary city of Cairo.

for four days giving up all hope for life. We were without sails or oars, the steering rudder and the sailyards were broken, and the waves burst into the barge. We cried: "Allah, Allah," for our ship was a mere riverboat, small as a ferry. We threw part of the cargo overboard, and I gave up all hope for my life and goods. I vowed 1 dinar from the proceeds of the silk. Finally, God in his glory and majesty granted us to reach Caesarea, but my clothes and goods were completely soaked. I did not find a place to stay and to spread out my things, So I took domicile [lodging] in the synagogue, where I remained for five days. . . .

When I arrived in Ramle, I had to pay customs to a degree I am unable to describe. The price in Ramle of the Cyprus silk, which I carry with me, is 2 dinars per little pound. Please inform me of its price and advise me whether I should sell it here or carry it with me to you in Misr (Fustat), in case it is fetching a good price there. By God, answer me quickly, I have no other business here in Ramle except awaiting answers to my letters. About 3 dinars worth of goods of mine were jettisoned from the barge; may God, the exalted, restore the loss. If you want me to carry the silk with me, instruct Makhluf b. Muhsina (write him!) to pay me 2–3 dinars, or have Abu Barhun write to his brother Ya'qub (Jacob) to give me this sum so that I do not have to sell my clothing or the silk.* A man like you does not need to be urged. I know that my money and yours are one. Moreover, you have a share in this. I need not stress the urgency of a reply concerning the price of silk from Sham (Syria-Lebanon) and from Cyprus, and whether I should sell it here or carry it with me. . . .

I wrote you from Tripoli and informed you that I had sent four bundles of cotton and twenty-one pieces [bundles] of figs to Alexandria. I wrote to M. Marduk, asking him to receive this shipment. With Yahya b. al-Zaffat I sent two bags and one basket with wheat, red earth [used for writing on bales], and two baskets with raisins and figs. I instructed him to deliver these to Marduk. Your share in the basket (of wheat) and the figs is 8 dinars, and your share in the silk also 8 dinars. I hope you have written to Alexandria instructing Marduk to take care of the matter, and also to attend to the sacking. Also write him to send you either the proceeds, or the goods to be bought for them, or broken dinars.† And by God, answer. I have no business other than waiting for your letter. By God, do not neglect this. By the bread (we have eaten together), as soon as this letter arrives, send the answer to the warehouse of the representative of the merchants, Abu 'l-Barakat Ibn al-Hulaybi. A man like you needs no urging.

Describe to me the prices in the city (Fustat), and especially with regard to wheat and bread—I need not urge you to write me about this—as well as concerning the state of my father and the family. Special regards to you, and also to those who ask about me. Please honor me with any concern you might have. Regards also to Joseph and his mother. How are they? Regards also to our friends. And Peace. . . .

---

*Merchants in this time did not carry much gold or silver with them during their travels. Instead they relied upon the sale of their goods to provide them with cash. Between the loss of his goods and the high taxes, the author does not have enough to cover his expenses.

†Broken coins could be sold back to the mint in Fustat.

A LETTER FROM ADEN TO SOUTHWEST INDIA
(1139 CE)

In Your name, O Merciful.

The letter of your excellency, the illustrious elder has arrived, may God pro-long your life and make permanent your honored position, and rank. . . . May he never deprive your dwelling-place and court of any good. May he bestow upon you that which is most suitable of all he usually confers. May he subdue those that are envious of you and crush your enemies, and may all your affairs be complet-ed successfully. . . .

I took notice, my master, of your announcement of the sending of "refur-bished" iron in the boat of the nakhoda (shipowner) Ibn Abi 'l-Kata'ib. The ship-ment has arrived and I received from him two bahars and one-third,* as you noticed. . . . As to your shipment, my master, forwarded from Fandarayna [on the Indian coast] in the ship of the Fatan Swami [the chief of the merchant guild] through the Sheikh Abu l'-hasan b. Ja'far:

His smaller ship arrived and I took delivery from it of one and a quarter and an eighth bahar of pepper, as was stated in your memo to my master, the illustrious Madmun, as well as of a bahar of amlas [smooth] iron.

The bigger ship, however, arrived near Berbera [in Somalia], when its captain got into trouble with it until it was thrust against Bab al-Mandeb [the southern tip of the Arabian peninsula], where it foundered. The pepper was lost completely; God did not save anything of it. As to iron, mariners were brought from Aden, who were engaged to dive for it and salvage it. They salvaged about one-half the iron, and, while I am writing this letter, they are bringing it out of the Furda [the cus-toms house] to the storehouse of our illustrious elder, my master Madmun b. al-Hasan. All the expenses incurred for the diving and for transport will be deducted from whatever will be realized for that iron and the rest will be divided propor-tionally, each taking his proper share.

I regret your losses very much. But the Holy One, be he blessed, will com-pensate you and me presently. . . .

I sent to you five mann [approximately 10 pounds] of good silk on my account, for I saw that my master, the illustrious elder Madmun, had sent some to Ben 'Adlan and to others and it was reported in his name that it is selling well in Malabar. Therefore, I thought it was preferable to send, instead of gold, mer-chandise which might bring some profit. Thus, kindly sell it for me for whatev-er price God, the exalted, assigns and send it to me in any ship, without any responsibility for any risk on land or sea. If there is an opportunity to buy betel-nut or cardamom, kindly do so, but you, my master, need no instructions for you are competent. Indeed, I cause you trouble every year; but, you, my mas-ter, do excuse me, as it has always been your habit, past and present [to do so]. . . .

---

*Each bahar weighed approximately 300 pounds.

THE ACCOUNT OF AN OVERSEAS TRADER
(1045–6 CE)

In the Name of the Great God.

Account submitted to my lord Abi Ishaq Barhun, son of Ishaq, may the memory of the righteous be blessed, [for the period between 14 September 1045 and 3 September 1046] when the ships sailed.

Remainder of the Account. . . .

[A. Cash in the Hands of the Agent.]

This was sold after the sailing of the ships:
    Two baskets with [powdered] antimony° weighing 3 (hundred pounds)

> 11⅓ din[ars]

Less expenses for the [antimony] which was on your private account. . . .

> 5 din., 5 qir.

> Balance: 6⅛ din.

Short shawls, less commission, 9 din. less ⅛,. . . ²¼, ⅛ were kept back. They will be listed when collected.

> Balance: 6½ din.

331 linings, less commission and discount

> 16½ din.

Collected from the price of the other 300 (linings) sold previously. . . .

> 1½ din.

Leather mantles used as covers for beads

> ½ din.

1¼ units (of corals) on strings, less commission and discount

> 3 din.

Collected by me in Qayrawan before leaving:

> 6 din.

in number and weight

> 6 din. less ⅙

———————————————

°A metallic element used to make medicinal compounds.

Obtained, through God's bounty, for the silk which I bought in al-Mahdiyya

19 din. less 2 qir.

Hide good as cover for baskets

½ din.

500 single (coral) strings

⅓ din.

Received from Surur b. al-Hatib . . .

6 din. less 5 qir.

Grand Total:*   65½, ¼ din., 1 qir.

[B. Due from the Employer.]

From this is to be deducted:

Balance (in my favor) of the previous account, submitted [for the previous year]. . . .

39¼ din.

Expenses for the packages of (coral) beads carried by me

9½ din., 2 qir.

Expenses for the prepaid shipment which arrived in the Shami boat

1¼, ⅛ din., ½ qir.

Balance due for my late sister—may god have mercy upon her—for her passage

1 din., ½ qir.

Expenses for the porcelain beads which you charged against me for Alexandria and Misr (Fustat) and which I actually paid

16¼, ⅛ din.

Living expenses for fourteen months from Elu to Tishri (July/August 1044–September/October 1045)

22½ din.

Grand Total: 90⅙ din.

Owed by you and covered by what I owe (you) in your house†

24 din.

---

*Some of the smaller items have been deleted; the amounts will not total exactly.
†In other words, while the expenses of the trader (24 dinars) exceed what the merchant has paid him, they are covered by a separate debt owed to the merchant by the trader.

44 The Arabian Slave Trade

G.S.P. Freeman-Grenville, ed. *The East African Coast: Select Documents from the First to the Earlier Nineteenth Century.* Oxford, England: Clarendon Press, 1962. 9–13.

A tenth-century sailor named Buzurg Ibn Shahriyar of Ramhormuz collected seafaring tales; many of them are fictitious, but contain important kernels of truth about trade in the Arabian Peninsula and surrounding areas. In this story, Arabian merchants are driven by a storm to the shores of eastern Africa, possibly in Somalia or Kenya. There they encounter a king who encourages them to trade in his land and shows them every courtesy possible, but when the merchants leave they kidnap the king and some of his followers and sell them into slavery in Oman. Years later, the merchants are forced to seek safe harbor in the same kingdom, only to discover that the king has escaped bondage and returned to rule his people. As you will discover, this story is not only about the king's escape from slavery, but about the spread of Islam in Africa.

Ismailawaih told me, and several sailors who were with him, that in the year [922 CE] he left Oman in his ship to go to Kanbalu. A storm drove him towards Sofala on the Zanj coast. Seeing the coast where we were, the captain said, and realizing that we were falling among cannibal negroes and were certain to perish, we made the ritual ablutions and turned our hearts towards God, saying for each other the prayers for the dead. The canoes of the negroes surrounded us and brought us into the harbor; we cast anchor and disembarked on the land. They led us to their king. He was a young negro, handsome and well made. He asked who we were, and where we were going. We answered that the object of our voyage was his own land.

"You lie," he said. "It was not in our land that you intended to disembark. It is only that the winds have driven you thither in spite of yourselves."

When we had admitted that he spoke the truth, he said: "Disembark your goods. Sell and buy, you have nothing to fear."

We brought all our packages to the land and began to trade, a trade which was excellent for us, without any obstacles or customs dues. We made the king a number of presents to which he replied with gifts of equal worth or ones even more valuable. When the time to depart came, we asked his permission to go, and he agreed immediately. The goods we had bought were loaded and business was wound up. When everything was in order, and the king knew of our intention to sail, he accompanied us to the shore with several of his people, got into one of the boats and came out to the ship with us. He even came on board with seven of his companions.

When I saw them there, I said to myself: "In the Oman market this young king would certainly fetch thirty dinars, and seven companions sixty dinars. Their clothes alone are not worth less than twenty dinars. One way and another this would give us a profit of at least 3,000 dirhams, and without any trouble."

Reflecting thus, I gave the crew their orders. They raised the sails and weighed anchor.

In the meantime the king was most agreeable to us, making us promise to come back again and promising us a good welcome when we did. When he saw the sails fill with the wind and the ship begin to move, he wished to embark in the canoes which were tied up to the side. But we cut the ropes, and said to him: "You will remain with us, we shall take you to our land. There we shall reward you for all of the kindnesses you have shown us.

"Strangers," he said, "when you fell upon our beaches, my people wished to eat you and pillage your goods, as they have already done to others like you. But I protected you, and asked nothing from you. As a token of my goodwill I even came down to bid you farewell in your own ship. Treat me then as justice demands, and let me return to my own land."

But no one paid any heed to his words; no notice was taken of them. As the wind got up, the coast was not slow to disappear from sight. Then night enfolded us in its shrouds and we reached the open sea.

When the day came, the king and his companions were put with the other slaves whose number reached about 200 head. He was not treated differently from his companions in captivity. The king said not a word and did not even open his mouth. He behaved as if we were unknown to him and as if we did not know him. When he got to Oman, the slaves were sold, and the king with them.

Now several years after, sailing from Oman towards Kanbalu, the wind again drove us towards the coasts of Sofala on the Zanj coast, and we arrived at precisely the same place. The negroes saw us, and their canoes surrounded us, and we recognized each other. Fully certain we should perish this time, terror struck us dumb. We made the ritual ablutions in silence, repeated the prayer of death, and said farewell to each other. The negroes seized us, and took us to the king's dwelling and made us go in. Imagine our surprise; it was the same king that we had known, seated on his throne, just as if we had left him there. We prostrated ourselves before him, overcome, and had not the strength to raise ourselves up.

"Ah!" said he, "here are my old friends." Not one of us was capable of replying. He went on: "Come, raise your heads, I give you safe conduct for yourselves and your goods." Some raised their heads, others had not the strength, and were overcome with shame. But he showed himself gentle and gracious until we had all raised our heads, but without daring to look him in the face, so much were we moved to remorse and fear. But when we had been reassured by his safe conduct, we finally came to our senses, and he said: "Ah! Traitors! How you have treated me after all I did for you!" And each one of us called out: "Mercy, oh King! be merciful to us!"

"I will be merciful to you," he said. "Go on, as you did last time, with your business of selling and buying. You may trade in full liberty." We could not believe our ears; we feared it was nothing but a trick to make us bring our goods on shore. None the less we disembarked them, and came and brought him a present of enormous value. But he refused it and said: "You are not worthy for me to accept a present from you. I will not sully my property with anything that comes from you."

After that we did our business in peace. When the time to go came, we asked permission to embark. He gave it. At the moment of departure, I went to tell him so. "Go," he said, "and may God Protect you!" "Oh King," I replied, "you have showered your bounty upon us, and we have been ungrateful and traitorous to you. But how did you escape and return to your country?"

He answered: "After you had sold me in Oman, my purchaser took me to a town called Basrah, and he described it. There I learnt to pray and to fast, and certain parts of the Koran. My master sold me to another man who took me to the country of the king of the Arabs, called Baghdad—and he described Baghdad. In this town I learnt to speak correctly. I completed my knowledge of the Koran and prayed with the men in the mosques. I saw the Caliph [ruler], who is called al-Muqtadir [reigned 908–932]. I was in Baghdad for a year or more, when there came a party of men mounted on camels. Seeing a large crowd, I asked where all these people were going. I was told: 'To Mecca.' 'What is Mecca?' I asked. 'There,' I was answered, 'is the House of God to which Muslims make the Pilgrimage.' And I was told the history of the temple. My master, to whom I told all this, did not wish to go with them or to let me go. But I found a way to escape his watchfulness and to mix in the crowd of pilgrims. On the road I became a servant to them. They gave me food to eat and got for me the cloths needed for the *ihram* [the ritual garments used for the pilgrimage]. Finally, they instructing me, I performed all the ceremonies of the pilgrimage.

Not daring to go back to Baghdad, for fear that my master would take away my life, I joined up with another caravan which was going to Cairo. I offered my services to the travellers, who carried me on their camels and shared their provisions with me. When I got to Cairo I saw the great river which is called the Nile. I asked: 'Where does it come from?' They answered: 'Its source is in the land of the Zanj.' 'On which side?' 'On the side of a large town called Aswan, which is on the frontier of the land of the blacks.'

With this information, I followed the banks of the Nile, going from one town to another, asking alms, which was not refused me. I fell, however, among a company of blacks who gave me a bad welcome. They seized on me, and put me among the servants with a load which was too heavy for me to carry. I fled and fell into the hands of another company which seized me and sold me. I escaped again, and went on in this manner, until, after a series of similar adventures, I found myself in the country which adjoins the land of the Zanj. Of all the terrors I had experienced since I left Cairo, there was none equal to that which I felt as I approached my own land. For I said to myself, a new king has no doubt taken my place on the throne and commands my army. To regain power is not an easy thing. If I make myself known or if anyone recognizes me, I shall be seized upon, taken to the new king and killed at once. Or perhaps one of his favorites will cut off my head to gain his favor.

So, in prey to mortal terror, I went on my way by night, and stayed hid during the day. When I reached the sea, I embarked on a ship; and, after stopping at various places, I disembarked one night on the shore of my country. I asked an old woman: 'Is the king who rules here a just king?' She answered: 'My son, we have no king but God.' And the good woman told me how the king had been carried off. I pretended the greatest astonishment at her story, as if it had not concerned me and events which I knew very well. The people of the kingdom, she said, have agreed not to have another king until they have certain news of the former one. For the diviners have told them that he is alive and in [good] health, and safe in the land of the Arabs.

When the day came, I went into town and walked towards my palace. I found my family just as I had left them, but plunged into grief. My people listened to the account of my story, and it surprised them and filled them with joy. Like myself, they embraced the religion of Islam. Thus I returned into possession of my sovereignty, a month before you came. And here I am, happy and satisfied with the grace God has given me and mine, of knowing the precepts of Islam, the faith, prayers, fasting, the pilgrimage, and what is permitted and what is forbidden: for no man else in the land of the Zanj has obtained a similar favor. And if I have forgiven you, it is because you were the first cause of the purity of my religion. But there is still one sin on my conscience which I pray God to take away from me."

"What is this thing, oh King?" I asked. "It is," he said, "that I left my master, when I left Baghdad, without asking him his permission, and that I did not return to him. If I were to meet an honest man, I would ask him to take the price of my purchase to my master. If there were among you a really good man, if you were truly upright men, I would give you a sum of money to give him, a sum ten times what he paid as damages for the delay. But you are nothing but traitors and tricksters."

We said farewell to him. "Go," he said, "and if you return, I shall not treat you otherwise than I have done. You will receive the best welcome. And the Muslims may know that they may come here to us, as to brothers, Muslims like themselves. As for accompanying you to your ship, I have reasons for not doing so." And so on that we parted.

45 Chinese Observations of Trade

Chau [Chao] Ju-kua. *Chau Ju-kua: His Work on the Chinese and Arab Trade in the Twelfth and Thirteenth Centuries, Entitled Chu-fan-chï.* Translated by Friedrich Hirth and W.W. Rockhill. St. Petersburg, Russia: Imperial Academy of Sciences, 1911. 77–78, 115–116, 161–162, 166–168.

Chinese traders had connections throughout Asia and as far away as the Mediterranean. The thirteenth-century chronicle of Chao Ju-kua describes in detail the places visited by traders, including information on customs, architecture, and religious beliefs, as well as trade. Chao was a customs inspector in the Chinese port city of Fujian [Fukien]. Basing his description on written sources and upon details provided by traders, Chao wrote about all of the places connected to China by trade, including Java and Sumatra (in present-day Indonesia), India, Egypt, Sicily (in Italy), and Spain. Traders to China paid import duties in kind, transferring on average between 10 and 30 percent of their goods to customs officials.* An earlier chronicle written in the twelfth century stated that, the "Great World-encircling Ocean Sea bounds the Barbarians' countries; in every quarter there are kingdoms of them, each has its peculiar products, each its trading center from which it derives prosperity."

JAVA

The dwellings are of imposing appearance and painted in greenish tints. Traders going there are put up in visitors' lodges, where food and drink both plentiful and good are supplied them. The natives dress their hair and wear clothes which are girt around their chest and reach down to their knees. When they are sick, they take no medicines, but simply pray to their local gods or to the Buddha. . . . It is a broad and level country, well suited to agriculture. It produces rice, hemp, millet, beans, but no wheat. Ploughing is done with buffaloes. The people pay a tithe-rent. They make salt by boiling sea water. The country also abounds in fish, turtles, fowls, ducks, goats, and they kill horses and buffaloes for food. The fruits comprise big gourds, coconuts, bananas, sugar-cane and taro. They have also elephants' tusks, rhinoceros horns, pearls, camphor, tortoise-shell, sandalwood, aniseed, cloves, cardamoms, cubebs, laka-wood, mats, foreign sword blades, pepper, betel nuts, saffron, sapan-wood and parrots. They also pay attention to the raising of silk-worms and the weaving of silk; they have various brocaded silks, [damasks and cotton cloth]. No tea is raised in this country. . . .

Foreign merchants use in trading gold and silver of various degrees of fine-ness, vessels [containers] made of gold and silver, silk stuffs, black damasks, orris-root, cinnabar, copperas, alum, borax, arsenic, lacquer-ware, iron tripods and green and white porcelain ware. There is a vast store of pepper in this foreign country and the merchant ships, in view of the profit they derive from that trade, are in the habit of smuggling out of China copper cash for bartering purposes. Our Court has repeatedly forbidden all trade with this country, but the foreign traders, for the purpose of deceiving the government, changed its name and referred to it as Su-ki-tan.

EGYPT AND EAST AFRICA†

The capital of the country, called Mi-sü-li, is an important center for the trade of foreign peoples. . . . The streets of the capital are more than fifty feet broad; in the middle is a roadway twenty feet broad and four feet high for the use of camels, horses, and oxen carrying goods about. On either side, for the convenience of pedestrians' business, there are sidewalks paved with green and black flagstones of

---

*Luxury items, such as pearls, were taxed at 10 percent. Other goods were taxed at 30 percent.
†The author devotes a length passage to the "country" of the Muslims, which appears to refer to present-day Egypt.

surpassing beauty. . . . Very rich persons use a measure instead of scales in business transactions in gold or silver. The markets are noisy and bustling, and are filled with great store of gold and silver damasks, brocades, [etc.]

The peasants work their fields without fear of inundations or droughts; a sufficiency of water for irrigation is supplied by a river whose source is not known. During the season when no cultivation is in progress, the level of the river remains even with the banks; with the beginning of cultivation it rises day by day. Then it is that an official is appointed to watch the river and to await the highest water level, when he summons the people, who then plough and sow their fields. When they have had enough water, the river returns to its former level.

There is a great harbor in this country, over two hundred feet deep, which opens to the southeast on the sea, and has branches connecting with all quarters of the country. On either bank of the harbor the people have their dwellings and here daily are held fairs, where crowded boats, wagons, all loaded with hemp, wheat, millet, beans, sugar, meal, oil, firewood, fowls, sheep, geese, ducks, fish, shrimp, date-cakes, grapes and other fruits.

The products of the country consist in pearls, ivory, rhinoceros horns, frankincense, . . . cloves, nutmegs, . . . and foreign satins.*

THE PHILIPPINE ISLANDS

Whenever foreign traders arrive at any of the settlements, they live on board ship before venturing to go on shore, their ships being moored in midstream, announcing their presence to the natives by beating drums. Upon this the . . . traders race for the ship in small boats, carrying cotton, yellow wax, native cloth, coconut-heart mats, which they offer for barter. If the prices of goods they wish to purchase cannot be agreed upon, the chief of the local traders must go in person, in order to come to an understanding, which being reached the natives are offered presents of silk umbrellas, porcelain, and rattan baskets; but the foreigners still retain on board one or two natives as hostages. After they go on shore to traffic [trade], which being ended they return the hostages. A ship will not remain at anchor longer than three or four days, after which it proceeds to another place. . . .

KOREA

The soil of this country is well adapted to the growing of rice and there are no camels or buffalo. . . . They use no cash, but merely barter with rice. Their household vessels and other implements are all made of copper. . . . The products of this country are ginseng, quicksilver [mercury], musk, pine-seeds, hazel-nuts, . . . cotton cloth of all sizes, . . . bronze temple bells, porcelain, straw mats, and writing

---

*Not all of the products listed here are produced in Egypt. Cloves, for instance, were imported from present-day Indonesia.

brushes made of rats' hair. Trading ships barter in exchange for these articles colored silk [goods], calendars, and books.

46 Visual Document: The Map of Abraham de Cresques

This fourteenth-century map of Abraham de Cresques depicts the trade connections between Iberia (present-day Spain and Portugal) and North Africa. The kingdom of Mali controlled much of the Niger River valley reaching almost to the shores of the Atlantic Ocean. Mali achieved wealth because of its tremendous repositories of gold, a mineral used as currency throughout the Mediterranean world. The king depicted in the illustration is Mansa Kankan Musa, an early fourteenth-century Islamic king of Mali whose famous pilgrimage to Mecca in 1324 flooded the markets of Egypt with so much gold that it devalued the local currency. Examine the map carefully. What does the mapmaker want you to know about the role of Mansa Musa and his kingdom in trade networks? What does the map tell you about trade in North Africa, and trade between North Africa and Iberia?

DISCUSSION QUESTIONS

1. What is the role of trade in the different societies you have encountered in this chapter?

2. How do governments of different societies regard trade? How and to what degree are they involved? What factors determine the extent of their involvement?

3. How are merchants viewed by different societies? What are the different facets of a merchant's career?

4. What factors are involved in long-distance trade? How was long-distance trade carried out?

5. How did merchants decide which goods to buy and sell? What factors influenced their decisions?

6. What role did religion play in trade networks?

Chapter 9

Regulating Behavior

Why do people behave the way they do? What governs the day-to-day activities of people? In all societies there are rules for everyday behavior. These rules may be explicit, as in the case of a religious text or law code, or implicit, as in the case of customs and popular beliefs. Many customs and beliefs do not adhere to a particular written text, and can only be discerned through observation. Indeed, prescriptive literature (i.e., written texts that prescribe how people should behave) was only available to elites in society who could read, or have texts read to them. From written texts it is often possible to understand how elites wanted all members of society to behave, but it is difficult to know whether people behaved as those elites intended. This section combines different kinds of documents about the behavior of elites and commoners, women and men, young and old. Some of those documents describe how people are supposed to behave, while others describe how people actually did act in their daily lives.

The first excerpt below contains the observations of a fifteenth-century sailor named Ma Huan. Ma traveled throughout Asia, and wrote extensive commentaries on people in Vietnam, Java, and also Mecca. The second selection consists of excerpts from the Quran, a collection of the teachings of the Islamic prophet Muhammad. The third selection, excerpts from the fourteenth-century *Piers the Ploughman,* includes Christian prescriptive literature comparable to that contained within the Quran. The fourth excerpt is taken from the Catholic Inquisition in France during the thirteenth century. The fifth excerpt is taken from an eleventh-century Japanese novel entitled *The Tale of Genji;* it describes life in the Japanese royal court. In contrast, the sixth and final selection in this chapter describes how the Inca empire in South America organized its population to perform all the tasks necessary to the society.

141

47 A Chinese Explorer in Asia and the Mediterranean

Ma Huan, *Ying-Yai Sheng-Lan: The Overall Survey of the Ocean's Shores.* Cambridge, England: Cambridge University Press, 1970. 82–83, 95–96, 173–175.

Between 1405 and 1433, the Chinese emperor financed seven naval expeditions to the West led by Cheng Ho [Zheng He]. These voyages, completed decades before those of Christopher Columbus, took Cheng to many places, including Java [in present-day Indonesia], Thailand, India, and the city of Mecca. These voyages were not the first contacts between China and their western neighbors: an extensive trade network existed between Chinese ports and others in Asia. Ma may also have learned much from his father, who was a Muslim who had performed the pilgrimage to Mecca. Ma Huan first traveled with Cheng in 1413 as an official translator. After this voyage, he began to keep a written record which he updated after subsequent voyages. For each place that the Chinese ships visited, Ma recorded information about the people and cultures he encountered. Although Ma Huan may not have visited Mecca or Medina in person, he was certainly familiar with the two cities and described holy sites in both cities in considerable detail.

VIETNAM

When men and women marry, the only requirement is that the man should first go to the woman's house, and consummate the marriage. Ten days or half a moon later, the man's father and mother, with their relatives and friends, to the accompaniment of drums and music, escort husband and wife back to [the paternal] home; then they prepare wine and play music. . . . As to their writing: they have no paper or pen; they use [either] goat-skin beaten thin or tree-bark smoked black; and they fold it into the form of a classical book, [in which], with white chalk, they write characters that serve for records.

As to the punishable offenses [in this] country: for light [offenses], they employ thrashing on the back with a rattan stick; for serious [offenses], they cut off the nose; for robbery, they sever a hand; for the offense of adultery, the man and woman are branded on the face so as to make a scar; for the most heinous offenses, they take a hard wood [stick], cut a sharp point to it, and set it up on a [log of] wood which resembles a small boat; [this] they put in the water; [and] they make the offender sit on the wood spike; the wood [stick] protrudes from his mouth and he dies; [and] then [the body] is left on the water as a warning to the public. . . .

• • •

JAVA

As to their marriage-rites: the man first goes to the woman's family house, and the marriage is consummated; three days later the man escorts his bride [home]; whereupon the man's family beat brass drums and brass gongs, blow on coconut-shell pipes, strike drums made of bamboo tubes, and let off firecrackers, while in front and behind they are surrounded by men with short knives and round shields. The woman has dishevelled hair, uncovered limbs, and bare feet. Around her she fastens a kerchief with silk embroidery; at her neck she puts on an ornament of gold beads strung together; [and] on her wrists she wears a bracelet ornamented with gold, silver, and other precious things. Relations, friends, and neighbors decorate a boat with such things as areca-nuts, betel-leaves, and sewn strings of grasses and flowers, and form a party to escort the bridal pair in accordance with their rite of congratulating [the newlyweds] on the happy [event]. When they reach the groom's house, they strike gongs, beat drums, drink wine, and play music. After a few days they disperse.

. . . [W]hen rich men and chiefs and persons of high standing are about to die, the most intimate serving-girls and concubines under their care first take an oath to their lords, saying "In death we go with you"; after the death, on the day of the funeral, they build a high wooden framework, under which they pile a heap of fire-wood; [and] they set fire to this and burn the coffin. The two or three serving-girls and concubines who originally took the oath wait till the moment when the blaze is at its height; then, wearing grasses and flowers all over their heads, their bodies clad in kerchiefs with designs of the five colors, they mount the framework and dance about, wailing, for a considerable time; [then] they cast themselves down into the flames, and are consumed in the fire with the corpse of their lord, in accordance with their rite of sacrificing the living with the dead. . . .

• • •

MECCA

They profess the Muslim religion. A holy man first expounded and spread the doctrine of his teaching in this country, and right down to the present day the people of the country all observe the regulations of the doctrine in their actions, not daring to commit the slightest transgression. . . . The menfolk bind up their heads; they wear long garments; [and] on their feet they put leather shoes. The women all wear a covering over their heads, and you cannot see their faces. . . . The law prohibits wine-drinking. The customs of the people are pacific and admirable. . . . They all observe the precepts of their religion, and law-breakers are few. It is in truth a most happy country. . . . The Hall [Kaaba]° is built with layers of five-colored stones; in shape it is square and flat-topped. . . . Over [the Hall] is a covering

---

°The Kaaba is a small, cube-shaped building that sits in the courtyard of the Great Mosque in Mecca.

of black hemp-silk. Every year on the tenth day of the twelfth moon all the foreign Muslims—in extreme cases making a long journey of one or two years—come to worship inside the Hall. Everyone cuts off a piece of the hemp-silk covering as a memento before he goes away. When it has been completely cut away, the king covers over [the Hall] again with another covering woven in advance; this happens again and again, year after year, without intermission. . . .

If you go west again and travel for one day, you reach a city named Mo-ti-na [Medina]; the tomb of their holy man Ma-ha-ma [Muhammad] is situated exactly in the city; [and] right down to the present day a bright light rises day and night from the top of the grave and penetrates the clouds.

48 Islamic Law

> *Al-Quran: A Contemporary Translation.* Karachi, India: Akrash Publishing, 1984. 90, 97–98, 102–103, 109, 284, 508, 545.

The following selections are taken from the Quran, the holy book of the Islamic faith. The Quran is a collection of the teachings of the prophet Muhammad, compiled by his disciples after his death. As with many such religious texts, the contents provide important clues about how people were expected to behave in society. The passages selected below focus upon a few themes: the relationship between believers and non-believers within Islamic society, prescriptions for behavior, the place of women, and the pilgrimage to Mecca.

BELIEVERS AND NON-BELIEVERS

But he who performs good deeds, whether man or a woman, and is a believer, will surely enter Paradise, and shall not be deprived even of an iota of his reward.

• • •

. . . [W]hosoever kills a human being, except as punishment for murder, or for spreading corruption in the land, it shall be like killing all humanity; and whosoever saves a life, saves the entire human race. Our apostles brought clear proofs to them; but even after that most of them committed excesses in the land. The punishment for those who wage war against God and His Prophet, and perpetrate disorders in the land, is to kill or crucify them, or have a hand on one side and a foot on the other amputated, or banish them from the land. Such is their disgrace in the worlds, and in the Hereafter their doom shall be dreadful. But those who repent before they are subdued should know that God is forgiving and kind.

• • •

We sent down the Torah which contains guidance and light, in accordance with which the prophets who had submitted (to God) gave instructions to the Jews, as did the rabbis and priests, for they were the custodians and witnesses of God's writ. So therefore, do not fear men, fear me, and barter not My messages away for a paltry gain. Those who do not judge by God's revelations are infidels indeed. And there (in the Torah) We had ordained a life for a life, and an eye for an eye, and a nose for a nose, and an ear for an ear, and a tooth for a tooth, and for wounds retribution, though he who forgets it out of charity, atones for his sins. And those who do not judge by God's revelations are unjust. Later in the train of the prophets, we sent Jesus, son of Mary, confirming the Torah which had been (sent down) before him, and gave him the Gospel containing guidance and light which corroborated the earlier Torah, a guidance and warning, for those who preserve themselves from evil follow the straight path.

· · ·

O believer, do not hold Jews and Christians as your allies. They are allies of one another; and anyone who makes them his friends is surely one of them; and God does not guide the unjust.

· · ·

O believers, any one of you who turns back on his faith (should remember) that God could verily bring (in your place) another people whom He would love as they would love Him, gentle with believers, unbending with infidels, who would strive in the way of God, unafraid of blame by any slanderer. . . . Your only friends are God and His Messenger, and those who believe and are steadfast in devotion, who pay the zakat [charitable tax] and bow in homage (before God). And those who take God and His Prophet and the faithful as their friends are indeed men of God, who will surely be victorious.

O Prophet, announce what has reached you from your Lord, for if you do not, you will not have delivered His message. God will preserve you from (the mischief of) men; for God does not guide those who do not believe. Say to them: "O people of the Book, you have no ground (for argument) until you follow the Torah and the Gospel and what has been revealed to you by your Lord." But what has been revealed to you by your Lord will surely increase rebellion and unbelief in many; so do not grieve for those who do not believe. All those who believe, and the Jews and the Sabians and the Christians, in fact any one who believes in God and the Last Day, and performs good deeds, will have nothing to fear or regret. We had taken a solemn pledge from the children of Israel, and sent messengers to them; but whenever an apostle came to them bringing what did not suit their mood, they called one imposter, another they slew, and imagined that no trials would befall them; and they turned deaf and blind (to the truth). But God still turned to them; yet many of them turned blind and deaf again; but God sees every thing they do. They are surely infidels who say: "God is the Christ, son of Mary." But the Christ had only said: "O children of Israel, worship God who is my Lord and your Lord." Whosoever associates a compeer with God, will have Paradise denied to him by God, and his abode shall be Hell; and the sinners will have none to help them. Disbelievers are they surely who say, "God is the third of the trinity; but there is no god other than God the one." And if they do not desist from saying what they say, then indeed those among them who persist in disbelief will suffer painful punishment. Why do they not turn to God and ask His forgiveness? God is forgiving and kind. The Christ, son of Mary, was but an apostle, and many apostles had (come and) gone before him; and his mother was a woman of truth. They both ate the (same) food (as men.) Behold, how We show men clear signs, and behold, how they wand[er] astray!

• • •

Tell them: "O people of the Book, do not overstep the bounds of truth in your beliefs, and follow not the wishes of a people who had erred before, and led many others astray, and wandered away from the right path."

WOMEN IN ISLAMIC SOCIETY

. . . God has given you instructions about [women]. You also read them in the Book concerning orphaned women [in your charge] to whom you deny their ordained rights and yet wish to take them in marriage, as well as in respect of helpless children, that you should be just in the matter of orphans. The good you do is known to God. If a woman fears ill treatment from her husband, or his tiring of her, there is no harm if they make a peaceful settlement, and peace is an excellent thing. Yet avarice is part of man's nature. If you do good and fear God, God is cognizant of all that you do. Howsoever you may try you will never be able to treat your wives equally. But do not incline (to one) exclusively and leave (the other) suspended (as it were). Yet if you do the right thing and are just, God is verily forgiving and kind. If both (decide to) separate, God in his largess will provide for them, for God is infinite and all-wise.

PRESCRIPTIONS FOR BEHAVIOR

O You who believe, fulfil your obligations. Made lawful (as food) for you are animals except those mentioned (here); but unlawful during Pilgrimage is game. . . . Forbidden you is carrion and blood, and the flesh of the swine, and whatsoever has been killed in the name of some other than God, . . . or killed . . . unless slaughtered while still alive; and that which has been slaughtered at altars is forbidden, . . . all this is sinful.

• • •

O believers, when you stand up for prayer, wash your faces and hands up to the elbows, and also wipe your heads and wash your feet up to the ankles. If you are in a state of seminal pollution, then bathe and purify yourself well. But in case you are ill or are travelling, or you have satisfied the call of nature, or have slept with a woman and you cannot find water, then take wholesome dust, and pass it over your face and your hands. . . .

• • •

O believers, . . . do not transgress. God does not love transgressors. . . . The expiation (for breaking an oath) is feeding ten persons who are poor, with food that you give your own families, or clothing them, or freeing a slave. But he who cannot do so should fast for three days. . . . O believers, this wine and gambling, these idols, and these arrows you use for divination, are all acts of Satan; so keep away from them ... [:] Satan only wishes to create among you enmity and hatred through wine and gambling, and to divert you from the remembrance of God and prayer. . . .

THE PILGRIMAGE

Announce the Pilgrimage to the people. They will come to you on foot and riding along distant roads on lean and slender beasts . . . let them then attend to their persons and complete the rites of pilgrimage, fulfil their vows and circuit round the ancient House.

49 Christian Mores in England

> William Langland. *Piers the Ploughman*. Translated with an introduction by J.F. Goodridge. London: Penguin Books, 1966. 77–82, 84.

William Langland was an obscure English priest who lived during the fourteenth century. Around 1370, he began to compose a lengthy allegory about the human condition and the search for moral purity. In the excerpt below, the king and his nobles are told by Reason to seek the person of Truth. Piers the Ploughman declares to the nobles that he can show the way to Truth if, in return for his help, the nobles will help to plow his field. As Piers describes the landmarks on the journey, he explains the path to Christian righteousness.

"Do you know anything about a saint called Truth?" they said. "Can you tell us where to find him?"

"Good Heavens, no!" said the man. . . .

"By Saint Peter!" said a plowman, pushing his way through the crowd, "I know Him, as well as a scholar knows his books. Conscience and Common Sense showed me the way to His place, and they made me swear to serve Him forever, and do His sowing and planting for as long as I can work. I've been his man for the last fifty years; I've sown His seed and herded His beasts, and looked after all His affairs, indoors and out. I ditch and dig, sow and thresh, and do whatever Truth tells me—tailoring and tinkering, spinning and weaving—I put my hand to anything He bids me. And Truth is pleased with my work, though I say it myself. He pays me well, and sometimes gives me extra; for He's as ready with His wages as any poor man could wish, and never fails to pay His men each night. Besides, He's as mild as a lamb, and always speaks to you kindly. So if you would like to know where He lives, I'll put you on the track in no time."

"Thank you, Piers old fellow," the pilgrims said; and they offered him money to guide them to Truth's castle.

"No, by my soul!" swore Piers, "I wouldn't take a farthing [money] not for all the riches in St. Thomas' shrine! Truth would find it hard to forgive me for that! But if you want to go the right way, listen now, while I set you on Truth's path.

You must all set out through *Meekness,* men and women alike, and continue until you come to *Conscience;* for Christ may know by this that you love God above all things, and your neighbor next, and treat others as you would like them to treat you. Then turn down by the stream *Be-gentle-in-speech,* till you come to a ford [shallow crossing], *Honor-thy-father-and-mother.* There you must wade into the water and wash yourselves thoroughly, then you'll step more lightly for the rest of your life. Next, you will see a place called *Swear-not-without-necessity-and-above-all-take-not-the-name-of-the-Lord-thy-God-in-vain.* After that, you will pass by a farm where you must not trespass on any account, for its name is *Thou-shalt-not-covet-thy-neighbor's-cattle-nor-his-wives-nor-any-of-his-servants-lest-you-do-him-an-injury.* So take care not to break any branches there, unless they are on your property.

You will also see two pairs of stocks;† but do not stop, for they are *Steal-not* and *Kill-not.* Go round and leave them on your left, and don't look back at them. And remember to observe Holy Days, and keep them holy from morning till nightfall. Then you will come to a hill, *Bear-no-false-witness.* Turn right away from it, for it is thickly wooded with bribes, and bristling with florins [money]. At all costs gather no blossoms there, or you will lose your soul. And so you will arrive at a place called *Speak-the-truth-and-mean-it-and-never-swerve-from-the-truth-for-any-man.* From there you will see a mansion as bright as the sun, surrounded by a moat of *Mercy,* with walls of *Wisdom,* to keep out passion. It has battlements of *Christendom* to save mankind, and is buttressed with *Believe-or-you-cannot-be-saved.*

And all the buildings, halls, and chambers are roofed, not with lead, but with *Love,* and are covered with the *Lowly-speech-of-brothers.* The drawbridge is of *Ask-and-you-shall-receive,* and each pillar is built of penance and prayers to the saints, and all the gates are hung on hinges of almsdeeds. The doorkeeper's name is Grace, a good man, who has a servant, Amendment, well known among men. And this is the password you must give him so that Truth may know you are honest: 'I have done penance which the priest gave me; I am very sorry for my sins, I always shall be whenever I think of them, and still should be even if I were Pope!'

Then you must ask Amendment to beg his Master to open the wicket-gate that Eve shut in the beginning, when she and Adam ate the sour apples. For 'Through Eve the door was closed to all men, and through the Virgin Mary it was opened again.' So Mary always has the key, even when the King is sleeping. And if Grace gives you leave to enter by this gate, you will find Truth dwelling in your heart, hung on a chain of charity. And you will submit to Him as a child to its father, never opposing His will.

But then beware of the villain Wrath, who envies Him who dwells in your heart. For he will push Pride in your way and make you feel so pleased with your-

---

†A "stock" was a device for the public punishment of criminals. It consisted of a wooden frame that held both head and hands in place.

self that you are blinded by the glory of your own good deeds. So you will be driven out 'as the early dew,' the door will be locked and bolted against you, and it may be a hundred years before you enter again. Thus by thinking too much of yourself, you may lose God's love, and enter His courts no more, unless His grace intervenes.

But there are also seven sisters, the eternal servants of Truth, who keep the postern-gates of the castle. These are Abstinence and Humility, Chastity and Charity. His chief maidens, Patience and Peace, who help many people, and the Lady Bountiful, who opens the gates to still more, and has helped thousands out of the Devil's pound. Anyone related to these seven is wonderfully welcome there, and received with honor. But if you are kin to none of them, it is very hard for you to get in at all, except by the special mercy of God."

• • •

Then the people complained to Piers and said, "This is a grim way you've described to us. We should need a guide for every step of the road." "Now look," said Piers the Plowman, "I have half an acre of land here by the highway. Once I can get it plowed and sown, I will go with you and show you the way myself." "We should have a long time to wait," said a veiled lady. "What work could we women be doing to pass the time?"

"Why, some of you can sew up the sacks," said Piers, "to keep the seed from spilling. And you fair ladies with slender fingers—you have plenty of silks and fine stuffs to sew. Make some vestments for priests, while you've got the time, and lend a hand in beautifying the churches. And those of you who are married or widows can spin flax and make some cloth, and teach your daughters to do it too. For Truth commands us to take care of the needy and clothe the naked. I'll give them food myself, so long as the harvest doesn't fail. For if I don't mind working all my life for the love of God, to provide meat and bread for the rich and poor. So come along now, all you men who live by food and drink—lend a hand to the man who provides you with it, and we will finish the job quickly."

"By Heavens!" said a knight, "this fellow knows what's good for us! But to tell the truth, I've never handled a team of oxen. Give me a lesson, Piers, and I'll do my best by God!" "That's a fair offer," said Piers. "And for my part, I'll sweat and toil for both of us as long as I live, and gladly do any job you want. But you must promise in return to guard over [the] Holy Church, and protect me from the thieves and wasters who ruin the world. And you'll have to hunt down all the hares and foxes and boars and badgers that break down my hedges, and tame falcons to kill the wild birds that crop my wheat."

Then the knight answered courteously and said, "I give you my word, Piers, as I am a true knight; and I'll keep this promise through thick and thin and protect you to the end of my days."

"Ah, but there's one thing more I must ask you," said Piers. "Never ill-treat your tenants, and see that you punish them only when Truth compels you to—even then, let Mercy assess the fine, and be ruled by Meekness. . . . And take care also that you never ill-use your serfs. It will be better for you in the long run, for though they are your underlings here on earth, they may be above you in Heaven, in greater happiness, unless you lead a better life than they do."

• • •

And now Piers and his pilgrims have gone to the plough, and many folk are helping him to till his half acre. Ditchers and diggers are turning up the headlands, and others, to please Piers, are hoeing up the weeds, while he is delighted with their labors and quick to praise them. They are all eager to work, and every man finds something useful to do. Then at nine o'clock in the morning Piers left his plough in order to see how things were going, and pick out the best workers to hire again at harvest-time. At this, some of them sat down to drink their ale and sing songs. . . .

"By the Lord!" said Piers, bursting with rage, "Get up and go back to work at once—or you'll get no bread to sing about when famine comes. You can starve to death, and to hell with the lot of you!"

50 The European Inquisition

Walter L. Wakefield. *Heresy, Crusade and Inquisition in Southern France, 1100–1250.* London: George Allen & Unwin Ltd., 1974. 209.

To encourage religious conformity, the Catholic Church in Europe used a tribunal called the Inquisition to investigate religious heresy. Although most commonly associated with sixteenth-century Spain, the Inquisition actually originated in the Roman empire, and was used in many places in Western Europe. The reading below examines the Inquisition in Toulouse, France, in the thirteenth century. William Pelhison, an inquisitor and member of the Dominican monastic order, chronicled this investigation of heretical behavior. Although popular contemporary notions of the Inquisition stress the secrecy and power of the institution, this selection shows a community attempting to restrict inquisitorial actions, with some degree of success.

One day one of our friars, while preaching, declared in his sermon that heretics lived in the town and that they held assemblies and disseminated their heresies there. The people of the town became very disturbed and agitated at hearing this. Hence, the consuls of the town summoned the prior to the town hall and ordered him to tell the friars not to dare to preach such things in the future and said that they would take it very ill if it were said that there were heretics there, since no one among them, so they insisted, was any such thing. These and other remarks to the same effect they uttered as threats. When Master Roland heard the story . . . he replied . . . "Surely it behooves us now to preach more and more against heretics and their believers." This he did. . . .

• • •

At that time there died in the bourg [town] a certain heretic, Galvan by name, a leading figure among the Waldenses. The fact did not escape Master Roland, who announced it publicly in a sermon, and, when the friars, clergy, and some of the people had assembled, they went boldly to the house where the aforesaid heretic died and razed it to the ground, making a refuse-pit of it. They dug up that Galvan and took him from the cemetery . . . then in a great procession dragged his body through the town and burned it in the common field outside the town. This was one in praise of our Lord Jesus Christ and the Blessed Dominic and to the honor of the Roman and Catholic church, our mother, in the year of the Lord 1231.

• • •

The . . . archbishop of Vienna, . . . made Arnold Catalan, who was then of the convent at Toulousse, and inquisitor against heretics in the diocese of Albi, . . . However, the believers of the heretics would say nothing at that time, rather, they united in denials; yet he did sentence two living heretics . . . and both were burned but at different times. He condemned certain other deceased persons and had them dragged away and burned. Disturbed by this, the people of Albi sought to throw him into the River Tarn, but at the insistence of some among them released him, beaten, his clothing torn to shreds, his face bloody; yet even while being dragged along he cried out, "Blessed be the Lord Jesu Christ!"

• • •

Moreover, in that land in those days Catholics were harassed and in several localities those who searched out heretics were killed, although Lord Raymond, the count, had promised in the treaty of peace that over a period of five years, for every heretic, male or female, he would give two silver marks to the one who seized them and after five years one mark. This happened many times. But the chief men of the region, together with the greater nobles and the burghers and others, protected and hid the heretics. They beat, wounded, and killed those who pursued them, for the prince's entourage was notably corrupted in the faith. . . .

• • •

At that time the inquisitors made their inquisition in Tailless and summoned many people of the town before them. Among them was a man from the bourg, John Textor by name. He . . . had many of the important heretical sympathizers of the town to defend him. Now this wicked John spoke out before everyone: "Gentlemen, listen to me! I am not a heretic, for I have a wife and I sleep with her. I have sons, I eat meat, and I lie and swear, and I am a faithful Christian. So don't let them say these things about me, for I truly believe in God. They can accuse you as well as me. Look out for yourselves, for these wicked men want to ruin the town and honest men and take the town away from its lord." Then the case was pressed . . . and . . . he was condemned. But when the vicar . . . sought to drag him away to the stake, those who defended the man raised an outcry against his doing any such thing, and everyone was muttering against the friars and the vicar. So the aforesaid John was . . . put into prison. . . .

The town was now very much stirred up against the friars; there were even more threats and speeches against them than usual, and many heretical persons incited the people to stone the friars and destroy their houses because, the cry was, they were unjustly accusing decent married men of heresy.

• • •

At the same town the consuls [secular administrators] made proclamation throughout the town . . . that, on penalty of corporal punishment and fine, no one was to give, sell or lend anything whatever or to give assistance in any form to the Friars Preachers. . . . We friars did have the essentials in sufficient supply from friends and Catholics who, despite the danger, handed us bread, cheese, and eggs over the garden walls . . . when the consuls . . . learned of this, they set their guards at our gates and also on the garden, watching the house day and night to prevent any necessities being brought in. They even cut us off completely from the water of the Garonne. . . .

51 Courtly Manners in Japan

Murasaki Shikibu. *The Tale of Genji*. Translated by Arthur Waley. Boston and New York: Houghton Mifflin Company, 1929. 211–214.

Court life in eleventh-century Japan was governed by elaborate rituals designed to celebrate and reinforce the position of the nobility. Within the closed world of the imperial palace, the Emperor presided over the pursuit of aesthetic beauty that governed the day-to-day life of nobles like Prince Genji whose personal story was chronicled by Lady Murasaki Shikibu around 1000 CE. *The Tale of Genji* is a memorial to the carefully crafted gestures, poetry, and ceremonies that regulated the behavior of the most powerful members of Japanese society. The imperial court had for centuries been influenced by cultural and religious developments on the Asian continent: as Genji indicates below, knowledge of Chinese and Korean culture was highly prized. Yet despite the social conventions that governed court life, *The Tale of Genji* suggests that members of the court—like Prince Genji and the Emperor's consort Fujitsubo who together have a clandestine love affair—often circumvent these customs. In this passage, Genji must perform a festival dance before the Emperor and the ladies of the palace without betraying his love for Fujitsubo.

[The Festival of the Red Leaves] was to be a more magnificent sight this year than it had ever been before and the ladies of the Palace were very disappointed that they could not be present.° The Emperor could not bear that Fujitsubo should miss the spectacle, and he decided to hold a grand rehearsal in the Palace. Prince Genji danced the "Waves of the Blue Sea." To no Chujo was his partner; but though both in skill and beauty he far surpassed the common run of performers, yet beside Genji he seemed like a mountain fir growing beside a cherry-tree in bloom. There was a wonderful moment when the rays of the setting sun fell upon him and the music grew suddenly louder. Never had the onlookers seen feet tread so delicately nor head so exquisitely poised; and in the song which follows the first movement of the dance his voice was as sweet as the song of [the bird that sings in Paradise] whose music is Buddha's Law. So moving and beautiful was this dance that at the end of it the Emperor's eyes were wet, and all the princes and great

---

°Ladies within the Imperial Court were not permitted to leave the palace compound.

gentlemen wept aloud. When the song was over and, straightening his long dancer's sleeves, he stood waiting for the music to begin again and at last the more lively tune of the second movement struck up,—then indeed, with his flushed and eager face, he merited more than ever his name of Genji the Shining One. The Princess Kokiden did not at all like to see her stepson's beauty arousing so much enthusiasm and she said sarcastically, "He is altogether too beautiful. Presently we shall have a god coming down from the sky to fetch him away." Her young [ladies-in-waiting] noticed the spiteful tone in which the remark was made and felt somewhat embarrassed. As for Fujitsubo, she kept on telling herself that were it not for the guilty secret which was shared between them the dance she was now witnessing would be filling her with wonder and delight. As it was, she sat as though in a dream, hardly knowing what went on around her.

Now she was back in her own room. The Emperor was with her. "At today's rehearsal," he said, "The Waves of the Blue Sea went perfectly." Then, noticing that she made no response, "What did you think of it?" "Yes, it was very good," she managed to say at last. "The partner did not seem to me bad either," he went on; "there is always something about the way a gentleman moves and uses his hands which distinguishes his dancing from that of professionals. Some of our crack dancing-masters have certainly made very clever performers of their own children; but they never have the same freshness, the same charm as the young people of our class. They expended so much effort on the rehearsal that I am afraid the festival itself may seem a very poor affair. No doubt they took all this trouble because they knew that you were here at the rehearsal and would not see the real performance."

Next morning she received a letter from Genji: "What of the rehearsal? How little the people who watched me knew of the turmoil that all the while was seething in my brain!" And to this he added the poem: "When sick with love I yet sprang to my feet and [danced] with the rest, knew you what meant the fevered waving of my long dancing-sleeve?" Next he enjoined secrecy and prudence upon her, and so his letter ended. Her answer showed that despite her agitation she had not been wholly insensible to what had fascinated all other eyes: "Though from far off a man of China waved his long dancing-sleeves, yet did his every motion fill my heart with wonder and delight."

To receive such a letter from her was indeed a surprise. It charmed him that her knowledge should extend even to the Court customs of a land beyond the sea. Already there was a regal note in her words. Yes, that was the end to which she was destined. Smiling to himself with pleasure he spread the letter out before him, grasping it tightly in both hands as a priest holds the holy book, and gazed at it for a long while.

On the day of the festival, the royal princes and all the great gentlemen of the Court were in attendance. Even the Heir Apparent went with the procession. After the music-boats had rowed round the lake dance upon dance was performed, both Korean and of the land beyond the sea [China]. The Emperor insisted upon treating Genji's performance at the rehearsal as a kind of miracle or religious portent, and ordered special services to be read in every temple. . . . The Ring° was by

---

°The circle of men who stand around the dancers while they switch costumes.

the Emperor's order composed indifferently of commoners and noblemen chosen out of the whole realm for their skill and grace. The two Masters of Ceremony, Sayemon no Kami and Uyemon no Kami, were in charge of the left and right wings of the orchestra. Dancing-masters and others were entrusted with the task of seeking out performers of unusual merit and training them for the festival in their own houses. When at last under the red leafage of tall autumn trees forty men stood [in a circle] with their flutes and to the music that they made[,] a strong wind from the hills sweeping the pine-woods added its fierce harmonies, while from amid a wreckage of whirling and scattered leaves the Dance of the Blue Waves suddenly broke out in all its glittering splendor,—a rapture seized the onlookers that was akin to fear.

The maple-wreath that Genji wore had suffered in the wind and thinking that the few red leaves which clung to it had a desolate air the Minister of the Left plucked a bunch of chrysanthemums from among those that grew before the Emperor's seat and twined them in the dancer's wreath.

At sunset the sky clouded over and it looked like rain. But even the weather seemed conscious that such sights as this would not for a long while be seen again, and till all was over not a drop fell. His [Genji's] Exit Dance, crowned as he was with this unspeakably beautiful wreath of many colored flowers, was even more astonishing than that wonderful moment on the day of the rehearsal and seemed to the thrilled onlookers like the vision of another world. Humble and ignorant folk sitting afar on tree-roots or beneath some rock, or half-buried in deep banks of fallen leaves—few were so hardened that they did not shed a tear. . . .

52 An Inca Census

Huaman Poma. *Letter to a King: A Peruvian Chief's Account of Life Under the Incas and Under Spanish Rule.* Translated by Christopher Dilke. New York: E.P. Dutton, 1978. 54–59.

Guaman Poma was an Inca noble who was born after the Spanish conquest of the Inca empire. The Inca empire, a successor state to Huari, arose in the fourteenth century in the Andes Mountains. Poma wrote an elaborate letter to the Spanish king in which he protested the cruelties of Spanish administrators and clergy in the Inca highlands. Although the letter was written between 1567 and 1615, after the Spanish conquest, Poma offered a glimpse of preconquest society to illustrate, by comparison, the failings of Spanish rule. In this passage, he discusses how the Inca state organized the population to ensure the livelihood of all. Within this description, Poma also comments on what behavior was expected from people at the different stages of their life. The passage describes a semiannual census of the population that categorized people by age, gender, and productivity.

A . . . general inspection used to be made by the Inca and the nobles belonging to the Council of the Realm. The people, whether male or female, were separated into ten categories in order to facilitate counting them. Each person was employed in the calling for which he or she was best suited and laziness was discouraged. In no other way could the bare subsistence of the Indians, the greater state kept by their nobles and their majesty of the Inca have been maintained. . . .

The ritual of the visits occurred unalterably every six months, and it was then that the people moved up from one age-group to another and adopted their new duties.

• • •

The first category consisted of new born babies . . . being rocked in the cradle by their mothers, who are the proper source of milk and affection for these tiny creatures. The relations might assist, but it was on the mother that the full load of responsibility was placed by the law. This load was all the heavier if the baby was nobly born or if it had lost its father in war.

To the second category belong the children . . . learning to walk. These . . . were often put in the care of elder children so that they should not . . . come to any . . . harm. They were still considered as the responsibility of their mothers, but special provision was made for twins . . . [that] obliged both the father and the mother to care for these personally for a period of two years.

If the little children were orphans, from the moment of birth they had a right to a certain area of cultivated land. Thus the whole community, and not just the parents, was concerned about their support and supervision. . . .

Children . . . between five and nine . . . the third category, began to be disciplined by their parents with frequent beatings. . . . They were used to look after the younger children or to rock the cradles of the newly born.

The girls of the same age were sometimes able to do jobs about the house or to learn a skill such as spinning fine thread. Some of them gathered herbs, helped to make maize spirit or looked after babies. It was an important part of their education that they were taught to be clean in person and useful to their parents.

The fourth category was composed of boys and girls between the ages of 9 and 12. The boys were employed in trapping small birds which were sometimes brilliantly colored, like humming-birds, sometimes ash-colored, and sometimes linnets or ring-doves. The skins of these birds were treated as leather, the flesh was prepared for eating and the feathers were used to decorate shields or make tufts round lances for the Inca and his warriors.

Boys got their education in the fields and were not sent to any other school. It was considered inadvisable to train them for a job, since they would only have treated the job as a game until they were grown up. Only small tasks like watching the flocks, carrying wood, weaving and twisting thread were entrusted to them.

The main occupation of the girls in this category was picking the large variety of wild flowers in the countryside. These flowers were used for dyeing the fine cloth called *cunbe*, among other purposes. The girls also gathered nutritious herbs which were dried and stored for a period of up to one year.

It was part of their ritual duty to assist in sacrifices and invocations to the Sun. The turban which the Inca wore . . . owed its delicate colors to their ministrations, as did other clothing such as headbands, sashes, belts and sandals.

In the fifth category were all those between the ages of about 12 and 18. The boys' main duty was to watch the flocks of mountain sheep. Whilst so occupied, they learned to catch or kill a wide variety of animal life with the help of lassoes, traps and catapults.

Even before the Incas took power, boys of this age were employed in the personal service of the rulers and their divinities.

The young girls with cropped hair, who belonged to this age-group, performed various useful jobs in and out-of-doors for their parents and grandparents, such as cooking and cleaning the house or helping about the farm. Being submissive and respectful, they quickly learned whatever was expected of them. Along with their short hair they went barefoot and wore short dresses without any pretence of elegance until they reached the age of marriage. Even then, they continued to lead the same life of poverty and service until the change from the single to the married state was ordered by the Inca or someone acting in his name. It was forbidden on pain of death for any of these girls to anticipate the order by giving themselves to a man and this was so well understood that punishment seldom had to be imposed.

In the sixth category, the young men between the ages of 18 to 20 were given the name of *sayapayac,* which means "ready to obey commands." They served as messengers, travelling between villages or places within the same valley. They also looked after the herds, carried the rations for the army and attended upon the chiefs. They kept to a simple diet, avoidance of alcohol, and chaste habits. All they needed was a little tea, some boiled maize, a shirt and a warm coat. The boys of noble birth lived all the more austerely, were harshly treated and seldom allowed to rest, and were deprived of women until they were older.

The female counterparts were the girls who were ready for marriage. These young and pretty creatures were still expected to remain virgins until the actual ceremony. Indeed, some of them were chosen to be perpetual virgins in the service of the Sun, the Moon, the Day-Star and other divinities. Some were also distributed among the Inca and the great nobles, or people of special merit. The distribution was carried out with absolute impartiality, even when the Inca was concerned. Nobody was permitted to take a woman according to his own will or desire. Even the Inca was subject to the penalties of the law, including death for crimes against the virtue of girls and women. This respect for virginity was one of the noblest features of our country. Some women, while living a perfectly free life in their homes and fields, were never touched in their whole lifetime and died as pure as on the day when they were born.

It was a wonderful provision of our law to separate those girls who were to marry from those who were to remain intact all their days.

The seventh and most important category included all the brave men capable of service in war and aged between 25 and 50. On reaching the age of 33 they were regarded as fully trained and kept in readiness for battle or whatever other duties might be assigned to them. Some of them were designated as . . . settlers. They were sent to populate other provinces where they were allotted farms of a size big enough for the support of a family. Local girls were enlisted as wives for them. This policy enabled the Inca to assure the security of distant and uncertain provinces, where the settlers acted as his trustworthy informants.

Members of this category, who were in general called . . . men of war, were also employed in agriculture and the mines, and in duties at court. Likewise girls of the same age were primarily regarded as suitable wives for fighting men, but in their girlhood they were given the task of making clothes for the nobility. They had to weave the thick cloth . . . and spin the fine and delicate *cunbe*. They were not regarded as free agents at the inspection because they were already firmly destined to become soldiers' wives. As soon as a particular man was designated as the husband, the girl passed under his control.

Girls of good family were carefully shielded against marrying men of no consequence or adventurers. If any girl succeeded in breaking this rule she was degraded to the same level as the man. Once properly married, a woman received the title of Mama and was honored in her capacity as a mother of children.

The sick and handicapped, who were in the eighth category, included the dumb, the blind, the chronically unfit, the crippled and deformed and those lacking a limb. Some of them, especially the dwarfs, hunchbacks and those with split noses, made a pastime out of their skill in telling jokes and stories. Others were employed according to their actual capacities. If they had legs they were used for coming and going. If they had hands they were trained to weave; or they might be given jobs as stewards and accountants.

The female unfortunates were usually very skilful in handiwork of all kinds, such as the making of fine cloth, cooking and fermenting. As with the men, the amusing ones found a place as entertainers of the nobility. . . .

In all cases the handicapped were encouraged or obliged to marry their counterparts. A blind man was paired off with a blind woman, a dumb man with a dumb woman, a cripple with a cripple, a hunchback with a hunchback and a dwarf with a dwarf. In this way, under a dispensation made for them by the Inca, they were allowed to multiply their own kind. Handicapped women who failed to find husbands took lovers so that they should not remain childless.

These sick and deformed Indians owned their own houses and property and stood in need of no charity, being adequately provided for under the law.

The ninth category was composed of those beyond their prime but still fairly active, who worked on the farms, carried wood and straw or acted as servants to the nobility. After the age of 50 they were relieved from military service and from any obligation to live away from home, but remained at the beck and call of the rulers.

The women over 50 often resumed their old occupation of weaving. Others attended upon the great ladies or upon the sacred virgins, carrying out whatever duties were entrusted to them including carrying a *quipu* for the keeping of accounts.°

Not all the women in this class were advanced in age, since widows were included, however young, on the grounds that they were not virgins any more. Such widows were considered as lost lives and of no particular value to the community, although later they might be respected for their old age.

The tenth and last category was left for the dull and sleepy old people, usually deaf as well, over the age of 80. Being so very ancient, they were not expected to

---

°The *quipu* is a cord tied with elaborate knots to record statistical information. The color of the threads and the distance between the knots, represent numbers.

do much more than eat and sleep. Some few of them were still able to make ropes, weave blankets, spin thread, act as doorkeepers and look after rabbits and ducks. A number of old women might be more or less usefully occupied in a household of some consequence.

The aged were greatly respected and honored. Value was attached to their influence over the young, their advice and their capacity to hand down the knowledge of religion with their little remaining understanding. They were clothed free of charge and allowed to have their own garden plots, which were cultivated under a communal system called *minga*. One couple, a man and a woman, undertook to take care of each old person, to whom they made many gifts. Thus it was unnecessary to maintain any hospitals for the aged.

53 Visual Document: *Codex Mendoza*

The *Codex Mendoza* is a remarkable pictorial manuscript that was prepared by the Nahua (Aztec) Indians under the direction of the Spanish around 1541. It seems that the Viceroy of Mexico, Antonio de Mendoza, asked an Indian artist named Francisco Gualpuyogualcal to prepare a text indicating the conquests, tribute, military and political affairs, and customs of the Aztecs before the Spanish conquest. The pictures prepared by the artist were then annotated in Spanish. The manuscript was eventually acquired by the French historian and geographer Andre Thevet in the late sixteenth century after the Spanish ship carrying it had been captured by French pirates. At Thevet's death it was sold to the English ambassador, and it finally came to rest at Oxford University. Perhaps influenced by the Spanish under whom it was compiled, the *Codex Mendoza* is nevertheless a remarkable document that reveals much about the Aztec empire and its people. What do the illustrations tell you about the roles of children in Aztec family life? How do those roles differ based on age and gender?

Please note that the upper two pairs in the illustration are facsimile images from the *Codex Mendoza*. An English translation appears below.

These eleven blue dots
mean eleven years

Father of the children
in this row

One and a half *tortillas*

An 11-year-old boy is being
punished by his father, with
dry chile¹ smoke in his nostrils

Fumes or smoke
of chiles¹

Mother of the children
in this row

One and a half *tortillas*

An 11-year-old girl is being threatened
by her mother, with dry
chile¹ smoke in her nostrils

Chile¹ fumes

12 years

Father of the children
in this row

One and a half *tortillas*

A 12-year-old boy tied hand and foot,
stretched out all day on damp ground

This picture represents the night

Mother of the children
in this row

One and a half *tortillas*

A 12-year-old girl goes
sweeping at night

13 years   Two *tortillas*

DISCUSSION QUESTIONS

1. How do religions govern people's behavior? What similarities and differences do you see in the Islamic and Christian documents?

2. Looking closely at the readings, how do prescriptions for behavior differ for people of higher and lower status? In other words, what class differences exist in the ways in which behavior is described?

3. Compare and contrast the behavior of elites in *The Tale of Genji* with those in *Piers the Ploughman*. What information is the author of each respective reading conveying about the behavior of the nobles in Japan and England?

4. Ceremony and ritual play a large part in each of your readings. How might the different ceremonies—for example, marriage rites in Ma Huan's chronicle or the Inquisition in William Pelhison's account—bind together, or tear apart, the belief of people in their communities?

5. Compare the Inca census with the other readings you have done for this chapter. How is Inca society, and the regulation of people's behavior, different from, or similar to, that of other societies? How do Inca and Aztec societies compare?

6. What similarities exist between the Quran and the allegorical journey of English nobles to find "Truth"?

Chapter
10

The Spread of Religions and Cultures

*T*he spread of religions both united and divided societies in this era. Religions were diffused by a number of different means, including commerce, conversion efforts by traveling missionaries, war, language, or adoption by the elites of the society. The adoption of a particular religion often involved much more than the mere acceptance of spiritual beliefs or a sacred text. Language, particularly that used to write the sacred texts, and cultural practices such as dress, restrictions of food, and the performance of hygienic procedures were often transmitted as an integral part of religious practice. In this way, religion played a large role in deter-mining fundamental parts of everyday life in societies following their tenets.

The following selections include a wide variety of religions that spread among different regions, or that spread from one society to its neighbors through conquest, trade, or conversion. It is important to note that popular religious prac-tices may have varied significantly from those practiced in court circles. The first excerpt, from the *Nihongi*, describes the inauspicious beginning of Buddhism in Japan. By contrast, the second reading discusses the arrival of a variant type of Buddhism, called Theravada, in grandiose, mythical terms. The third selection concerns the religion of the Aztecs. Originally a nomadic group, they settled in the central valley of Mexico, and the peoples they conquered became subject to their religious and cosmographical views. The fourth and fifth readings present Christian and Muslim views of the Crusades in the west Asian region considered holy in both faiths. The chapter ends with a contemporary account of the pilgrim-age to Mecca of the fabulously wealthy Muslim king of Mali.

54 The Spread of Buddhism to Japan

Nihongi. *Chronicles of Japan from the Earliest Times to AD 697.* Translated by W. G. Aston. Rutland, Vt. Charles E. Tuttle, 1972. 65–68.

This selection details the peaceful arrival of Buddhism to Japan. In this seventh-century version, written some 150 years later, embassies were sent from Korea to bring Buddhist doctrine to the Japanese royal court. Buddhism was adopted voluntarily on a trial basis by one elite family. Its arrival and early history were not favorable, and Buddhism was subsequently banned. Nevertheless, it did eventually become a major, though not exclusive, religion in Japan in the following centuries.

Winter, 10th month. King Syong-myong of Pekche sent Kwi-si of the Western Division, and the Tal-sol, Nu-ri Sachhi-hye, with a present to the Emperor[;] . . . he presented a memorial in which he lauded the merit of diffusing abroad religious worship, saying:—"This doctrine is amongst all doctrines the most excellent. But it is hard to explain, and hard to comprehend. Even . . . Confucius had not attained to a knowledge of it. This doctrine can create religious merit and retribution without measure and without bounds, and so lead on to a full appreciation of the highest wisdom . . . every prayer is fulfilled and naught is wanting. Moreover, from distant India it has extended hither . . . where there are none who do not receive it with reverence as it is preached to them.

The servant, therefore, Myong, King of Pekche, has humbly despatched his retainer . . . to transmit it to the Imperial Country, and to diffuse it abroad throughout the home provinces, so as to fulfil the recorded saying of Buddha: "My law shall spread to the East."

This day the Emperor . . . leaped for joy, and gave command to the envoys, saying:—"Never from former days until now have we had the opportunity of listening to so wonderful a doctrine. We are unable, however, to decide of ourselves." Accordingly he inquired of his Ministers one after another, saying:—"The countenance of this Buddha which has been presented by the Western frontier State is of a severe dignity, such as we have never at all seen before. Ought it to be worshipped or not?" Soga no Oho-omi, Iname no Sukune, addressed the Emperor, saying:—"All the Western frontier lands without exception do it worship. Shall Akitsu Yamato alone refuse to do so?" [Others] addressed the Emperor jointly, saying:—"Those who have ruled the empire in this our State have always made it their care to worship in Spring, Summer, Autumn and Winter the 180 Gods of Heaven and Earth, and the Gods of the Land and of Grain. If just at this time we were to worship in their stead foreign Deities, it may be feared that we should incur the wrath of our National Gods."

The Emperor said:—"Let it be given to Iname no Sukune, who has shown his willingness to take it, and, as an experiment make him to worship it."

The Oho-omi knelt down and received it with joy. He enthroned it in his house at Oharda, where he diligently carried out the rites of retirement from the world, and on that score purified his house . . . and made it a Temple. After this a pestilence was rife in the Land, from which the people died prematurely. As time went on it became worse and worse, and there was no remedy. Okoshi . . . and Kamako . . . addressed the Emperor jointly, saying:—"It was because thy servants' advice on a former day was not approved that the people are dying thus of disease. If thou dost not retrace thy steps before matters have gone too far, joy will hardly be the result! It will be well promptly to fling it away, and diligently to seek happiness in the future."

The Emperor said: "Let it be done as you advise." Accordingly officials took the image of Buddha and abandoned it to the current of the Canal. . . . They also set fire to the Temple, and burnt it so that nothing was left. Hereupon, there being in the Heavens neither clouds nor wind, a sudden conflagration consumed the Great Hall (of the Palace).

· · ·

[6 months later]

The following report was received from the province of Kahachi: "From within the sea . . . there is heard a voice of Buddhist chants, which re-echoes like the sound of thunder, and a glory shines like the radiance of the sun." In his heart the emperor wondered at this and sent Unate . . . to go upon the sea and investigate the matter.

This month Unate no Atahe went upon the sea, and the result was that he discovered a log of camphor-wood shining brightly as it floated on the surface. At length he took it, and presented it to the emperor, who gave orders to an artist to make of it two images of Buddha. These are the radiant camphor-wood images now in the Temple of Yoshino.

55 The Spread of Buddhism in South Asia

The Mahavamsa or the Great Chronicle of Ceylon. Translated by Wilhem Geiger. Colombo, Ceylon [Sri Lanka]: Ceylon Government, 1950. 84–7.

The last passage described the initially inauspicious arrival of Buddhism in Japan. In this excerpt, missions were sent from Indian kingdoms to what is now Sri Lanka, and from there to Burma, Thailand, Laos, and Cambodia. The form of the religion dominant in Southeast Asia is Theravada Buddhism, a form of Buddhism that maintains that everything in the universe is constantly in flux. Inevitable sorrow results from this lack of permanence, and salvation can only be obtained by rejecting the sense of individuality, to reach a state called Nirvana. In contrast to the method of conversion seen in the Japanese piece, this conversion involves several tests of the religion's powers. Its adoption results largely from its proven ability to overcome evil and benefit its adherents.

. . . The great thera [a religious teacher] Mahinda, the theras Itthiya, Uttiya, Sambala and Bhaddasala his disciples, these . . . he sent forth with the charge: Ye shall found in the lovely island of Lanka the lovely religion of the conqueror.

• • •

. . . [T]he naga-king of wondrous power, Aravala, used the rain called "Hail" to pour down upon the ripe crops and cruelly did he overwhelm everything with a flood. The thera Majjhantika went thither with all speed, passing through the air, and wrought (miracles such as) walking on the surface of the water in Aravala's lake. . . . When the nagas beheld it they told their king with fury about this thing.

Then full of fury the naga-king brought [several] terrors to pass; fierce winds blew, a cloud gave forth thunder and rain, thunder strokes crashed, and lightning flashed here and there, trees and mountain-tops were hurled down. . . .

Then to him, humbled by these words the thera preached the doctrine, and thereupon the naga-king came unto the refuges and the precepts of duty, . . .

"Henceforth let no anger arise as of old; work no more harm to the harvest, for living beings love their happiness; cherish love for beings, let men live in happiness." Thus were they taught by him and they did according to (this teaching). . . . The conversion of eighty thousand persons took place. . . .

• • •

The wise Majjhima preached in the Himalaya region whither he had gone with four theras. . . . The five theras separately converted five kingdoms; from each of them a hundred thousand persons received the . . . doctrine. . . .

Together with the thera Uttara the thera Sona of wondrous might went to Suvannabhumi [lower Burma or Bengal]. Now at this time, whenever a boy was born in the king's palace, a fearsome female demon who came forth out of the sea was wont to devour [him] and vanish again. And at that very moment a prince was born in the king's palace. When the people saw the theras they thought: "There are companions of the demons," and they came armed to kill them. And the theras asked: "What does this mean?". . . . Then the demon came forth from the ocean with her following, and when the people saw them they raised a great outcry. But the thera created twice as many terrifying demons and therewith surrounded the demon and her following on every side. She thought: This [country] is come into possession of these [people] and, panic-stricken, she took to flight.

When the thera had made a bulwark round the country he pronounced in the assembly the [doctrine.]

. . . [S]ixty thousand were converted to the true faith.

56 Religious Ritual in the Central Valley of Mexico

Fray Bernardino de Sahagún. *The Florentine Codex. General History of the Things of New Spain: Book 2—The Ceremonies.* Translated by Arthur J. O. Anderson and Charles E. Dibble. Santa Fe, N. Mex: The School of American Research, 1951. 197, 216–217.

As the Aztec society expanded, it imposed its religion on the peoples it conquered in the central valley of Mexico (estimated to have held twenty-five million people at the time of European contact in 1519). Aztec society worshiped the sun. Part of the ritual of worship involved the offering of sacrifices, in which the spilling of human and animal blood played an important role. These rites, and their role in the worship of the sun, are described in the following passage.

Although human sacrifice is the feature of Aztec religion that garners most attention from modern scholars, there were limits placed on this practice. Normally men from enemy or conquered groups were sacrificed on specific days of religious significance within the complicated Aztec calendar. This sacrifice, the Aztecs believed, was required in order for the sun to continue to conquer the night at dawn each day.

When captives and slaves died, [they] were called, "Those who have died for the god."

Thus they took [the captive] up [to the pyramid temple] . . . [the priests] going holding him by his hands. And he who was known as the arranger [of captives] . . . laid him out upon the sacrificial stone.

And [then] . . . four men stretched him out, [grasping] his arms and legs. And already in the hand of the fire priest lay the knife, with which he was to slash open the breast of the . . . captive.

And then . . . he at once seized his heart. And he whose breast he laid open was quite alive. And when [the priest] had seized his heart, he dedicated it to the sun.

• • •

Each day, when the sun arose, quail were slain and incense was offered. . . .

And they invoked [the sun], saying:

"The sun hath come forth—the shafts of heat, the turquoise child, the soaring eagle. And how he will go on, or how he may tarry [we know not]. . . .

Reprinted by permission, from *The Florentine Codex: General History of the Things in Spain* by Fray Bernardino de Sahagún. Book 2: The Ceremonies, pp. 197, 216–217. Translated by Arthur J. O. Anderson and Charles E. Dibble. Copyright © 1981 by the School of American Research, Santa Fe.

They said unto him: "Work; perform thy office [for us], O our lord."

And this each day was thus done when the sun rose. . . .

And thus was incense offered four times during the day, and five times during the night: The first time [was] when the sun burst forth. The second time [was] when [it was] time to eat [the first meal]. And the third time [was] at midday; and the fourth time [was] when already the sun had set.

And at night, thus was incense offered: the first time, when it was dark; the second time, when it was time to sleep; the third time, when the shell trumpets were sounded; the fourth time, at midnight; and the fifth time, near dawn. And when it was dark, incense was offered and a supplication was made to the night. It was said:

"The Lord of the Night, he of the sharp nose, hath unfolded, and we know not how his office will end."

And his feast day came upon the day . . . called *naui ollin,* every two hundred and three days. And when the day had come, all did penances; all fasted for four days. And when they reached the day of the day-count, at noon, shell trumpets were blown, and straws were passed through the flesh to draw blood. And they cut the ears of little children lying in their cradles. And all the people bloodied themselves, and no supplications were then made. But everyone drew blood; straws were passed through tongue or ear-lobe, and incense was offered. Everyone [did so]; none were negligent.

And there was the image of that one, [the sun, at a pyramid temple] called Quauhxicallii. There was erected his image, his image was designed as if it had the mask of a man [but] with [the sun's] rays streaming from it. His sun ornament was round, circled with feathers. . . . Here in his presence was the fasting done, and the passing of straws through the flesh, the laying of offerings, and the slaying of quail.

And upon his feast day, also many captives died, and these were also called, "those who died in war." These went to the house of the sun and dwelt with the sun.

57 The Beginning of the Crusades

James A. Brundage. *The Crusades: A Documentary Survey.*
Milwaukee, Wis.: Marquette University Press, 1962. 17–20.

The Christian Crusades into Islamic kingdoms were inspired by increasing military threats to Byzantium, and in particular, to its capital, Constantinople. In 1095 the ruler of Byzantium appealed to Pope Urban II for aid. The following excerpt comes from an account written by Robert the Monk. It describes Urban's sermon delivered in France to rally support to stop the spread of Islam. The motivation for the Crusades was first and foremost religious—to conquer or reconquer formerly Christian lands and especially the Christian holy sites in Jerusalem, such as the Church of the Holy Sepulchre. For Pope Urban II there were important political considerations as well: successful campaigns might reunite the Catholic Church, reassert the authority of the papacy in western Europe, and put a halt to military conflicts within Europe. The crusade inaugurated by Urban II was the first of four military campaigns between 1095 and 1291. For the Catholic armies, the high point of the Crusades was the capture of Jerusalem in 1099, although the city ultimately was lost to the armies of Saladin in 1187.

In the year of the Incarnation of Our Lord 1095, a great council was held in the Auvergne region of Gaul, in the city of Clermont. . . . There the pope addressed the whole gathering in these words:

"Frenchmen! You who come from across the Alps; you who have been singled out by God and who are loved by him—as is shown by your many accomplishments; you who are set apart from all other peoples by the location of your country, by your Catholic faith, and by the honor of the Holy Church; we address these words, this sermon, to you!

We want you to know the melancholy reasons which have brought us among you and the peril which threatens you and all the faithful. Distressing news has come to us (as has often happened) from the region of Jerusalem and from the city of Constantinople; news that the people of the Persian kingdom, an alien people, a race completely foreign to God, a 'generation of false aims, of a spirit that broke faith with God' has invaded Christian territory and has devastated this territory with pillage, fire, and the sword. The Persians have taken some of these Christians as captives into their own country; they have destroyed others with cruel tortures. They have completely destroyed some of God's churches and they have converted others to the uses of their own cult. They ruin altars with filth and defilement. They circumcise Christians and smear blood from the circumcision over the altars or throw it into the baptismal fonts. They are pleased to kill others by cutting open their bellies, extracting the end of their intestines, and tying it to a stake. Then, with flogging, they drive their victims around the stake until, when their viscera have spilled out, they fall dead on the ground. . . . And what shall I say about the shocking rape of women? On this subject it would, perhaps, be worse to speak than to keep silent. . . .

Who is to revenge all this, who is to repair this damage, if you do not do it? . . . Rise up and remember the manly deeds of your ancestor, the prowess and greatness of Charlemagne, of his son Louis, of your other kings, who destroyed pagan kingdoms and planted the holy church in their territories. You should be especially aroused by the fact that the Holy Sepulchre of the Lord our Savior is in the hands of these unclean people, who shamefully mistreat and sacrilegiously defile the Holy Places with their filth. Oh, most valiant knights! Descendants of unconquered ancestors! Remember the courage of your forefathers and do not dishonor them!

But if your affection for your beloved children, wives, and parents would hold you back, remember what the Lord says in the Gospel: 'He who loves father or mother more than me is not worthy of me.' 'Everyone who has left house, or brothers, or father, or mother, or wife, or children, or lands, for my name's sake, shall receive a hundredfold, and shall possess life everlasting.'° Do not allow any possession or any solicitude for family affairs detain you.

This land in which you live, surrounded on one side by the sea and on the other side by mountain peaks, can scarcely contain so many of you. It does not abound in wealth; indeed, it scarcely provides enough food for those who cultivate it. Because of this you murder and devour one another, you wage wars, and you frequently wound and kill one another. Let this mutual hatred stop; let these quarrels abate; let these wars cease; and let all these conflicts and controversies be put to rest. Begin the journey to the Holy Sepulchre; conquer the land which the wicked have seized, the land which was given by God to the children of Israel. . . .

Jerusalem is the navel of the world, a land which is more fruitful than any other, a land which is like another paradise of delights. This is the land which the Redeemer of mankind [Jesus Christ] illuminated by his coming, adorned by his life, consecrated by his passion, redeemed by his death, and sealed by his burial. This royal city, situated in the middle of the world, is now held captive by his enemies and is made a servant, by those who know not God, for the ceremonies of the heathen. . . ."

When Pope Urban had said these and many similar things in his urbane sermon, those who were present were so moved that, as one man, all of them together shouted: "God wills it! God wills it!" When the venerable pontiff heard this, he turned his eyes toward heaven and gave thanks to God. He then waved his hand for silence, and said:

"Dearly beloved brethren! . . . If the Lord God had not been present in your minds, you would not all have cried out the same thing, for although all of you shouted, your cries had but one origin. I tell you, therefore, that God placed this shout in your breasts and that God brought it out. Since this shout came from God, let it be your battle cry. When you make an armed attack on the enemy, let all those on God's side cry out together, 'God wills it!'"

58 Saladin Conquers Jerusalem

Arab Historians of the Crusades. Selected and translated from Arabic by Francesco Gabrieli; translated from Italian by E.J. Costello. Berkeley and Los Angeles: University of California Press, 1969. 139–146. [Originally published in Italy as *Storici Arabi delle Crociate.*]

°From the New Testament, Matthew 10:37; 29:29.

Figure 10.1 A symbolic portrayal of the fall of Jerusalem in which Saladin seizes the "True Cross" from the Frankish king.

The conquest of Jerusalem in 1099 was celebrated throughout Christian Europe, but in 1187 the city fell to Muslim forces under the command of Saladin. Ibn al-Athīr, the author of the account below, was an eyewitness to the reconquest of Jerusalem and later wrote a history of the events. In his chronicle, al-Athīr wrote that when western Europeans (the Franks) captured Jerusalem, they desecrated the Dome of the Rock,* and put thousands— including Muslim scholars—to death. For this reason, Saladin is initially unwilling to negotiate the surrender of Jerusalem, preferring to threaten retribution for atrocities committed in the past. In the end, a negotiated settlement allows those within Jerusalem to ransom themselves provided that they have the money to do so.

When Saladin had completed his conquest of Ascalon and the surrounding regions he sent for the Egyptian fleet and a large detachment of troops. . . . This force set out by sea, intercepting Frankish communications; every Frankish vessel they sighted they attacked, and captured every galley. When they arrived and Saladin could rely on their support, he marched from Ascalon to Jerusalem. . . . The inhabitants of that region, Ascalon and elsewhere had also gathered in Jerusalem, so there was a great concourse of people there, each of whom would choose death rather than see the Muslims in power in their city; the sacrifice of life, possessions and sons was for them a part of their duty to defend the city. During that interval they fortified it by every means to hand, and then all mounted the walls, resolved to defend them with all their might, and showed determination to fight to the limit of their ability in the defense of Jerusalem. They mounted catapults to ward off attempts to approach the city and besiege it. . . .

---

*The Dome houses the rock from which Muslims believe that Muhammad ascended to heaven.

Then began the fiercest struggle imaginable; each side looked on the fight as an absolute religious obligation. There was no need for superior authority to drive them on: they restrained the enemy without restraint, and drove them off without being driven back. Every morning the Frankish cavalry made sorties to fight and provoke the enemy to battle; several of both sides fell in these encounters. . . . [The Muslims] charged like one man, dislodged the Franks from their positions and drove them back into the city. When the Muslims reached the moat they crossed it, came up under the walls and began to breach them, protected by their archers and by continuous artillery fire which kept the walls clear of Franks and enabled the Muslims to make a breach. . . .

When the Franks saw how violently the Muslims were attacking, how continuous and effective was the fire from the ballistas° and how busily the [diggers] were breaching the walls, meeting no resistance, they grew desperate, and their leaders assembled to take counsel. They decided to ask for safe conduct out of the city and to hand Jerusalem over to Saladin. They sent a deputation of their lords and nobles to ask for terms, but when they spoke of it to Saladin he refused to grant their request. "We shall deal with you," he said, "just as you dealt with the population of Jerusalem when you took it in [1099], with murder and enslavement and other such savageries!" The messengers returned empty-handed. Then Baliān ibn Barzān asked for safe conduct for himself so that he might appear before Saladin to discuss developments. Consent was given, and he presented himself and once again began asking for a general amnesty in return for surrender. The Sultan still refused his requests and entreaties to show mercy. Finally, despairing of this approach, Baliān said: "Know, O Sultan, that there are very many of us in this city, God alone knows how many. At the moment we are fighting half-heartedly in the hope of saving our lives, hoping to be spared by you as you have spared others; this is because of our horror of death and our love of life. But if we see that death is inevitable, then by God we shall kill our children and our wives, burn our possessions, so as not to leave you with a *dinar* or a *drachma* [money] or a single man or woman to enslave. When this is done, we shall pull down the Sanctuary of the Rock and the Masjid al-Aqsa and the other sacred places, slaughtering the Muslim prisoners we hold—5,000 of them—and killing every horse and animal we possess. Then we shall come out to fight you like men fighting for their lives, when each man, before he falls dead, kills his equals; we shall die with honor, or win a noble victory!"

Then Saladin took counsel with his advisers, all of whom were in favor of his granting the assurances requested by the Franks, without forcing them to take extreme measures whose outcome could not be foreseen. "Let us consider them as being already our prisoners," they said, "and allow them to ransom themselves on terms agreed between us." The Sultan agreed to give the Franks assurances of safety on the understanding that each man, rich and poor alike, should pay ten *dinar*, children of both sexes two *dinar* and women five *dinar*. All who paid this sum within forty days should go free, and those who had not paid at the end of the

---

°A device similar to a large crossbow used for firing stones or other projectiles at the enemy.

time should be enslaved. Baliān ibn Barzān offered 30,000 *dinar* as ransom for the poor, which was accepted, and the city surrendered on [2 October 1187], a memorable day on which the Muslim flags were hoisted over the walls of Jerusalem. At every gate, Saladin sen amirs [officials] in charge of taxation to claim the appropriate ransom from the inhabitants. But they cheated in carrying out their duties, and divided among themselves money that would otherwise have filled the State treasury to the benefit of all. . . .

. . .

Once the city was taken and the infidels had left, Saladin ordered that the shrines should be restored to their original state. The Templars [an order of Christian knights] had built their living-quarters against al-Aqsa, with storerooms and latrines and other necessary offices, taking up part of the area of al-Aqsa. This was all restored to its former state. The Sultan ordered that the Dome of the Rock should be cleansed of all pollution, and this was done. . . . To hide the pictures that covered the wall, the Franks had set slabs of marble over the Rock, concealing it from sight, and Saladin had them removed. It had been covered with the marble because the priests had sold a good part of it to the Franks who came from abroad on pilgrimages and bought pieces for their weight in gold in the hope of benefitting by its health-giving influences. Each of them, on his return home with a piece of this stone, would build a church for it and enclose it in the altar. One of the Frankish Kings of Jerusalem, afraid that it would all disappear, had it covered with a slab of marble to preserve it. When it was uncovered Saladin had some beautiful Qurans brought to the mosque, and magnificent copies of the sections of the Holy Book for use in worship. . . .

The Frankish population of Jerusalem who had not departed began to sell at very low prices their possessions, treasures and whatever they could not carry with them. The merchants from the army and the non-Frankish Christians in Jerusalem bought their goods from them. The latter had asked Saladin's permission to remain in their homes if they paid the tax, and he had granted them this, so they stayed and bought up Frankish property. What they could not sell, beds and boxes and casks, the Franks left behind; even superb columns of marble and slabs of marble and mosaics in large quantities. Thus they departed.

59 The Pilgrimage of Mansa Musa

J.F. P. Hopkins, ed. *Corpus of Early Arabic Sources*. Cambridge, England: Cambridge University Press, 1981. 267–274.

Al-'Umari was born in Damascus in 1301, and died in the same city in 1349. He spent much of his life in Cairo, where his father was a senior political official. In this selection, Al 'Umari discusses the state of Mali, in West Africa, and its famous leader, Mansa Musa, who fulfilled a requirement of the

Muslim religion by undertaking a pilgrimage to Mecca in 1324. His visit illustrates the spread of Islam far beyond its area of origin. In addition, on his return to Mali, the king spent so much gold that he devalued the Egyptian gold market for years afterward. Tales of his fabulous wealth traveled as far as Europe, and sparked Europeans' interest in attempting to reach West Africa and its fabled sources of gold.

Sultan Musa the king of [Mali] . . . came to Egypt on the Pilgrimage. He was staying in [the] Qarafa [district of Cairo] and Ibn Amir Hajib was governor of Old Cairo and Qarafa at that time. A friendship grew up between them and this sultan Musa told him a great deal about himself and his country and the people of the Sudan who were his neighbors. One of the things which he told him was that his country was very extensive and contiguous with the Ocean. By his sword and his armies he had conquered 24 cities each with its surrounding district with villages and estates. . . . He has a truce with the gold-plant people, who pay him tribute.

Ibn Amir Hajib said that he asked him about the gold-plant, and he said: "It is found in two forms. One is found in the spring and blossoms after the rains in open country. It has leaves like . . . grass and its roots are gold. The other kind is found all the year round at known sites on the banks of the Nile and is dug up. There are holes there and roots of gold are found like stones or gravel and gathered up. . . ." Sultan Musa told Ibn Amir Hajib that gold was his prerogative and he collected the crop as a tribute except for what the people of that country took by theft.

But . . . in fact he is given only a part of it as a present by way of gaining this favor, and he makes a profit on the sale of it, for they have none in their country. . . .

• • •

It is a custom of his people that if one of them should have reared a beautiful daughter he offers her to the king as a concubine and he possesses her without a marriage ceremony as slaves are possessed, and this in spite of the fact that Islam has triumphed among them and that . . . this sultan Musa was pious and assiduous in prayer, Koran reading, and mentioning God.

"I said to him (said Ibn Amer Hajib) that this was not permissible for a Muslim, whether in law or reason, and he said: 'Not even for kings?' and I replied: 'No! Not even for kings! Ask the scholars!' He said: 'By God, I did not know that. I hereby leave it and abandon it utterly.'

I saw that this sultan Musa loved virtue and people of virtue. He left his kingdom and appointed as his deputy there his son Muhammad and emigrated to God and His Messenger. He accomplished the obligations of the Pilgrimage, visited [the tomb of] the Prophet [at Medina] (God's blessing and peace be upon him!) and returned to his country with the intention of handing over his sovereignty to his son and abandoning it entirely to him and returning to Mecca the Venerated to remain there as a dweller near the sanctuary; but death overtook him, may God (who is great) have mercy upon him."

• • •

Ibn Amir Hajib continued; "I asked sultan Musa how the kingdom fell to him, and he said: 'We belong to a house which hands on the king by inheritance. The king who was my predecessor did not believe that it was impossible to discover the furthest limit of the Atlantic Ocean and wished vehemently to do so. So he equipped 200 ships filled with men and the same number equipped with gold, water, and provisions enough to last them for years, and said to the man [chosen] to lead them: "Do not return until you reach the end of it or your provisions and water give out." They departed and a long time passed before anyone came back. Then one ship returned and we asked the captain what news they brought. He said: "Yes O Sultan, we travelled for a long time until there appeared in the open sea [as it were] a river with a powerful current. Mine was the last of those ships. The [other] ships went on ahead but when they reached that place they did not return and no more was seen of them and we do not know what became of them. As for me, I went about at once and did not enter that river." But the sultan disbelieved him.

Then that sultan got ready 2,000 ships, 1,000 for himself and the men whom he took with him and 1,000 for water and provisions. He left me to deputize for him and embarked on the Atlantic Ocean with his men. That was the last we saw of him and all those who were with him, and so I became king in my own right.'

This sultan Musa, during his stay in Egypt both before and after his journey to the Noble Hijaz, maintained a uniform attitude of worship and turning towards God. It was as though he were standing before Him because of His continual presence in his mind. He and all those with him behaved in the same manner and were well-dressed, grave, and dignified. He was noble and generous and performed many acts of charity and kindness. He had left his country with 100 loads of gold which he spent during his Pilgrimage on the tribes who lay along his route from his country to Egypt, while he was in Egypt, and again from Egypt to the Noble Hijaz and back. As a consequence he needed to borrow money in Egypt and pledged his credit with the merchants at a very high rate of gain so that they made 700 dinars profit on 300. Later he paid them back amply. He sent to me 500 mithqals of gold by way of honorarium. ["]

. . .

... ["T]he emir Abu l'Abbas Ahmad b. al-Hak . . . told me of the opulence, manly virtues and piety of this sultan. 'When I went out to meet him (he said) . . . he did me extreme honor and treated me with the greatest courtesy. He addressed me, however, only through an interpreter despite his perfect ability to speak in the Arabic tongue. . . . I tried to persuade him to go up to the Citadel to meet the sultan, but he refused persistently, saying: "I came for the Pilgrimage and nothing else. I do not wish to mix anything else with my Pilgrimage." . . . I realized that the audience was repugnant to him because he would be obliged to kiss the ground and the sultan's hand. I continued to cajole him and he continued to make excuses but the sultan's protocol demanded that I should bring him into the royal presence, so I kept on at him till he agreed.

When we came in the sultan's presence we said to him: "Kiss the ground!" but he refused outright saying: "How may this be?" Then an intelligent man who was with him whispered to him something we could not understand and he said: "I make obeisance to God who created me!" then he prostrated himself and went forward to the sultan. The sultan half rose to greet him and sat him by his side. They conversed here together for a long time. . . . [']

. . .

This man flooded Cairo with his benefactions. He left no court emir nor hold-er of a royal office without the gift of a load of gold. The Cairenes made incalcula-ble profits out of him and his suite in buying and selling and giving and taking. They exchanged gold until they depressed its value in Egypt and caused its price to fall. ["]

. . .

Merchants of Misr and Cairo have told me of the profits which they made from the Africans, saying that one of them might buy a shirt or cloak or robe or other garment for five dinars when it was not worth one. Such was their sim-plicity and trustfulness that it was possible to practice any deception on them. They greeted anything that was said to them with credulous acceptance. But later they formed the very poorest opinion of the Egyptians because of the obvi-ous falseness of everything they said to them and their outrageous behavior in fixing the prices of the provisions and other goods which were sold to them, so much so that were they to encounter today the most learned doctor of religious science and he were to say that he was Egyptian they would be rude to him and view him with disfavor because of the ill treatment which they had experienced at their hands.

. . . [W]hen he made the Pilgrimage . . . the sultan was very open-handed towards the pilgrims and the inhabitants of the Holy Places. He and his compan-ions maintained great pomp and dressed magnificently during the journey. He gave away much wealth in alms.

. . .

Gold was at a high price in Egypt until they came in that year. The mithqal did not go below 25 dirhams and was generally above, but from that time its value fell and it cheapened in price and has remained cheap till now. The mithqal does not exceed 22 dirhams or less. This has been the state of affairs for about twelve years until this day by reason of the large amount of gold which they brought into Egypt and spent there.

60 Visual Document: A Portrayal of the Buddha

Although no records exist that show what the Buddha actually looked like, a myriad of visual representations of the Buddha have been produced. These images vary and take on different characteristics, in different areas. This one, from Japan, portrays the Buddha as female. What does the portrayal of the Buddha as female suggest to you? What features of the representation seem particularly important or striking?

DISCUSSION QUESTIONS

1. By what means are religions spread?
2. Is the spread of religions such as Buddhism, Islam, or Christianity solely based upon religious doctrine? What are the cultural and political dimensions of this process?
3. Does religion unite or divide communities? Why?
4. How does religious practice affect daily life?
5. How might you compare Mansa Musa's expression of faith with that of the Japanese emperor? How do the two texts on the crusades in West Asia compare?

Chapter
11

Labor in the World

*I*n all societies people work to provide themselves with food and shelter. The work that people do, the way that their labor is organized, and who controls that labor, are all crucial aspects of human history. Yet, the variety of work performed within the world's societies is truly dizzying. In the Andes Mountains of the Americas, the Inca empire organized male workers into a seasonal labor draft called the *mita* to mine silver ore. In Java, women and men carefully tended flooded fields in which rice was grown. In China, educated young men studied Confucius in preparation for the *jinshi* (*chin-shih*) examination that would provide them with a prestigious administrative post if they passed.

How do societies organize work? One way to understand the complexity of labor is to distinguish between those tasks necessary to maintain the well-being of the community from that work which is performed for the benefit of someone else. In other words, some work provides necessities for human life—providing food for one's extended family, and caring for the very young and old within that family. Other labor is performed for rulers or the society at large. This work may take different forms, from providing a portion of the harvest for local rulers, or simply paying one's taxes.

Who performs the different tasks necessary to maintain the community? For example, all societies have a gender division of labor that regulates what work women and men perform. Childrearing and the care of the elderly are usually tasks reserved for women, while at the same time women are often excluded from active roles in politics. Settled agricultural societies also contain class distinctions that distinguish between wealthy nobles, such as the Aztec *pipiltin*, and a working class, such as European peasants. Other distinctions within society may also play a role in determining who performs what tasks. The Indian caste system with *brahmins* at the top of society and so-called "untouchables" at the bottom is not just organized by class, but also by the ethnic differences between the indigenous inhabitants of the Indian peninsula and the Aryan peoples who migrated there.

61 Labor In Medieval Russia

George Vernadsky, trans. and ed. *Medieval Russian Laws.* New York: Octagon Books, Inc., 1965. 39–40, 46–48, 51, 54–56, 69–70, 77.

As Russian medieval states grew in complexity, each set down fundamental laws to govern the day-to-day activities of the people, from slaves to the nobles. The regulation of workers plays a prominent part in all such law codes. As the articles below demonstrate, the state was governing not just the behavior of the workers (whether agricultural or craft), but the access of landlords to their labor. In other words, one important interest of state rulers was to minimize conflict among landlords over access to, and control of, workers. The following passages are taken from two different states, Russia in the 1100s and Pskov (in Novgorod) between 1397 and 1467.

RUSSIAN LAW (12th c.)

Article 32. And if a slave should conceal himself, and the owner announces it in the market place, and for three days nobody brings him in, and [the owner] should find him on the third day, he may take his slave and he [who concealed the slave] pays three *grivna* fine. . . .

• • •

Article 56. If an indentured laborer runs away from his lord, he becomes the latter's slave. But if he departs openly, to sue for his money [and goes] to the prince, or to the judges, to complain of the injustice on the part of the lord, they do not reduce him to slavery but give him justice.

Article 57. If an agricultural indentured laborer ruins a war horse, he does not pay for it. But if the lord from whom he received money entrusts to him [a work horse to work with] plow and harrow and he ruins it, he has to pay for it. But if the lord sends him away for some business of his [that is the lord's], and [the work horse] perishes, he [the laborer] need not pay for it.

Article 58. If [others] steal [cattle] from [the lord's] stable, the laborer does not have to pay for it. But if [the laborer] loses cattle on the field because he failed to drive them to the yard and did not lock them where the lord ordered him, or because he worked for himself and neglected working for the lord, then he has to pay.

Article 59. If the lord offends the indentured laborer and seizes his money or movables [personal property], he has to return all this and pay 60 *kuna* for the offense.

Article 60. If the lord transfers the indenture on the laborer [to a third person] for money, [the transaction is annulled and] the [first] lord has to return the money he accepted and pay a three *grivna* fine.

Article 61. If the lord sells the indentured laborer into slavery, the laborer is free from all obligations for the money [he received from the lord], and the lord pays a 12 *grivna* fine.

Article 62. If the lord beats the indentured laborer for good reason, he is without fault; but if he beats the indentured laborer foolishly, being drunk, and without any fault on the part of the indentured laborer, he has to pay for the offense to the indentured laborer the same fine as it would be to a freeman.

Article 63. If a full slave steals another's horse, [the owner of the slave] has to pay 2 *grivna*.

Article 64. If an indentured laborer steals [a horse] or some other [beast], his lord is responsible for him. And when they find him, the lord first pays for the horse or anything else that he stole, and [the indentured laborer] is his full slave. And if the lord does not want to pay in behalf of [his indentured laborer], he sells him, and first reimburses [the owner] for the horse, or the ox, or cattle, whatever was stolen, and keeps the balance.

Article 65. If a slave strikes a freeman and hides in the house, and his lord will not surrender him, the lord pays for him a 12 *grivna* [fine]; and then whenever the injured man meets the offender, who struck him, [Prince] Iaroslav [allowed the injured man] to kill the offender, but [Iaroslav's] sons, after their father's death, ordered the matter to be settled with the alternative of payment: either to bind the slave [to a post] and beat him, or to accept 1 *grivna* for the offense to his honor. . . .

• • •

Article 90. If a peasant dies [without male descendants] his estate goes to the prince; if there are daughters left in the house, each receives a portion [of the estate]; if they are married, they receive no portion. . . .

• • •

Article 110. Full slavery is of three kinds: [first] if anyone buys [a man] willing [to sell himself into slavery], for not less than half a *grivna*, and produces witnesses and pays [the fee of] 1 *nogata* in the presence of the slave himself. And the second kind of slavery is this: if anyone marries a female slave without special agreement [with her lord]; if he marries her with a special agreement, what he agreed to, stands. And this is the third kind of slavery: if anyone becomes [another's] steward or housekeeper without a special agreement; if there has been an agreement, what has been agreed upon, stands.

Article 111. And the recipient of a [money] grant is not a slave. And one cannot make a man one's slave because [he received] a grant-in-aid in grain, or [failed to furnish] additional grain [when repaying the grant]; if he fails to complete the term of work [for the grant], he has to return the grant; if he completes the term, he stands cleared.

Article 112. If a slave runs away and his owner makes due announcement, and someone else, having heard the announcement or knowing about it and understanding that the man is a fugitive slave, gives him some bread or shows him the way [to escape], he has to pay for the male slave 5 *grivna* and for the female slave 6 *grivna*.

Article 113. If anyone apprehends another's slave and informs the owner, he receives 1 *grivna* for the arrest [of the slave]; if he lets him escape, he has to pay 4 *grivna* but keeps the fifth *grivna* [as his remuneration for the attempted] arrest; in case of a female slave, [he pays] 5 *grivna* and [keeps] the sixth *grivna* for the [attempted] arrest.

Article 114. If anyone finds by himself his runaway slave in some town the mayor of which did not know about [that slave], he informs the mayor, and the latter sends a clerk with him, and they go and bind the slave, and he gives the clerk 10 *kuna* binding fee, but no remuneration for the arrest. If the slave escapes when he drives him home, that is his loss, nobody has to pay him, since the slave had not been arrested [by any authority, but on the owner's initiative].

Article 115. If anyone meets another's slave, not knowing that he is such, and gives him information [about travelling,] or keeps him in his own house, and then [that slave] leaves him, he has to swear that he did not know that the man was another's slave, and he is not required to pay [the owner].

Article 116. If a slave should receive [from anyone] money under false pretense, and the creditor lent it not knowing [that the man was a slave], the owner [of the slave] has to redeem or lose him. If the creditor lent the money knowing [that the man was a slave] he loses his money.

Article 117. If anyone authorizes his slave to trade and the latter should fall in debt, the owner redeems him but does not lose him.

Article 118. If anyone buys another man's slave without knowing it, the original owner takes the slave and the buyer receives his money back after swearing that he had bought him without knowing [who he was].

Article 119. [If a runaway slave obtains goods on credit,] the owner takes back the slave, [and assumes his debt,] and also takes the goods.

Article 120. If [a slave] runs away and takes any neighbor's property or goods, his owner pays the damages.

Article 121. If a slave robs a man, the owner may redeem or surrender him, as well as those who participated with him in the robbery, but not [the slave's] wife and children unless they helped him to rob, or hid [the stolen goods]; in such a case he [the owner of the slave] surrenders them, or else he redeems them all. If freemen participated in the robbery, they are liable for the payment of the fine to the prince.

THE CHARTER OF THE CITY OF PSKOV (1397–1467)

Article 39. And if a master carpenter or a hired craftsman accomplishes the work [and the employer refuses to pay him], he may sue the employer for his pay through an announcement [in the marketplace].

Article 40. And if a hired worker about the homestead [farm] leaves his employer before the completion of his appointed work, he receives wages in accordance with the amount [of time he worked]. And a worker may sue his employer for his wages only within one year after leaving the work; if he stayed with his employer for five or ten years and did not receive his wages, he may claim his wages for all that period. But after the expiration of one year [after the worker's discharge] a worker may not sue his employer.

Article 41. And if a hired carpenter sues his employer for his wages, and that carpenter has left without having completed his work; and if [facing the court], the carpenter says to his employer, "I have completed all my work for thee"; and the employer says, "Thou hast not completed thy work"—then, if there has been no written agreement between them, the employer shall deposit the amount sued for before the cross, [letting the employee take the oath]; or the employer himself takes the oath.

Article 42. And if the landlord wants to terminate the lease of his tenant farmer, or vegetable gardener, or fisherman, the term for ending such leases is the day of the beginning of St. Philip's fast; likewise, if the farmer wants to terminate the lease on the farm, or the vegetable gardener, or the fisherman [wants to terminate the lease], the term is the same, and there shall be no other term, either for the landlord, or for the farmer, or the fisherman, or the vegetable gardener. And if the farmer, or the vegetable gardener, or the fisherman refuses to leave because of the [unlawful] term set by the landlord, he wins, and the landlord loses his customary quarter [of farm products], or his portion of the vegetables, or his portion of fish from the fishery.

Article 43. And if the lessee of a fishery misses the spring catch of fish, he shall pay the landlord according to the yield the landlord got from his other fisheries.

Article 44. And at the termination of the lease, either by the landlord or by the lessee, the landlord may sue his farmer, or vegetable farmer, or fisherman for the amount of money or grain [he may have loaned him], stating kinds of grain, specifically, such as spring wheat, or winter wheat, through an announcement in the market place. . . .

. . .

Article 84. And if a tenant farmer dies and there is no wife, or children, or a brother, or any relative left, the landlord is entitled to sell the movable [i.e., the personal property] in order to recover his subsidy; [and if] later on any descendants of the deceased, or a brother of his, appear, they may not sue the landlord for [the tenant's] movables.

Article 85. And if a tenant farmer dies, and the landlord has his note on the subsidy, and if there are wife and children left, even if they have not been mentioned in the note [as comakers] they may not deny their liability but must repay the subsidy according to the note. And if there is no note, the case is tried according to the Pskov customary law.

Article 86. And if after a tenant farmer's death his brother or other descendants are left and claim his movables, the landlord may sue them for the subsidy [previously accepted by the deceased]. [On the other hand], the brother and descendants of the deceased may not hold the landlord responsible for the loss of a basket or keg; but as to a horse, or a cow, they may sue the landlord for it.

Article 87. And if a tenant farmer sues the landlord for some movables and the landlord supplies sufficient evidence that the object in question [is his own property], and it is known to outsiders as well as to the neighbors that the object belongs to the landlord, then the tenant loses the suit, and the landlord is right. . . .

62 Crafts in the Islamic World

Ibn Khaldun. *The Muqaddimah: An Introduction to History.*
Bollingen Series 43. Translated by Franz Rosenthal. Princeton,
N.J.: Princeton University Press, 1967. 3 vols., 2:355–395.

The fourteenth-century *Muqaddimah* of Ibn Khaldun is a wide-ranging
chronicle that covers virtually all aspects of the North African Islamic world. In
the following passages, Ibn Khaldun enumerates both "necessary" and
"noble" crafts. For him, the necessary crafts are those skills that produce
food, dwellings, and clothing for people, whereas the noble crafts include
medicine, midwifery, as well as the arts of calligraphy, book-making, and
music. For Ibn Khaldun, these crafts existed in their highest form only within
cities, or within what he terms "civilization."

It should be known that the crafts practiced by the human species are numerous,
because so much labor is continually available in civilization. They are so numerous as to defy complete enumeration. However, some of them are necessary in
civilization or occupy noble position because of their object. We shall single these
two kinds out for mention and leave all the others.

Necessary crafts are agriculture, architecture, tailoring, carpentry, and weaving. Crafts noble because of their object are midwifery, the art of writing, book production, singing, and medicine. . . .

• • •

THE CRAFT OF AGRICULTURE

The fruit of this craft is the obtainment of foodstuffs and grains. People must
undertake to stir the earth, sow, cultivate the plants, see to it that they are watered
and that they grow until they reach their full growth, then, harvest the ears, and get
the grain out of the husks. . . . Agriculture is the oldest of all the crafts, in as much
as it provides the food that is the main factor in perfecting human life, since man
can exist without anything else but not without food. . . .

• • •

THE CRAFT OF ARCHITECTURE

This is the first and oldest craft of sedentary civilization. It is the knowledge of how
to go about using houses and mansions for cover and shelter. This is because man
has the natural disposition to reflect upon the outcome of things. Thus, it is
unavoidable that he must reflect upon how to avert the harm arising from heat and
cold by using houses which have walls and roofs to intervene between him and
those things on all sides. . . .

• • •

THE CRAFT OF CARPENTRY

This craft is one of the necessities of civilization. Its material is wood. This is as follows: God made all created things useful for man, so as to supply his necessities and needs. Trees belong among these things. They have innumerable uses known to everybody. One of their uses is their use as wood when they are dry. The first use of wood is as wood for fires, which man needs to live; as sticks for support, protection of flocks, and other necessities; and as supports for loads that one fears might topple over. After that, wood has other uses, for the inhabitants of the desert as well as for those of settled areas. . . .

The master of this craft must first split the wood into smaller pieces or into boards. Then, he puts these pieces together in the required form. In this connection, he attempts with the aid of his craft to prepare these pieces by the proper arrangement for their becoming parts of the desired particular shape. The man in charge of this craft is the carpenter. He is necessary to civilization. Then, when sedentary culture increases and luxury makes its appearance and people want to use elegant types of roofs, doors, chairs, and furniture, these things come to be produced in a most elegant way through the mastery of remarkable techniques. . . . Carpentry is also needed for the construction of ships, which are made of boards and nails. . . .

. . .

THE CRAFT OF WEAVING AND TAILORING

It should be known that people who are temperate in their humanity cannot avoid giving some thought to keeping warm, as they do shelter. One manages to keep warm by using woven material as protective cover against both heat and cold. This requires the interlacing of yarn, until it turns out to be a complete garment. This is spinning and weaving. . . . The purpose of tailoring is to give woven material a certain form in accordance with the many different shapes and customs that may occur in this connection. . . . The tailoring of clothes, the cutting, fitting, and sewing of the material, is one of the various methods and aspects of sedentary culture.

This should be understood, in order to understand the reason why the wearing of sewn garments is forbidden on the pilgrimage. According to the religious law, the pilgrimage requires, among other things, the discarding of all worldly attachments and the return to God as He created us in the beginning. . . . He should come to the pilgrimage as if he were going to the Last Judgment, humble in his heart, sincerely devoted to his Lord. . . .

. . .

THE CRAFT OF MIDWIFERY

Midwifery is a craft that shows how to proceed in bringing the newborn child gently out of the womb of his mother and how to prepare the things that go with that. It also shows what is good for a newborn child, after it is born, as we shall mention. The craft is as a rule restricted to women, since they, as women, may see the [genitals] of other women. . . . When the embryo has gone through all its stages and is completely and perfectly formed in the womb—the period God determined for its remaining in the womb is as a rule nine months—it seeks to come out, because God implanted such a desire in unborn children. But the opening is too narrow for it, and it is difficult for the embryo to come out. It often splits one of the walls of the vagina by its pressure. . . . All this is painful and hurts very much. This is the meaning of labor pains. In this connection, the midwife may offer some [relief] by massaging the back, the buttocks, and the lower extremities adjacent to the uterus. . . . When the embryo has come out, it remains connected with the uterus by the umbilical cord at its stomach, through which it was fed. That cord is a superfluous special limb for feeding the child. The midwife cuts it but so that she does not go beyond the place where it starts to be superfluous and does not harm the stomach of the child or the uterus of the mother. She then treats the place of the operation with cauterization or whatever other treatments she sees fit. . . .

• • •

One can see that this craft is necessary to the human species in civilization. Without it, the individuals of the species could not, as a rule, come into being. . . .

• • •

THE CRAFT OF MEDICINE

This craft is necessary in towns and cities because of its recognized usefulness. Its fruit is the preservation of health among those who are healthy, and the repulsion of illness among those who are ill, with the help of medical treatment, until they are cured of their illnesses.

• • •

CALLIGRAPHY, THE ART OF WRITING

Writing is the outlining and shaping of letters to indicate audible words which, in turn, indicate what is in the soul. . . . It is a noble craft, since it is one of the special qualities of man by which he distinguishes himself from the animals. Furthermore, it reveals what is in people's minds. It enables the intention of a person to be carried to distant places, and, thus, the needs of that person may be executed without him personally taking care of them. It enables people to become acquainted with science, learning, with the books of the ancients, and with the sciences and information written down by them. . . .

• • •

THE CRAFT OF BOOK PRODUCTION

Formerly, people were concerned with scholarly writings and official records. These were copied, bound, and corrected with the help of a transmission technique and with accuracy. The reason for this was the importance of the ruling dynasty and the existence of the things that depend on sedentary culture. All that has disappeared at the present time is the result of the disappearance of the dynasties and the decrease of civilization. In Islam it had formerly reached tremendous proportions in [Iraq] and in Spain. All of it depends on civilization, on the extent of the ruling dynasties, and on the demand existing in the dynasties for it. Thus, scholarly works and writings were formerly numerous. People were desirous of transmitting them everywhere and at any time. They were copied and bound. The craft of book producers, thus, made its appearance. They are the craftsmen concerned with copying, correcting, and binding books, and with all the other matters pertaining to books and writings. The craft of book production was restricted to cities of a large civilization.

. . .

THE CRAFT OF SINGING AND MUSIC

This craft is concerned with the setting of poems to music. This is done by scanning the sounds according to well-known fixed proportions, which causes any sound . . . thus scanned to constitute a tune, a rhythmic mode. . . . The result is pleasant to listen to because of its harmony and the quality that harmony gives to the sounds. This is as follows: As explained in the science of music, sounds are in certain proportions (intervals) to each other. A sound may be one-half, one-quarter, one-fifth, or one-eleventh of another sound. The difference in interval between sounds that reach the ear transforms them from simple sounds to combinations of sounds. But every combination is pleasant to listen to. . . .

63 An Aztec Tribute List

The Codex Mendoza. Translated by Frances F. Berdan and Patricia Rieff Anawalt. Berkeley, Calif.: University of California Press, 1992. 4 vols., 4:7, 34–35, 42, 76.

The following passage describes the migration of the Aztecs, and their expansion in the central valley of Mexico. Over the course of the fifteenth century, they progressively conquered virtually all of their neighbors. They required tribute payments of these subjugated peoples. As seen below, the tribute consisted of specific goods produced in each of the conquered areas. These payments were an implicit requisition of the labor power of each of the subjected societies, because requiring finished products meant requisitioning the time, energy, and labor needed to produce them.

In the year 1324, . . . the Mexicans arrived at the site of the city of Mexico. . . . And almost at the center and middle of the site . . . the Mexicans found a great stone or rocky hill, on top of which flourished a large prickly pear cactus, where a red-tailed eagle had its aerie and feeding ground. . . .

And since they explored the entire region and found it fertile and full of game birds, fish, and shellfish with which they could sustain themselves and profit in their trading with nearby towns, and because the water [provided] a defense [so] that their neighbors could not harm them . . . [they settled.]

In the course of some years, the inhabitants were multiplying and so the city was named Mexico, a name derived from the Mexicans. . . . And as the people had developed as daring and warlike, they gave vent to their spirit by overcoming their neighbors. Thus by force of arms they subject[ed] . . . vassals and tributaries. . . .

• • •

After having succeeded to the said lordship, Moctecuhzoma conquered . . . forty-four towns . . . and subjected them to his lordship and empire. And in acknowledgment of vassalage, during his entire lifetime they paid him many and large tributes. . . .

• • •

The quantity, value and amount of the tribute that his subjects paid him will be seen and understood later. . . . He demanded that they pay much in tribute, and that they always comply; and for this he put his . . . stewards in all the towns of his subjects, as governors . . . and since they were so feared, no one dared counter-mand or overstep his will and order. But [his will] was entirely kept and obeyed, because he was inexorable in the execution and punishment of rebels.

• • •

[I]n tribute . . . the people of Tlatelolco . . . had to keep in constant repair the temple called Huitznahuac . . . and provide forty large baskets of cacao ground with maize flour . . . each basket contained one thousand six hundred cacao beans . . . eight hundred loads of large cloaks; also eight warrior costumes of ordinary feathers, and another eighty shields, likewise of ordinary feathers. . . .

• • •

The number of towns of the hot lands contained and named on the following page [gave] . . . four hundred loads of women's skirts and tunics; also one thousand two hundred loads of small casks of soft henequen, which they gave in tribute every six months; and also two hundred little pitchers of bees' honey; . . . one thousand two hundred yellow varnished gourd bowls; four hundred little baskets of white copal for incense. . . .

64 Chinese Agricultural Labor

Jacques Gernet. *Daily Life in China on the Eve of the Mongol Invasion, 1250–1276.* Translated by H.M. Wright. New York: The Macmillan Company, 1962. 103–104.

These selections reveal the circumstances that peasants in China experienced throughout this period. Whether they were peasants owning and cultivating small plots of land, tenant farmers in renting or sharecropping arrangements, or agricultural laborers hired for a season, they all lived in permanent fear of starvation. Even good harvests barely met their basic needs. In bad years, their only recourse to stave off starvation was to sell off what little land or equipment they owned, or to sell their children or themselves into debt servitude. Loans could provide short-term relief, although interest rates were very high, up to twenty percent a month for cash loans, or fifty percent for cereals during the harvest. The following example of a loan agreement from the ninth and tenth centuries concerns cloth, which served as a currency in Central Asia at that time.

On the first day of the third moon of the year [marked by the cyclical signs] *chia-tzu*, Fan Huai-t'ung and his brothers, whose family is in need of a little cloth, have borrowed from the monk Li a piece of white silk 38 feet long and two feet and half an inch wide. In the autumn, they will pay as interest 40 bushels of corn [wheat] and millet. As regards the capital, they will repay it [in the form of a piece of silk of the same quality and size] before the end of the second moon of the following year. If they do not repay it, interest equivalent to that paid at the time of the loan [that is, 40 bushels of cereals] shall be paid monthly. The two parties having agreed to this loan in the presence of each other shall not act in any way contrary to their agreement. The borrowers: Wen-ta, Huai-ta, Huai-chu and their elder brother Huai-t'ng.

The following document, dating from the same period, concerns the sale of an agricultural laborer.

Contract agreed on the third day of the 11th moon of the year yi-wei. The monumental-stonemason Chao Seng-tzu, because. . . . he is short of commodities and cannot procure them by any other means, sells today, with the option of repurchase, his own son Chiu-tzu to his relation [by agreement] the lord Li Ch'ien-ting. The sale price has been fixed at 200 bushels of corn and 200 bushels of millet. Once the sale has been concluded, there will neither be anything paid for the hire of the man, nor interest paid on the commodities. If it should happen that the man sold, Chiu-tzu, should fall ill and die, his elder brother will be held responsible for repaying the part of the goods [corresponding to the period of hire which had not been completed]. If Chiu-tzu should steal anything of small or great value from a third person, either in the country or in town, it is Chiu-tzu himself [and not his employer] from whom reparation will be demanded. . . . The earliest time-limit for the repurchase of Chiu-tzu has been fixed at the sixth year. It is only when this amount of time has elapsed that his relations are authorized to repurchase him. Lest a higher price should then be asked for him, this contract has been drawn up to establish proof of the agreement.

65 A Chinese Weaver

Patricia Ebrey, ed. *Chinese Civilization and Society: A Sourcebook*. New York: The Free Press, 1981. 141–142.

By the time of the Ming dynasty (1368–1644), the production of textiles was a major industry. While cotton cloth was woven by peasants as a means of earning extra income, silks were woven in commercial workplaces by salaried weavers. The following selection was written around 1400 by the scholar Hsu I-k'uei. Although he clearly intended it as a moral lesson to regulate workers' behavior, the conditions he discusses provide an accurate reflection of conditions in these workshops. Note that while in comparison to unskilled agricultural laborers, skilled weavers of luxury cloth did enjoy considerably better conditions, the work was still hard and advancement according to individual skill was discouraged. The author of this tale wishes to convey that ambition on the part of workers is dangerous: people should be content with their place in society.

When I lived in Hsiang-an Ward in Ch'ien-t'ang, I had a wealthy neighbor who employed live-in weavers. Late every evening one of them would start to sing and the rest would join in. From the sound of their voices, they seemed to be cheerful. "How happy they are!" I sighed.

One morning I walked over there and found it to be just a rickety old house. There were four or five looms in a room, arranged in a row from the north to south, and about ten workers, all of whom were laboring with both hands and feet. They looked pale and spiritless. I called one worker over and said, "From what I have seen, your work is very hard. Why are you still so happy?"

The worker replied, "Happiness is determined by the thoughts in a person's mind. If he isn't greedy, he can be happy with very little. But those who are greedy may earn a thousand strings of cash a day and still always feel unhappy. Though my job is a humble one, I can earn two hundred strings of cash a day. The master provides me with food and clothes, so I can use my wages to support my parents, wife, and children. We are far from having delicious food, yet neither are we suffering from hunger or cold. I consider my life a normal one; I am not discontent, and the material I weave is very beautiful and highly valued by people. Thus, the master can easily sell the products and we are able to earn our wages easily. Since this is all we really want, our inner contentment naturally comes out in our voices as we sing together. We do not think of the hardship of the work.

Not long ago, there was a weaver employed in another workshop. He earned approximately the same amount of money as we do. Yet, after working for a while, he started to complain: 'I am a more skillful weaver than anyone else, but I still get the same wages. I am going to work for someone who will pay me twice as much.' Later on, one workshop owner did offer him double. The master examined his work and noticed that it was indeed superior, and the other weavers, after seeing his skill, also respected him highly. The master was very happy, thinking, 'This one weaver's work is better than that of ten others put together. It is well worth doubling his pay.' After working for a while, the weaver again became dissatisfied. He thought, 'I am such a superior weaver that if I leave this occupation and engage in another, I will undoubtedly be superior in that one, too. If I take employment under a high official, by playing up to him and serving him wholeheartedly, I will be able to gain great wealth and glory for myself. Why should I work in a weaving factory forever?'

Eventually he did take a position serving a high official. He worked among the slaves taking care of carriages and horses, and for five years did not find anything he could consider an opportunity for wealth and glory. Then one day, after another five years had passed, he provoked the official, who became infuriated and dismissed him and refused to see him ever again. By that time, the weaver had already forgotten his former trade. Moreover, people were disgusted with his arrogance and inability to be content, and no one wanted to hire him to weave. In the end he died of hunger and cold.

I took this person as a warning. How could I fail to feel content and happy?"

This worker is indeed content and exemplifies what Lao Tzu meant when he said, "One who knows how to be satisfied will always be satisfied." This is why I recorded his story. At the time of our conversation, there were about ten workers present. The one who talked to me was named Yao.

66 Controlling the English Peasantry

R.B. Dobson. *The Peasants' Revolt of 1381*. New York: St. Martin's Press, 1970. 63–67.

In feudal England, members of the gentry and nobility controlled the livelihood of peasants and laborers. In the aftermath of the Black Death (an outbreak of bubonic plague that struck England in 1348), there was a tremendous shortage of workers on English estates. This shortage of labor gave peasants, laborers, and craftsmen a chance to demand higher wages: in effect, the disastrous plague made landowners compete for scarce workers, driving their wages up. In an effort to control those wages, the English king, Edward III, and his council passed ordinances in 1349 and 1351 to return wages to their level before the plague struck. Opposition to the ordinances, among other labor grievances, eventually led to the English Peasants' Revolt of 1381. The following excerpts are taken from the statutes of 1351 and describe how landowners planned to control their workers, or servants.

Against the malice of servants who were idle and unwilling to serve after the pestilence without taking outrageous wages it was recently ordained by our lord the king, with the assent of the prelates, nobles, and others of his council, that such servants, both men and women, should be obliged to serve in return for the salaries and wages which were customary (in those places where they ought to serve) during the twentieth year of the present king's reign (1346–7). . . . ° It was also ordained that such servants who refused to serve in this way should be punished by imprisonment, as is more fully stated in the said ordinance. Accordingly commissions were made out to various people in every county to investigate and punish all those who offended against the ordinance. But now our lord king has been informed in this present parliament, by the petition of the commons [i.e., landholders], that such servants completely disregard the said ordinance in the interests of their own ease and greed and that they withhold their service to great men and others unless they have liveries and wages twice or three times as great as those they used to take in the said twentieth year of Edward III and earlier, to the serious damage of the great men and impoverishment of all members of the said commons. Therefore the commons ask for a remedy. Wherefore, in the said parliament and by the assent of the prelates, earls, barons and other magnates as well as that of the commons there assembled, the following things were ordained and established to prevent the malice of said servants.

1. First, that carters, ploughmen, leaders of the plough, shepherds, swineherds, domestic and all other servants shall receive the liveries and wages accustomed in the said twentieth year and four years previously; so that in areas where wheat used to be given, they shall take 10 [pence] for the bushel, or wheat at the will of the giver, until it is ordained otherwise. These servants shall be hired to serve by the entire year, or by the other usual terms, and not by the day. No one is to receive more than 1 [penny] a day at the time of weeding or hay-making. Mowers of meadows are not to be paid more than 5 [pence] an acre or 5 [pence] a day; and reapers of corn [wheat] are to be limited to 2 [pence] in the first week of August, 3 [pence] in the second week and so on to the end of August. Less is to be given in those areas where less used to be given and neither food nor any other favor is to be demanded, given or taken. All such workers are to bring their tools openly in their hands to the market town; and there they are to be hired in a public and not in a secret place.

2. Item, that no one is to receive more than 2½ [pence] for threshing a quarter of wheat or rye, and more than 1½ [pence] for threshing a quarter of barley, beans, peas, or oats, if so much used to be given. In those areas where reaping was repaid by means of certain sheaves and threshing by certain bushels [in other words, with a portion of the harvest], the servants shall take no more and in no other way than was usual in the said twentieth year and previously. These same servants are to be sworn twice every year before the lords, stewards, bailiffs and

---

°In other words, workers were to be paid at the wages they were paid prior to the Black Death.

constables of every [village] to keep and observe these ordinances. These servants are not to depart from the [villages] in which they live during the winter to serve elsewhere in the summer if they can find work in their own [villages] at the wages mentioned above; saving that the people of the counties of Stafford, Lancaster and Derby and those of Craven, the Marches of Wales and Scotland and elsewhere may come and work in other counties during August and then return safely, as they have been accustomed to do before this time. Those who refuse to take such an oath, or to fulfill what they have sworn or undertaken shall be put in the stocks for three days or more by the said lords, stewards, bailiffs and constables of the [villages] or sent to the nearest [jail], there to remain until they are willing to submit to justice. For this purpose stocks are to be constructed in every [village]. . . .

3. Item, that carpenters, masons, tilers and other roofers of houses shall not take more for their day's work than the accustomed amount; that is to say, a master carpenter 3 [pence] and other [carpenters] 2 [pence]; a master mason of free-stone 4 [pence] and other masons 3 [pence]; and their servants 1½ [pence]. Tilers are to receive 3 [pence] and their boys 1½ [pence]; thatchers of roofs in fern and straw 3 [pence] and their boys 1½ [pence]. Plasterers and other workers on mud walls, as well as their boys, are to receive payment in the same manner, without food or drink. These rates are to apply from Easter to Michaelmas [from spring to fall]: outside that period less should be paid according to the assessment and discretion of the justices assigned for the purpose. Those who perform carriage by land or water shall receive no more for such carriage than they used to do in the said twentieth year and four years before.

4. Item, that cordwainers [bootmakers] and shoemakers shall not sell boots, shoes, or anything else connected with their mystery [craft] otherwise than they did in the said twentieth year. Goldsmiths, saddlers, horse-smiths, spurriers [makers of spurs], tanners, curriers [leather workers], pelterers, tailors and all other workmen, artificers and laborers, as well as all other servants not specified here, shall be sworn before the said justices to conduct and employ their crafts and offices in the way they did in the said twentieth year and earlier, without refusing because of this ordinance. If any of the said servants, laborers, workmen or artificers infringe this ordinance after taking such an oath, they shall be punished by fine, ransom or imprisonment, according to the discretion of the said justices.

5. Item, that the said stewards, bailiff and constables of the [villages] shall be sworn before the same justices to inquire diligently, by all the good ways they can, concerning all those who infringe this ordinance. They are to certify the names of all these offenders to the justices whenever they arrive in a district to hold their sessions. And so the justices, having been notified of the names of such rebels by the stewards, bailiffs and constables, shall have them arrested, to appear before themselves to answer for such contempts; so that the offenders shall pay fine and ransom to the king if they are convicted. Moreover, the offenders shall be ordered to prison, where they shall remain until they have found surety [pledge] to serve, received their payments, perform their work and

sell their saleable goods in the manner prescribed above. And if any of the offenders breaks his oath, and is convicted of it, he shall be imprisoned for forty days. And if he is convicted another time, he shall be imprisoned for a quarter of a year, so that each time he offends and is convicted, he shall receive a double penalty. . . .

67 Visual Document: Plowing and Weaving in China

Most of the population of China were peasants, engaged in farming and the production of livestock. A class of artisans also existed, to which weavers belonged. In the pictures, who is performing the work? How is this work portrayed? Does it seem easy, or require a lot of skill? What can you tell about the attitude of the artist toward his subject?

插秧

長兩麥秋潤午風槐
夏原溪南與溪北綠
歌插新秧把擲不停
手左右無亂行我教
插秧馬代勞民莫怠

千畦水
澤正淶
瀰競挿
新秋旺
挽同忻
力作月
明歸去
莫暀
逛

DISCUSSION QUESTIONS

1. How are different occupations viewed in different societies?

2. What labor is considered appropriate for women, and for men? What reasons are given—implicitly or explicitly—for the gender division of labor?

3. How do states and rulers regulate workers? What kinds of formal and informal means exist in these societies for regulating work?

4. Do you think that the regulation of workers suggests that workers are powerless to affect their own situation, or does that regulation suggest that there is labor discontent?

5. What are the differences between craft labor and other kinds of work? What determines if work is considered "noble," to use Ibn Khaldun's term, or menial?

Chapter
12

Disasters and Society

*D*isasters, both natural and human-made, are an integral part of the relationship between human societies and the environment. Virtually all societies cope with disaster at some point, with greater or lesser degrees of success. How different societies conceive of and respond to catastrophe varies considerably. In this chapter, we look at an extreme form of human interaction with the environment: perceptions of, and responses to, disasters.

The following selections illustrate a number of disasters, including epidemic disease, famine, earthquakes, flood, and whirlwinds. First, Ibn Khaldun argues that there is a direct relationship between the occurrence of disasters and failures in political leadership. Next, an aboriginal myth from Australia reveals how this culture understood tornados. The third reading describes how the Aztec worldview incorporated disasters such as earthquakes. The fourth selection, from Giovanni Boccaccio, describes a European reaction to the Black Death, or bubonic plague, and a later reading provides a glimpse of the North African response to the same fourteenth-century epidemic. Disasters and state responses to them in the Mongol Empire are the focus for the fifth reading, while the next selection discusses Chinese attempts to cope with famine.

68 A North African View of Disasters

Ibn Khaldun. *The Muqaddimah: An Introduction to History.*
Translated by Franz Rosenthal. Bollingen Series 43. Princeton,
N.J.: Princeton University Press, 1967, 3 vols. 2:135–136.

The fourteenth-century Islamic scholar Ibn Khaldun was certainly familiar with the threat posed by infectious diseases, as the Black Death had passed through northern Africa during his lifetime. As a historian, Ibn Khaldun believed that the appearance of natural disasters such as disease or famine heralded the end of political dynasties. Unlike many of his contemporaries, he did not seek religious explanations for such events: he did not believe that they resulted from the actions of an angry god, but rather were natural events in the life cycle of dynasties and civilizations. Ibn Khaldun also knew, as did many of his contemporaries, that dense populations and poor sanitary conditions accelerated the spread of diseases.

In the previous discussion it has been established that, at the beginning, dynasties are inevitably kind in the exercise of their power and just in their administration. The reason is either their religion, when the dynasty is based upon religious propaganda, or their noble and benevolent attitude toward others, which is required by the desert attitude that is natural to dynasties at the beginning.

A kind and benevolent rule serves as an incentive to the subjects and gives them energy for cultural activities. Civilization will be abundant, and procreation will be vigorous. All this takes place gradually. The effects will become noticeable after one or two generations at best. At the end of two generations, the dynasty approaches the limit of its natural life. At that time, civilization has reached the limits of its abundance and growth.

It should not be objected that it was stated before that in the later years of a dynasty, there will be coercion of the subjects and bad government. This is correct, but it does not contradict what we have just said. Even though coercion makes its appearance at that time and the revenues decrease, the destructive influences of this situation on civilization will become noticeable only after some time, because things in nature all have a gradual development.

In the later years of dynasties, there occur attacks on property and tax revenue and, through customs duties, on trading. Or, trouble occurs as the result of the unrest of the subjects and the great number of rebels who are provoked by the senility of the dynasty to rebel. Therefore, as a rule, little grain is stored. The grain and harvest situation is not always good and stable from year to year. The amount of rainfall in the world differs by nature. The rainfall may be strong or weak, little or much. Grain, fruits, and the amount of milk given by animals varies correspondingly. Still, for their food requirements, people put their trust in what it is possible to store. If nothing is stored, people must expect famines. If for some years nothing is stored, hunger will be general.

The large number of pestilences [diseases] has its reason in the large number of famines just mentioned. Or, it has its reason in the many disturbances that result from the disintegration of the dynasty. There is much unrest and bloodshed, and plagues occur. The principal reason for the latter is the corruption of the air (climate) through too large a civilization (population). It results from the putrefaction [putrefication] and the many evil moistures with which the air has contact in a dense civilization. Now, air nourishes the animal spirit and is constantly with it. When it is corrupted, corruption affects the temper of the spirit. If the corruption is strong, the lung is infected with disease. This results in epidemics, which affect the lung in particular. Even if the corruption is not strong or great, putrefaction grows and multiplies under its influence, resulting in many fevers that affect the tempers, and the bodies become sick and perish. The reason for the growth of putrefaction and evil moistures is invariably a dense and abundant civilization such as exists in the later years of a dynasty. Such civilization is the result of the good government, the kindness, the safety, and the light taxation that existed at the beginning of the dynasty. This is obvious. Therefore, it has been clarified by science in the proper place that it is necessary to have empty spaces and water regions interspersed between civilized areas. This makes circulation of the air possible. It removes the corruption and putrefaction affecting the air after contact with living beings, and brings healthy air. This also is the reason why pestilences occur much more frequently in densely settled cities than elsewhere, as, for instance, in Cairo in the East and Fez in the Maghrib.

69 Whirlwinds and Aboriginal Society

Wise Women of the Dreamtime: Aboriginal Tales of the Ancestral Powers. Collected by K. Langloh Parker, ed. Johanna Lambert. Rochester, Vt.: Inner Traditions International, 1993. 61–66.

The following passage is part of an aboriginal oral tradition from Australia. This evidence allows us to see how disasters fit into the worldview of aboriginal peoples. Here, whirlwinds are associated with Mullee Mullees, or dream spirits over which shamans have asserted control. In this tale, the whirlwinds represent a punitive force, but the ultimate results are unexpected. Aborigines believed that boolees, whirlwinds inhabited by spirits, caused the birth of twins, an undesirable event. They were also considered messengers of death.

Bralgah Numbardee was very fond of going out hunting with her young daughter Bralgah. . . . All the camp were proud of young Bralgah. She was the merriest girl and the best dancer of all her tribe, whose women were for the most part content to click the boomerangs, beat their rolled-up opossum-skin rugs, and sing the corroborree songs in voices from shrill to sweet, while the men danced; but not so Bralgah. She must dance, too, and not only the dances she saw the rest dance, but new ones that she taught herself, for every song she heard she set to steps. Sometimes, with laughing eyes, she would whirl round like a boolee, or whirlwind. Then suddenly she would change to a stately measure. Then for variety's sake she would perform a series of swift gyrations, as if, indeed, a whirlwind devil had her in his grip.

The fame of her dancing spread abroad, and proud indeed was the tribe to whom she belonged; hence their anxiety for her safety, and their dread that the Wurrawilberoo would catch her.

The Wurrawilberoo were two cannibals who lived in the scrub alone.

• • •

One day they went out to camp for two or three days. Nothing hurt them the first night, but the next day the Wurrawilberoo surprised and captured them. They gave Bralgah Numbardee a severe blow. She fell down and feigned death. . . . The Wurrawilberoo picked her up to carry her off to their camp. They did not wish to hurt young Bralgah; they meant to keep her to dance for them. They . . . gave her their . . . stone knife to carry, telling her to fear nothing. . . .

She went with them, but when they were not looking, she threw the knife away.

As soon as they reached the camp, the Wurrawilberoo asked her for it. . . . Bralgah said she had . . . forgotten it.

They said, "We will go back and get it. You stay here.". . .

Bralgah watched them go away, then told her mother, who immediately jumped up. Off then went both mother and daughter as fast as they could to their own tribe, whom they told what had happened.

When the Wurrawilberoo came back, they were enraged. . . . No feast, no dance for them that night unless they recovered their victims. . . .

But the Daens [Bralgah's people] were out looking for them, fully armed, seeing which the Wurrawilberoo turned and fled. . . . But so wroth were they at the attempt to capture their prized Bralgah that a council was held and the destruction of the Wurrawilberoo determined. Two of the cleverest wirreenuns said they would send their Mullee Mullees in whirlwinds after the enemy to catch them. This they did. Whirling along went the boolees with the Mullee Mullees in them. Quickly they went along the track of the Wurrawilberoo. . . .

"We will go," said one Wurrawilberoo to the other, "back to the camp, ahead of these whirlwinds. We will seize the girl and her mother, and fly in another direction. . . ."

On, on they fled before the whirlwinds, which gained both size and pace as they followed them.

The Daens were so astonished at seeing the Wurrawilberoo returning straight toward them, the whirlwinds after them, that they never thought of arming themselves. Into the midst of them rushed the Wurrawilberoo. One seized Bralgah the mother, the other young Bralgah, and before the astonished Daens realized their coming, they had gone some distance along the edge of the plain.

"Bring your weapons," roared the Mullee Mullees in the whirlwinds to the Daens as they swirled through the camp after the enemy.

. . . Just in front of the [Wurrawilberoo] were two huge . . . trees. Feeling that the whirlwinds . . . were already lifting them from their feet, the Wurrawilberoo clung to the balah trees. . . .

• • •

Then as the whirlwinds howled round them, tearing up everything in a wild fury, the balah trees now in their grasp creaking and groaning, Wurrawilberoo muttered a sort of incantation and released young Bralgah. As she slipped from this grasp, came a shout of joy from the Daens. . . .

But their joy was short lived. The whirlwinds, wound round the balah trees to which the Wurrawilberoo clung, and dragged them from their roots before the men could [let] go. Up, up the whirlwinds carried the trees, the men still clinging to them, until they reached the sky; there they planted them not far from the milky way. . . .

When the Daens saw that their enemies were gone, they turned to get Bralgah; her mother was already with them.

. . . [Yet] she was gone. All round the plain they looked. They saw only a tall bird walking across it.

• • •

As soon as the Mullee Mullees, which had animated the whirlwinds, returned . . . the Daens asked them if they had left her there.

No, they said, Bralgah had not gone to the sky, . . .

• • •

After a while they noticed a number of birds like the one they had seen on the plain . . . and after feeding for a while, these birds would begin to corroboree [dance]—such a strange corroboree, of which one bird taller than the others was seemingly a leader.

This corroboree was so human and like no movements of any other birds . . . it [was] the dance of the lost Bralgah. . . .

• • •

When Bralgah Numbardee died, she was taken to the sky . . . there [she] learned that the Wurrawilberoo by his incantation had changed her daughter into the dancing bird, which shape she had to keep as long as she lived on earth.

Afterwards, if ever the Daens saw a boolee speeding along near their camp, the women would cry, "Wurrawilberoo," clutch their children, and bury their heads in their rugs; the men would seize their weapons and hurl them at the ever-feared and hated capturers of Bralgah.

70 Disasters in the Aztec Worldview

Jacques Soustelle. *L'Univers des Aztèques* (1979). As translated in Serge Gruzinski, *The Aztecs: Rise and Fall of an Empire.* New York: Harry N. Abrams, Inc., 1992. 133–137.

In the following selection, scholar Jacques Soustelle discusses the Aztec worldview as seen in its calendar. One of the most striking features of Aztec thought is the prominence of disaster and the precariousness of human existence. The Aztecs thought that the universe was extinguishable, and that constant appeal to their gods was necessary to prevent disasters from occurring. They lived in an environment where natural catastrophes such as earthquakes and drought were common. The influence of such events is evident in this passage.

In the traditions and chronicles written up after the conquest as well as in pre-Columbian manuscripts and in the bas-reliefs of some monuments, one encounters the idea that our world was preceded by four worlds or "suns" which ended in cataclysms. These vanished worlds are called the "Tiger Sun," "Wind Sun," "Rain Sun" and "Water Sun." The Rain Sun is also sometimes known as the "Fire Sun," because it was a rain of fire that destroyed the world at the end of this period.

These four ages are not always described in the same order of succession. . . . The *Historia de los Mexicanos por sus Pinturas* gives the following order: Tiger, Wind, Rain, Water, which is corroborated by the magnificent monument known as the "Aztec Calendar.". . .

. . . Our present world is marked on the Aztec Calendar by the date of . . . 4-Movement, or Earthquake, when our sun began moving, four days after its birth. In the ritual calendar, this is the festival of the sun and of the lords. But it is also probably the date when our world will end in earthquakes, the sign . . . symbolizing both the sun's movement and seismic shocks.

In the . . . divinatory calendar, all days bearing the number 4 are considered an ill omen. The day of 4-Ocelotl, end of the Tiger Sun, is a day of ill omen, dominated by the god Tezcatlipoca, . . . god of the north, of cold, and of night, [who] turned himself into a tiger . . . to throw down the sun. The first age . . . ended in cold and darkness, following an eclipse.

The date 4-Ecatl, end of the Wind Sun, is considered a day of enchantments and sorcery . . . it was by a vast magic operation that the second world ended: All men were turned into monkeys. At the same time a violent wind was blowing, the manifestation of Eecatl, god of the wind. . . .

The date 4-Quiauitl, end of the Rain Sun, is placed under the protection of Tlaloc, god of rain, and it is this god's mask, recognizable by its long teeth and enormous eyes, that is used as the sign of rain. The third world collapsed under a rain of fire. Tlaloc was not only god of rain, although this was his most usual function, but also god of fire that falls from the sky—lightning and thunder, and perhaps volcanic eruptions: this is the rain of fire. . . .

The date 4-Atl, end of the Water Sun, is represented on monuments mentioned above by the number 4 accompanied by the face of the goddess Chalchiuhtlicue, "she who wears a skirt of precious stone," a water divinity and companion of Tlaloc . . . the fourth world ended in inundations, in a kind of flood.

Thus, on four occasions, a world was born and collapsed in gigantic catastrophes. Today's world will suffer the same fate. The ancient Mexicans conceived this history of the universe as that of victories and defeats of the alternating principles, taking turns to rule over everything, then driven away and deprived of any grip on the real world. The first of the suns is . . . the age of cold, the night, the north. The second . . . is the period of sorcery and of the west. The third is . . . of rain [and] . . . the south. The fourth, of water and of . . . the east . . . today's sun, the fifth, . . . is the sun of the center because five is the number of the center; the divinity or the center is Xiuhetcutli, god of fire: Hence our sun is a fire sun, sometimes represented by the same symbol as fire, a butterfly. . . .

71 The Black Death in Europe

Giovanni Boccaccio. *The Decameron.* Translated by Mark Musa and Peter Bondanella. New York: Mentor Books, 1982. 6–11.

In the mid-fourteenth century, an outbreak of bubonic plague spread rapidly across Europe from east to west. So virulent was the "Black Death," as the plague of 1348 was called, that most died within a few days of contracting the disease. Perhaps one-quarter of the European population died in the 1300s from the plague. The Black Death was a social catastrophe that tore communities apart. The sick and dying were left untended as neither medicine nor faith in God could halt the spread of the disease. As the sickness affected both rich and poor alike, communities often lost important leaders as well as many of the workers that formed the foundation of society. In the excerpt following, Giovanni Boccaccio recounts the effect of the Black Death upon the city of Florence.

Let me say, then, that thirteen hundred and forty-eight years had already passed after the fruitful Incarnation of the Son of God when into the distinguished city of Florence, more noble than any other Italian city, there came a deadly pestilence. Either because of the influence of heavenly bodies or because of God's just wrath as punishment to mortals for our wicked deeds, the pestilence, originating some years earlier in the East, killed an infinite number of people as it spread relentlessly from one place to another until it had stretched its miserable length all over the West. And against this pestilence no human wisdom or foresight was of any avail; quantities of filth were removed from the city by officials charged with the task; the entry of any sick person into the city was prohibited; and many directives were issued concerning the maintenance of good health. Nor were the humble supplications rendered not once but many times by the pious to God, through public processions or by other means, in any way efficacious; for almost at the beginning of springtime of the year in question the plague began to show its sorrowful effects in an extraordinary manner. It did not assume the form it had in the East, where bleeding from the nose was a manifest sign of inevitable death, but rather it showed its first signs in men and women alike by means of swellings either in the groin or under the armpits, some of which grew to the size of an ordinary apple and others to the size of an egg (more or less), and the people called them *gavoccioli*. And from the two parts of the body already mentioned, in very little time, the said deadly *gavoccioli* began to spread indiscriminately over every part of the body; then, after this, the symptoms of the illness changed to black or livid spots appearing on the arms and thighs, and on every part of the body—sometimes there were large ones and other times a number of little ones scattered all around. And just as the *gavoccioli* were originally, and still are, a very definite indication of impending death, in like manner these spots came to mean the same thing for whoever contracted them. Neither a doctor's advice nor the strength of medicine could do anything to cure this illness; on the contrary, either the nature of the illness was such that they did not recognize its cause and, as a result, could not prescribe the proper remedy (in fact, the number of doctors, other than the well-trained, was increased by a large number of men and women who had never had any medical training); at any rate, few of the sick were ever cured, and almost all died after the third day of the appearance of the previously described symptoms (some sooner, others later), and most of them died without fever or any other side effects.

This pestilence was so powerful that it was transmitted to the healthy by contact with the sick, the way a fire close to dry or oily things will set them aflame. And the evil of the plague went even further: not only did talking to or being around the sick bring infection and a common death, but also touching the clothes of the sick or anything touched or used by them seemed to communicate this very disease to the person involved. What I am about to say is incredible to hear, and if I and others had not witnessed it with our own eyes, I should not dare believe it (let alone write about it), no matter how trustworthy a person I might have heard it from. Let me say, then, that the plague described here was of such virulence in spreading from one person to another that not only did it pass from one man to the next, but, what's more, it was often transmitted from the garments of a sick or dead man to animals that not only became contaminated by the disease but also died with a brief period of time. My own eyes, as I said earlier, were witness to such a thing one day: when the rags of a poor man who died of this disease were thrown into the public street, two pigs came upon then, and, as they are wont to do, first with their snouts and then with their teeth they took the rags and shook them around; and within a short time, after a number of convulsions, both pigs fell dead upon the ill-fated rags, as if they had been poisoned. From these and many similar or worse occurrences there came about such fear that almost all of them took a very cruel attitude in the matter; that is, they completely avoided the sick and their possessions, and in so doing, each one believed that he was protecting his own good health.

There were some people who thought that living moderately and avoiding any excess might help a great deal in resisting this disease, and so they gathered in small groups and lived entirely apart from everyone else. They shut themselves up in those houses where there were no sick people and where one could live well by eating the most delicate of foods and drinking the finest of wines (doing so always in moderation) allowing no one to speak about or listen to anything said about the sick and the dead outside; these people lived, entertaining themselves with music and other pleasures that they could arrange. Others thought the opposite: they believed that drinking excessively, enjoying life, going about singing and celebrating, satisfying in every way the appetites as best one could, laughing, and making light of everything that happened was the best medicine for such a disease; so they practiced to the fullest what they believed by going from one tavern to another all day and night, drinking to excess; and they would often make merry in private homes, doing everything that pleased or amused them most. This they were able to do easily, for everyone felt he was doomed to die, and, as a result, abandoned his property, so that most of the houses had become common property, and any stranger who came upon them used them as if he were the rightful owner. In addition to this bestial behavior, they always managed to avoid the sick as best they could. And in this great affliction and misery of our city the revered authority of the laws, both divine and human, had fallen and almost completely disappeared, for, like other men, the ministers and executors of the laws were either dead or sick or so short of help that it was impossible for them to fulfill their duties; and as a result, everybody was free to do as he pleased.

Many others adopted a middle course between the two attitudes just described: neither did they restrict their food or drink so much as the first group nor did they fall into such dissoluteness and drunkenness as the second; rather, they satisfied their appetites to a moderate degree. They did not shut themselves up, but went around carrying in their hands flowers, or sweet-smelling herbs, or various kinds of spices; and they would often put these things to their noses, believing that such smells were a wonderful means of purifying the brain, for all the air seemed infected with the stench of dead bodies, sickness, and medicines.

Others were of a crueler opinion (though it was, perhaps, a safer one): they maintained that there was no better medicine against the plague than to flee from it; convinced of this reasoning and caring only about themselves, men and women in great numbers abandoned their city, their houses, their farms, their relatives, and their possessions and sought other places, going at least as far away as the Florentine countryside—as if the wrath of God could not pursue them with this pestilence wherever they went but would only strike those it found within the walls of the city! Or perhaps they thought that Florence's last hour had come and that no one in the city would remain alive.

And not all those who adopted these diverse opinions died, nor did they all escape with their lives; on the contrary, many of those who thought this way were falling sick everywhere, and since they had given, when they were healthy, the bad example of avoiding the sick, they in turn were abandoned and left to languish away without care. The fact was that one citizen avoided another, that almost no one cared for his neighbor, and that relatives rarely or hardly ever visited each other—they stayed far apart. This disaster had struck such fear into the hearts of men and women that brother abandoned brother, uncle abandoned nephew, sister left brother, and very often wife abandoned husband, and—even worse, almost unbelievable—fathers and mothers neglected to tend and care for their children as if they were not their own.

Thus, for the countless multitude of men and women who fell sick, there remained no support except the charity of their friends (and these were few) or the greed of servants, who worked for inflated salaries without regard to the service they performed and who, in spite of this, were few and far between; and those few were men or women of little wit (most of them not trained for such service) who did little else but hand different things to the sick when requested to do so or watch over them while they died. . . . And so, many people died who, by chance, might have survived if they had been attended to. Between the lack of competent attendants that the sick were unable to obtain and the violence of the pestilence itself, so many, many people died in the city both day and night that it was incredible just to hear this described, not to mention seeing it! . . .

The plight of the lower class and, perhaps, a large part of the middle class was even more pathetic: most of them stayed in their homes or neighborhoods either because of their poverty or because of their hopes of remaining safe, and every day they fell sick by the thousands; and not having servants or attendants of any kind, they almost always died. Many ended their lives in the public streets, during the day or at night, while many others who died in their homes were discovered dead by their neighbors only by the smell of their decomposing bodies. The city was full of corpses. The dead were usually given the same treatment by their neighbors, who were moved more by the fear that the decomposing corpses would contaminate them than by any charity they might have felt toward the deceased: either by themselves or with the assistance of porters (when they were available), they would drag the corpse out of the house and place it in the front of the doorstep, where, usually in the morning, quantities of dead bodies could be seen by any passerby; then they were laid out on biers, or for lack of biers, on a plank. Nor did a bier carry only one corpse; sometimes it was used for two or three at a time. More than once, a single bier would serve for a wife and husband, two or three brothers, a father or son, or other relatives, all at the same time. And very often it happened that two priests, each with a cross, would be on their way to bury someone, when porters carrying three or four biers would just follow behind them; and whereas these priests thought they had just one dead man to bury, they had, in fact, six or eight and sometimes more. Moreover, the dead were honored with no tears or candles or funeral mourners: in fact, things had reached such a point that the people who died were cared for as we care for goats today. . .

72 Disaster and Response in the Mongol Empire

Li Chih-Ch'ang. *The Travels of an Alchemist*. London: Routledge and Sons, Ltd., 1931. 55–56, 58–59, 92–93, 114, 122–123, 134, 141–142.

Li Chih-Ch'ang was a disciple of Ch'ang Ch'un, a Taoist monk who traveled from China to Turkostan in the thirteenth century. Ch'ang was summoned by Chingiz Khan, the ruler of Mongols and architect of the Mongol Empire (which at its zenith was the largest empire in the world, including China, Russia and West Asia). While traveling, Li Chih-Ch'ang commented extensively on the lands they passed through, paying careful attention to climatic extremes and the fragile balance between human societies and the environment. He also comments on the influence of the perceived ability of religious specialists to exert control over the weather.

In the first decade of the fourth month . . . the faithful expressed the hope that he (Ch'ang Ch'un) would perform the ceremonies of the Full Moon in the T'ien-ch'ang temple . . . [he] consented.

There happened at the time to be a great drought. No sooner had the celebration of the Full Moon (May 18) begun, than rain fell heavily. The people were afraid it would interfere with the processions. But when, soon after midday, the Master approached the altar and began to officiate, the sky suddenly cleared. The crowd was delighted and exclaimed in astonishment: "He can cause rain and stop it at his will. Great indeed must be his power in the Way, that Nature should thus obey him!"

• • •

He celebrated the Full Moon of mid-autumn (September 13th) at home in the temple. In the afternoon he initiated his followers into the use of various spells and also received candidates from the priesthood. The huge crowd that had collected was obliged to sit all day in the open. It comprised old people and children, many of whom were severely affected by the heat. Suddenly a cloud, shaped like an umbrella, settled over the assembly and remained there for several hours, to the extreme relief and astonishment of those who sat under it. A second miracle happened in connection with the well-water, which was sufficient for a hundred people, but not for a crowd of over a thousand. . . . On the three days round the time of Full Moon the well brimmed with water right up to the top, and however much was drawn, remained at the same level, so great was the assistance that his virtue elicited from Heaven.

• • •

During the tenth month the Memorial Hall . . . was being decorated with wall-paintings; but the cold weather had put a stop to the work. The Master refused to let it be suspended, saying: "If ever the flute of such a one as Tsou Yen [a religious figure] could bring back the spring-time, surely you credit me with power enough over the elements to make this work possible?" Presently, in the middle of winter, the weather became as balmy as in spring; there were no dust-storms, and the painter was able to finish his work.

• • •

On the eighteenth day of the eleventh month (December 3, 1221) after crossing a great river, we reached the northern outskirts of the mighty city of Samarkand. . . .

The town is built along canals. As no rain falls during the summer and autumn, two rivers have been diverted so as to run along every street, thus giving a supply of water to all the inhabitants. Before the defeat of the Khwariszm Shah there was a fixed population here of more than 100,000 households; but now there is only about a quarter this number, of whom a very large proportion are native. . . . But these people are quite unable to manage their fields and orchards for themselves, and are obliged to call in Chinese, Itai and Tanguts. The administration of the town is also conducted by people of every various nationality. Chinese craftsmen are found everywhere. Within the city is a mound about a hundred feet high on which stands the Khwarizm Shah's new palace. The Mongol Governor at first resided here. But the local population was exasperated by famine and there was perpetual brigandage. Fearing trouble, the Governor went to live on the north side of the river. . . . [The Governor] sent [Ch'ang Ch'un] a monthly allowance of rice, corn-flour, salt, oil, fruits, vegetables and so on; he became every day more attentive and respectful.

• • •

At this season [November] a fine rain begins to fall and the grass becomes green again. Then, after the middle of the eleventh month, the rain becomes heav-ier, sometimes turning to snow, and the ground becomes saturated. From the time of the Master's first arrival in Samarkand it was his habit to give what grain we could spare to the poor and hungry of the city. Often, too, he would send hot rice-meal, and in this way saved a great number of lives.

On [December 30] we set out. On . . . [26 January 1223] there was a snow-storm and such intense cold that many oxen and horses were frozen to death on the road. After three days we . . . reached the Khan's camp. Here we learnt that on the twenty-eighth, in the middle of the night, the bridge of boats had broken loose and been swept away. The Khan asked the reason of calamities such as earthquakes, thunder and so on. The Master replied: "I have heard that in order to avoid the wrath of Heaven you forbid your countrymen to bathe in rivers during the sum-mer, wash their clothes, make fresh felt or gather mushrooms in the fields. But this is not the way to serve Heaven. It is said that of the three thousand sins the worst is ill-treatment of one's father and mother. Now in this respect I believe your sub-jects to be gravely at fault and it would be well if your Majesty would use your influence to reform them."

This pleased the Khan and he said: "Holy Immortal, your words are exceed-ingly true; such is indeed my own belief," and he bade those who were present write them down. . . . The Master asked that what he had said might be made known to the Khan's subjects in general, and this was agreed to. . . .

• • •

IN THE A-PU-HAN MOUNTAINS

To the south are high mountain ranges that are snow-covered even in the hottest weather. Concerning this district many strange facts are reported. A little to the west, by the side of a lake, there is a "wind-tomb." It is covered with white clay in which there are a number of cracks. In the second or third months when the wind is about to rise in the ranges to the south, a strange noise in these holes always gives warning beforehand of the approaching storm. When the wind first comes from inside the "tomb" it seems to move spirally, like a ram's horn. Final-ly thousands of these small spirals unite in one whirlwind, which sends the dust flying, rolls stones along the ground, uproots trees, blows off roofs, and beats upon the valleys till they shake. Then, retreating to the south-east, it suddenly dies away.

Beside a torrent to the south-east are three or four watermills. When the stream reaches level ground it gradually dries up and disappears. In the mountains there is a great deal of coal. To the east are two springs which in the winter months suddenly burst out, forming great rivers and lakes. For a while the water then runs underground, only to burst out again further on, fish and all. Often it floods the people's houses and it is only in the second month of spring that the waters gradually recede and the ground can be dug.

• • •

In the fifth month the Governor of Peking . . . several times sent letters begging him to take over the direction of the Ta T'ien-ch'ang Kuan, and on the twenty-second day he returned there and did as they suggested. . . . The members of all eight congregations all bowed and knelt down before him, paying him Taoist homage. There was indeed a change in the whole attitude of the people towards Taoism. The water in the well at the Yu-hsu Kuan had long been brackish. But in the years [1224–1225] . . . when there were collected here all the Taoists who had returned from the west, the water suddenly became sweet in taste. This, too, arose from the general trend towards piety.

• • •

In the fifth month [1226] there was a great drought in the Capital [Peking] The farmers could not sow and a disaster was foreseen. The authorities cleared the markets and set altars up in them. Prayers were offered week after week, but with no result. The Governor sent an envoy to the Master begging him to pray for rain. He performed the rites for three days and two nights, and on the night when the holy figures [statues of Taoist deities and patriarchs] were to be prayed to, clouds suddenly gathered on all sides, and rain began to fall, continuing from midnight till breakfast time next day. The Governor sent a messenger who burnt incense and tendered the thanks of the City, saying that the drought had nearly burnt up the fields, corn had not been sown and the people had small hope of surviving. But thanks to the magic power of the Master, the Pure Ones Above had been moved to pour down sweet balm upon the people, who with one accord called it "The adept's Rain." "This effect," answered the Master, "was produced by the Absolute Faith of His Excellency the Governor. What power have I to cause the Holy Ones above to show compassion and give the people life?"

A second messenger now came saying that though a certain amount of rain had fallen, it was not nearly enough to make up for so long a drought. A real downpour was needed. The Master said there was no need to worry. When the powers above had once been moved by Absolute Faith, they would not fail faithfully to repay. A heavy rain must be close at hand.

Sure enough, before the evening meal was over floods of rain began to stream down. The harvest was excellent, and various celebrities and scholars came with poems in which they congratulated the Master.

73 Famine Investigation in China

Yao Chen. "Ballad on the Investigation of a Disaster."
Translated by Victor H. Mair. In *The Columbia Anthology of Traditional Chinese Literature*. Victor H. Mair, ed. New York: Columbia University Press, 1994. 100–101.

This selection discusses the investigation of a famine by the Chinese government. As in other societies, the Chinese worldview held natural disasters to be a sign of poor or corrupt leadership. Blame for such disasters was placed on various levels of government, ranging from local through provincial, and to the Emperor himself. Nevertheless, as the following poem written by Yao Chen, a fourteenth-century writer, suggests, common people bore the brunt of famine. Governments continued to demand tax payments during such times, which compounded the disaster.

Having heard that an official was coming to investigate the disaster,
The starving people stood near the head of his horse.
"Are you starving?" asked the official.
"This is a rich village," replied his clerk.
"Our food is already exhausted," said the people.
"There is some extra grain," said the lictor.°

Hearing the words of his assistants,
He turned away, unwilling to enter the village.
Starvation and repletion depend upon clerks and lictors;
The official merely holds on to the register in his hand.
Before the investigation, in some cases the people had enough to eat,
Having stored up extra rice during the twelfth month of the previous year;
After the investigation, all the people were starving.

When an official passes by, tax money must be handed over completely;
When he leaves, he will report on his diligent labors—
While the starving people will be weeping together in the night.

74 The Black Death in Syria

Ibn Battuta. *Travels in Asia and Africa, 1325–1354.* Translated by H.A.R. Gibb. London: George Routledge & Sons, Ltd., 1929. 305–306.

Ibn Battuta was an Islamic jurist and chronicler born in Tangier, Morocco. In 1325, he left his birthplace for a twenty-nine year odyssey that took him to the far reaches of the Islamic world and beyond. His travels began with the 3,000-mile trip to Mecca to complete the pilgrimage, and continued until he had traveled 75,000 miles. During his return from China and India, Ibn Battuta passed through Syria during the bubonic plague known in Europe as "the Black Death." While his comments on the event are brief, they show the devastating effect on the populations of towns and cities caused by the plague.

Early in June we heard at Aleppo that the plague had broken out at Gaza, and the number of deaths there reached over a thousand a day. On travelling to Hims I

°A low-ranking administrative official.

found that the plague had broken out there: about three hundred persons died of it the day I arrived. So I went on to Damascus, and arrived there on a Thursday. The inhabitants had then been fasting for three days; on the Friday they went out to the mosque of the Footprints [south of Damascus]. . . , and God eased them of the plague. The number of deaths among them reached a maximum of 2,400 a day. Thereafter I journeyed to 'Ajalún and thence to Jerusalem, where I found that the ravages of the plague had ceased. We revisited Hebron, and then went to Gaza, the greater part of which we found deserted because of the number of those who died there of the plague. I was told by the qadí that the number of deaths there reached 1,100 a day. We continued our journey overland to Damietta, and on to Alexandria. Here we found that the plague was diminishing in intensity, though the number of deaths had previously reached a thousand and eighty a day. I then travelled to Cairo, where I was told that the number of deaths during the epidemic rose to twenty-one thousand a day. From Cairo I travelled through [Upper Egypt] to 'Aydháb, whence I took a ship to Judda, and thence reached Mecca on [the 16 November 1348].

75 Visual Document: The Four Horsemen of the Apocalypse

The German artist Albrecht Dürer (1471–1528) combined precise detail with a fascination for the human psyche. Dürer's most famous works were engravings and woodcuts, many of which were inspired by Christian texts and personae. The inspiration for *Apocalypse,* the woodcut portrayed here, was the last book of the New Testament, "The Revelation of John." In it are described four horsemen, one with a bow riding a white horse, one rider on a red horse carrying a great sword, one on a black horse carrying a set of scales, and a fourth rider, Death, riding a sickly horse, each an instrument of God's wrath on earth on judgement day. In this illustration with its religious theme, Dürer drew inspiration from religious conflicts, plagues, and famines. Examine the image closely. Who fell victim to the four horsemen? What might this woodcut say about the fortunes of ordinary people and kings? To what cause did the artist attribute the calamities of his time?

DISCUSSION QUESTIONS

1. How do different societies conceive of disasters?

2. How does the way in which societies see themselves in relation to nature and the environment influence their perceptions of and responses to disaster?

3. To what extent are "natural" disasters caused or influenced by human agency or actions such as warfare or neglect?

4. What range of responses to disaster exists within the readings? To what extent are states or religious communities involved in these responses? Do you see any relation to responses to disaster today?

5. How do natural disasters affect communities?

6. How would you compare the attitude of Florentine residents to the Black Death with that of Australian aborigines to whirlwinds? Or with the subjects of the Mongolian empire to the disasters they experienced?

Chapter
13
The World in 1450

*T*he world of the mid-fifteenth century possessed many of the same rhythms as earlier centuries. The practices and patterns of daily life, as opposed to those of elite politics and religion, were foremost in the minds of most people in the world. Their day-to-day activities, although rarely captured in contemporary chronicles, are the subject of this chapter. If one could observe this world from afar, these endeavors would predominate throughout the globe. This same observer might note that one hemisphere—the Americas—existed in isolation from other continents even though there were tremendous similarities between community life in each region.

However, the world of the mid-fifteenth century was mere decades away from the "Columbian exchange," the transfer of plants, animals, diseases, and ideas between the "New World" and the "Old" after the voyages of Christopher Columbus. In 1450 there was little to foreshadow sudden global integration, save for the tenuous explorations of Mediterranean and Iberian sailors on the African coast. Even within Europe and West Asia, the most significant political event of the period was the fall of Constantinople to the Seljuk Turks. Elsewhere, in the Americas, the Aztec empire rose suddenly and dramatically in the Valley of Mexico. The world of 1450, then, was a world on the eve of a profound transformation that brought together peoples that had not previously had contact with one another.

76 Life in the Aztec Empire

Fray Bernardino de Sahagún. *Florentine Codex: General History of the Things of New Spain. Book 6: Rhetoric and Moral Philosophy.* Translated by Charles E. Dibble and Arthur O.J. Anderson. Santa Fe, N. Mex.: The School of American Research and The University of Utah Press, 1969. 127–33.

Ceremonies and festivals were important components of daily life that bound societies together. The excerpt that follows describes a betrothal and wedding in the Aztec world before the Spanish conquest in 1521–22. The story is taken from an encyclopedia of Aztec culture compiled by a Spanish missionary named Bernardino de Sahagún in the mid-sixteenth century. Sahagún detested indigenous religion* but came to admire many aspects of Aztec culture: despite these feelings, his accounts meticulously detail the day-to-day events in Aztec life. The ceremonial aspects of the wedding reinforce the weight of responsibilities placed upon the couple, especially upon the wife. Through the dialogue, he depicts the humility children must show their elders because of the suffering the parents incurred in raising them. Yet despite the debts owed to one's parents, the prospective bride and groom are leaving their immediate families to begin their own. To display their humility and sense of obligation to an older generation, departing children refer to the impending marriage as if it were a plague visited upon their parents.

Here is related how the [Aztecs] sought wives. When one's mother, one's father already saw that their youth [son] was already matured, already strong, then they assembled, they consulted with one another.

[The father] said: "Poor is this, our youth. Let us seek a woman for him, lest he somewhere do something. He may somewhere molest a woman; he may commit adultery. For it is his nature; he is matured."

Thereupon they [the parents] summoned their youth; they placed him before them. [The father] said to him: "Thou art here, thou who art my youth. Behold, we talk because we are concerned regarding thee. Thou poor one, already thou art this way, for thou hast matured. We say: 'Let us find thee a woman. Seek permission: take leave. Let the masters of the youths, the rulers of the youths learn of it.'"

And their youth then replied to them: "Ye have shown me favor, ye have inclined your hearts; in my behalf ye have suffered anguish, in my behalf ye have suffered affliction. I shall inflict sickness upon you, I shall visit you with sickness and pestilence. May it happen as ye desire, for so also are the desires of my heart. Oh, may it be that my heart suffer pain, affliction! Oh, may it be that I behold the dangerous places on earth! Where shall I go to experience it?"

---

*Sahagún indeed added explicit references to the Christian god in his description of the marriage ceremony. These have been omitted here.

Then tamales were prepared, chocolate was ground, sauces were prepared. They bought youths' axes—cutters of wood, splitters of wood. Then they summoned the masters of the youths, the rulers of the youths. Then they served them food, served them drink, gave them smoking tubes. And when they had eaten, when they had taken drink, thereupon the [youth's] old men, the guardians of the quarters, the guardians of the boundaries seated themselves; and they placed the youths' axes before them.

Thereupon [one of] the old men spoke: he said [to the leaders of the youths]: "Ye are here present, ye who are our sons, ye who are youths, ye who have labored, ye who have worked. Your [son] will disquiet you, for he wisheth to withdraw; he wisheth to enter the company of women. Verily, here are the youths' axes in order that he be separated; thus is the judgment of the Mexicans."

Thereupon [the master of] the youths responded; he said: "Ye have shown favor to your sons. Here your sons comprehend all, hear all. This is enough. Verily, he leaveth forever the youths [and] the leaders with whom for a little time he hath worked, hath labored."

Then the masters of the youths departed bearing the axes.

Then, later, all the kinsmen [of the youth] assembled. There was consultation with one another; there was consideration as to which woman they would request. And when they had become of one accord as to which woman would be requested, the old women, the matchmakers, while it was yet early morning, passed to her home. They urgently solicited the parents of the maiden.

And when it was already the fourth day, the parents of the maiden said to them: "The maiden hath caused you trouble. To what purpose doth she deceive our humble man? For her uncles, her aunts, are in agreement. May then all learn what they will say, and may the maiden also hear of it. Once again on the morrow ye will come; ye will come to hear of her pleasure."

And the next day, when the matchmakers had gone, deliberately, in tranquility, there was consultation. There was no one who disputed; there was no one who spoiled the discourse. When an amicable agreement had been reached, thereupon the parents of the maiden said: "It is good. May it be consummated. Will she move the humble one, the unembittered one, the unseasoned one? And if at times they will be poor, [if] her heart will suffer pain and affliction, how will he regard the maiden? Will she perhaps perform something? Will she perhaps do something?"

Then they said to the parents of the youth: "Rest your bodies. Learn when the union can occur."

And the youth's old men then sought out when it would be, which one was a good day. And when they had learned the good day, then they went to give this information; they told the maiden's parents when this would be: the proper day. They said the good days were Reed, Monkey, Crocodile, Eagle, House. Thereupon there were preparations: the ashes were prepared, ground cacao was prepared, flowers were secured, smoking tubes were purchased, tubes of tobacco were prepared, sauce bowls and pottery cups and baskets were purchased. Then the maize was ground; leavening was set out in basins. Then tamales were prepared. All night they were occupied; perhaps three days or two nights the women made tamales. So they passed the night. That which transpired in their presence let them sleep very little.

And the day before [the marriage] was to take place, there were invitations to banquet: first those who were illustrious, the lords, the captains, the seasoned warriors, and those who guided the groom, and moderately matured youths, the rulers of the youths; then those who were all the kinsmen of the man and of the woman.

And when it had dawned, when the groom was to marry the bride, and the bride was to marry the groom, thereupon the invited guests entered. First the rulers of the youths, the masters of the youths entered. When they were fed, they drank only chocolate, for they drank no pulque [a fermented beverage made from a type of cactus]. And at midday all the old men, the old women entered. To each one it was undertaken to give food, to give drink, to give flowers, to give tubes of tobacco. And the women came bearing, some of them, maguey fiber capes; some of them, coarse maguey fiber capes; some of them, small capes; and we poor people only grains of maize. They placed all the gifts before the hearth. And this caused the old men, the old women to become [drunk]. And the drinking bowl with which they became [drunk] was very small: the little black bowl. Some drank three bowls, some four bowls, some five bowls. This was sufficient to drink in order for the old men, the old women to become [drunk]. And that which they drank was yellow pulque, honeyed pulque.

And when the sun went hanging low, then they bathed the woman; they washed her hair with soap; they pasted her, arm and leg with red feathers, and bedizened [decorated] her face with pyrites. But if one was still somewhat a girl, they bedizened her face with yellow. And when preparations had been completed, then they placed her before the hearth upon a reed mat. Thereupon the [youth's] old men addressed her, greeted her, animated her.

They said to her: "O my daughter, thou art here. For thy sake thy mothers, thy fathers have become old men, old women. Now thou approachest the old women; already thou commencest the life of an old woman. Forever now leave childishness, girlishness; no longer art thou to be like a child, no longer art thou to be like a girl. . . . By night look to, take care of sweeping, the laying of the fire. Arise in the deep of night. Do not embarrass us; do not reject us as old men, do not reject thy mothers as old women. And perchance thy grandfathers, thy grandmothers still acknowledge thee, for already they have gone beyond; already the lord of the near, of the nigh, hath hidden them.

Thou poor one, animate thyself, for already thou forever abandonest thy mother. No longer art thou to incline thy heart; no longer art thou to recognize thy mother, thy father, for thou abandonest them completely. Pay close attention. O my daughter."

Then the woman replied. She wept much; she was saddened. She said [to the one who had spoken]: "My lord, precious persons, ye have shown me favor, ye have inclined your hearts. I shall impose sickness upon you. I shall visit you with sickness and pestilence. Here I have enriched myself; I have prospered by your motherhood, your fatherhood. Ye have inclined your hearts, precious persons."

And when the day had ended, when there was yet a little sun, then older relatives of the youth came to take the daughter-in-law. All of them, were old women. When they had come to enter [the bride's house], then they said: "We shall cause you to be frightened, for we have come to take our daughter. May she undertake the journey."

Thereupon [the relatives of the maiden] broke up; there was agitation. And a woman whose task it was, one already strong, was to bear her upon her back. Then she took a black manta by the corners. The daughter-in-law knelt upon it, whereupon [the woman] took her upon her back. Then the torches were lighted to show that already she was borne to her man's place. They went ordered in two rows, one on each side, as they provided her with light. And all the woman's kinsmen went in concourse about her; they went surrounding her; it was as if the earth rumbled behind her. And as they accompanied her, it was as if all eyes were fixed upon her; all the people looked at her.

And some said to their daughters: "Oh, blessed is the maiden! Open thy miserable eyes. Thou canst not reflect. Thou art lazy in hearing stern words; thou art perverse in accepting the exhortations, the indoctrination, the responsibility. Blessed is this woman, for she is observant, she is reared, she understandeth; she does not dishonor, doth not reject her mothers, her fathers as aged."

And when this was done, when they had gone to take her to the home of the man, then they placed her before the hearth. And when the two were together, they placed the woman to the left, and they placed the man to the right of the woman. And the mother of the man then went to give gifts to her daughter-in-law. She placed the shift on her, but her skirt she placed before her. And the mother of the woman then also went to give gifts. She tied a cape on [the man], but his breech clout she placed before him.

And the elderly matchmakers then tied them together. They took the corner of the man's cape; also they drew up the woman's shift; then they tied these together. And the man's mother then went to wash her daughter-in-law's mouth. Then she set out tamales in a wooden bowl, and sauce, [called] *tlatonilli,* which went in a polished sauce bowl. Then she fed her four mouthfuls. The woman took the lead in eating four mouthfuls; thereafter she also fed the man four mouthfuls. Then the elderly female matchmakers stood them up, introduced them into a chamber, put them to bed, they shut them in. When the elderly matchmakers had shut them in, they came out, and [these] old women remained there; they remained guarding them, remained becoming [drunk]. They went to their respective homes; they just awaited the dawn there.

77 The Iroquois Confederacy

Daniel K. Richter. *The Ordeal of the Longhouse: The Peoples of the Iroquois League in the Era of European Colonization.* Durham, N.C.: University of North Carolina Press, 1992. 31–6.

The following selection discusses the founding and functioning of the Iroquois confederacy, a highly successful political and military alliance between five, later six, nations, in present-day Eastern Canada and New York state. The roots of the confederacy lay in the late fourteenth century, and originally formed around a doctrine of peace. However, by the time of European arrival, the League had unleashed a series of military campaigns throughout the northeast.

In contrast to European societies, indigenous nations did not attempt to regulate the behavior of their own members by the use of force or its threat. Instead, leaders relied on persuasion and negotiation, and class based on the unequal distribution of goods did not exist. However, enemies were given no quarter, partly as a means to strengthen and to unify the community.

This warfare on a massive scale had a great impact on the region through the seventeenth century, resulting in famine and large-scale migrations as peoples dispersed, fled, and reformed into new units. As warfare took its toll on the populations of the Six Nations, mechanisms for adopting new members into the group, at the behest of women, became increasingly important for the survival of the groups. The Six Nations still exist today, in what is now Ontario, Quebec, and New York state.

Appropriately, the paradox of war and peace pervades Iroquois traditions about the League's founding. [D]etails vary in the many versions of the tradition . . . most variants agree, however, that the events described took place in a period of incessant warfare among the peoples of the Five Nations. "Everywhere there was peril and everywhere mourning," observes one version. "Feuds with outer nations, feuds with brother nations, feuds of sister towns and feuds of families and of clans made every warrior a stealthy man who liked to kill." The continual cycle of warfare and death produced particular pain for a man called Hiawatha. The demise of all his daughters in rapid succession robbed him of his reason; in his rage and depression he wandered off into the forest, where he finally encountered a being of supernatural origins named Deganawidah, the Peacemaker. Born, like the principal figures in the cosmogonic Myth, of a virgin, the peacemaker—who was perhaps a reincarnation of the Good Twin—taught Hiawatha rituals, removed grief, and eased the mind. Offering strings of the shell beads called wampum [a form of currency], he spoke Words of Condolence: the first dried Hiawatha's weeping eyes, the second opened his ears, the third unstopped his throat, and so on until his sorrow was relieved and his reason restored. These Condolence ceremonies were at the core of a new gospel, the Good News of Peace and Power, that would make war unnecessary. "When men accept it," the Peacemaker said of his teachings, "they will stop killing, and bloodshed will cease from the land."

To begin to appreciate the meaning of the Good News . . . one must first probe the role warfare played in their culture . . . "fundamental laws" defined a cultural pattern known as the "mourning war," which the people of the Five Nations shared with many of their native neighbors. Through that pattern of intersocietal violence, Iroquois sought assurance of social continuity and consolation upon the deaths of loved ones.

The connection between war and mourning rested on beliefs about the spiritual power that animated all things. Because an individual's death diminished the collective power of a lineage, clan and village, Iroquois families conducted "Requickening" ceremonies in which the deceased's name, and with it the social role and duties it represented, was transferred to a successor. Such rites filled vacant positions in lineages and villages both literally and symbolically: they assured survivors that the social function and spiritual potency embodied in the departed's name had not disappeared and that the community would endure. In

Requickenings, people of high status were usually replaced from within the lineage, clan, or village, but at some point lower in the social scale an external source of surrogates inevitably became necessary. Here warfare made its contribution, for those adopted . . . were often captives taken in battle.

[M]ourners' emotions were directed into ritualized channels. Members of the deceased's household, "after having the hair cut, smearing the face with earth or charcoal and gotten themselves up in the most frightful negligence," embarked on ten days of "deep mourning," during which they were excused from every duty of civility and courtesy. For the next year the survivors engaged in less intense formalized grieving, beginning to resume their daily habits but continuing to disregard their personal appearance and many social amenities. [T]he principles of interclan reciprocity required members of another kin group to "cover" the grief of the bereaved by conducting funeral rituals, providing feasts, and bestowing gifts—including the special variety of Condolence present often misleadingly described as blood payments. . . . In addition to the symbolic acts of communal unity and spiritual power these acts . . . were designed to cleanse sorrowing hearts and to ease the survivors' return to normal life.

But if the grief of the bereaved remained unassuaged, women of the mourning household could demand the ultimate socially sanctioned release for their violent impulses: a raid to seek captives who, it was hoped, would ease their pain. The target of a mourning-war campaign was usually a people traditionally defined as enemies. . . . Members of the deceased person's household, lost in grief . . . did not ordinarily participate in such a raid; instead, young men who were related by marriage to the female survivors of the deceased but who lived in other longhouses were obliged to form a war party or face the women's public accusations of cowardice. . . .

On occasion, grieving women or male leaders of the village might request that noted chiefs organize massive efforts involving warriors from several villages in or outside the League. . . . Such large-scale campaigns seem frequently to have culminated in carefully planned, relatively bloodless, largely ceremonial confrontations between massed forces protected by wooden body armor and bedecked in elaborate headdresses.

Large or small, the battles usually ended with the taking of a few captives by one side or the other. When the victors returned home, village leaders apportioned the prisoners to grieving lineages, whose elder women then chose either to adopt or to execute them. The matrons' decision . . . apparently depended on the depth of the households' grief and the initial impression the captives made. . . . The lives of women and children were much more likely to be spared than those of adult males. But in the end rational considerations seem to have mixed with an emotional calculus of whether the family's spiritual and temporal power would be better replenished by the literal replacement of the deceased—with all the material benefits of their labor and potential marital connections—or by a communal ritual of execution. The two choices seem to have been alternate forms of adoption, of acquiring the power the prisoners represented.

Thus a captive slated for execution was nonetheless adopted into a family and subsequently addressed appropriately as "uncle" or "nephew." During the next few days the doomed man, his status marked by a distinctive red and black pattern of facial paint, gave a death feast, where his executioners saluted him and allowed him to recite his war honors. Then . . . his captors tied him with a short rope to a stake, and villagers of both sexes and all ages took turns wielding firebrands . . . to burn him systematically from the feet up. . . . The victim was expected to endure his sufferings stoically . . . but this seems to have been ideal rather than typical behavior. Before the prisoner expired, someone scalped him, another threw hot sand on his exposed skull, and finally a knife to his chest or a hatchet to his neck ended his torments. Then women disarticulated the corpse and threw it into cooking kettles, from which the whole village feasted[;] . . . this meal carried great religious significance that probably in some way symbolized a complex absorption of the captive's spiritual power. . . .

The collective nature of these rites of execution suggests that . . . all villagers who joined in the rituals were able to participate directly in the defeat of their foes. Warfare thus promoted group cohesion and dramatized Iroquois superiority over their enemies. At the same time, youths learned valuable lessons in the way to behave bravely should they ever be captured. And the raiders who brought home captives profited as well. . . . Participation in a war party was a benchmark episode in an Iroquois youth's development and later success in battle increased the young man's stature among his kin and fellow villagers while raising his prospects for an advantageous marriage.

78 Life and Labor in Japan

Mary Elizabeth Berry. *The Culture of Civil War in Kyoto.*
Berkeley, Calif.: University of California Press, 1994. 212–215.

The following discussion describes daily life and community organization in Kyoto, Japan, in the fifteenth century. It focuses on local organizations called blocks, a two-sided rectangle of adjacent properties that were the basic neighborhood unit. As the reading below discusses, as commoners came to own more land, businesses, and houses in their block, they gradually developed a sense of ownership of their block. By the late fifteenth century, this new confidence resulted in an assertiveness of the block's interests against those of traditional elites, and a cohesive response in the face of calamities and controversies such as crime, natural disasters, and resource allocation.

The more distant origins of the block lie sometime before the fifteenth century, when the street was reconceived as a binding agent rather than a boundary. In the classical and early medieval capital, land was allocated and administered in units framed, or set off, by the surrounding roadways. The increasing shift in orientation toward the street and its facing properties, apparent by the early fifteenth century, doubtless reflected a prior shift from a manorial to a more commercial attitude toward space; urban property that had once served as . . . residential lots for landed proprietors and their satellites had become . . . rental sites for craftspeople and merchants making the transition from household service for the elite to professional status in the market place. As the arteries of their trade, streets came to link the tradespeople who lined them and pushed into them with open frontages and portable displays.

The notion of blocks as units . . . is conveyed by the naming of these units as separate locales. . . . Some names derived from local landmarks, typically shrines and temples or natural features; others derived from notable local employments, and still others from popular deities or saintly figures. . . .

• • •

Coincident with a greater security of land tenure among commoners, the naming of blocks also coincided with the accelerating street actions that I have chronicled before. As if creating a public space that could be occupied and altered by persons without title or office, townspeople took to the streets after 1480 to resist invasions of rural debtors and to avenge the injuries of officials and criminals. . . . The conduct of townspeople . . . indicates a widening appropriation of physical places and a presumption that commoners had a role to play in urban politics. That role—a mixture of self-defense, self-redress, and alternating defiance of and alliance with the authorities—took changing and sometimes contradictory directions. Yet one constant in the activism of townspeople was its association with physical space.

GO-HOKOIN-KI. 1495, 10TH MONTH, 22D DAY

I hear that several score participants in the debtors' uprising were killed. . . . They say the people of the blocks. . . and the brokers fought together against them.

TOJI HYAKUGO MONJO. 1516, 9TH MONTH, 21ST DAY

In the matter of the recent dispute over water use in the area of Shichijo and Suzaku: Administrators of Tojiin assert that, since the time of the original quarrel at the water source, Toji has again gathered forces and sent them there . . . they asserted: "Matters did come to violence during the dispute over water. But when we attacked the residents of Suzaku, people from the surrounding areas . . . joined forces with both sides, faced off against each other, and joined the battle."

TOKITSUGU KYO-KI. 1529, 1ST MONTH, 10TH AND 11TH DAYS

Asserting that they were to collect a commissariat tax, two [military deputies] burst into the property of Lord Ichijo and, we heard, took his wife and children hostage. . . . Again the Kodo bell sounded. [People of] the blocks rose up . . . and surrounded [Lord Ichijo's residence].

TOKITSUGU KYO-KI. 11TH MONTH, 29TH DAY, AND 12TH MONTH, 1ST DAY

This morning about ten men from the gang of Awa invaded the house of the tatami maker of this neighborhood. The people of northern Kyoto, all the way from Nijo avenue, rose up and surrounded them with two or three thousand persons. . . . Again, in later afternoon they invaded [a courtier's] house. . . . And again, the people of the various blocks rose up and surrounded them, shouting and crying. . . . People here are building fortified gates for the block and hence asked me for bamboo. I gave them ten stalks. . . . I also sent over sake to the [people of the] block.

• • •

The actions described in these documents were communal rather than solitary; they were conducted openly and violently, rather than privately and litigiously; and they drew together actors linked primarily by geography—by their blocks, residences, neighboring places, water sources, and sectors of the city—rather than by their employments, religion, proprietary attachments or status. . . . The streets became the battleground of elemental fights for physical security against invaders. On occasion, they also became the arena for battles against tax collectors and police. Although tax problems typically inspire petitions or the withholding of dues by the aggrieved groups, belligerent officials could galvanize substantial bodies united only by proximity. What we might begin to think of as "neighborhoods" closed ranks against assault.

79 Great Zimbabwe

P. S. Garlake. *Great Zimbabwe.* London: Thames and Hudson, 1973. 193–199.

Between the thirteenth and fifteenth centuries, Great Zimbabwe was an important center for trade and craft production in southern Africa. Located on a plateau north of the Lundi River, the complex of stone structures and enclosures housed between 1000 and 2500 adults and their families. The site includes several structures, including the Elliptical Building with walls up to 17 feet thick and 32 feet high. The archaeological evidence demonstrates that Great Zimbabwe was an important site in the local economy: among the articles discovered at the site were soapstone figurines and pottery, as well as copper and gold jewelry. Some of the jewelry—glass beads from Persia and celadon pottery from China—prove that Great Zimbabwe played an important role connecting southern Africa to the Indian Ocean seafaring trades.

Yet despite overwhelming evidence to the contrary, European visitors to the site for centuries maintained that it could not have been built by Africans. Local oral traditions were dismissed. The obvious use of local building materials in the construction of Great Zimbabwe was ignored. Europeans proclaimed that the site must have been a far-flung outpost of Egypt, or

Figure 13.1
Elliptical Building at Great Zimbabwe.

perhaps, others speculated, it had been built by European craftsmen. Even the pioneering work of prominent archaeologist Gertrude Caton-Thompson in the 1930s, work that declared Great Zimbabwe to have "indigenous" origins, was dismissed. In the excerpt below, Peter Garlake (also an archaeologist) summarizes what is known about Great Zimbabwe's past.

The new wealth that came to Great Zimbabwe [from the gold trade] was reflected in almost every aspect of life. The Valley was fully settled and the first sections of the Elliptical Building erected. The [site] contained many objects that illustrated the new affluence. Gold, copper and bronze ornaments occurred in quantity, the products of skilled craftsmen working in established patterns. Spinning and weaving were introduced: complicated crafts that point to sufficiently close contacts with artisans from the Indian Ocean towns to enable people to learn [these] new skills. Near Eastern ceramics and glass vessels were imported and many more glass beads. Prosperity must have quickened the rate of change and development in all spheres [of life]. Thus the period saw increasing refinements in the indigenous ceramics, masonry skills and architectural style. . . . Building [at Great Zimbabwe] reached its culmination with the erection of the enormous Great Outer Wall and the Conical Tower.

One wonders how Great Zimbabwe managed to get control of trade so completely as to establish a virtual monopoly, for no other site in Rhodesia [now Zimbabwe] has yielded more than a minute proportion of the imports at Great Zimbabwe. . . . One can . . . safely assume that the same exchange network was used [later by the Mwene Mutapa kingdom] and that it was developed by the Great Zimbabwe people: one in which tribute in the form of gold, ivory, iron and cloth was brought in from subjects or client rulers to the central court and imported luxuries flowed out along the same channels. This trade affected the general populace little. It was however sufficient to attract and hold a large number of people at Great Zimbabwe itself. Wealth must have reached them directly or indirectly as a reward for their labor not only as food producers but in quarrying and transporting stones to the Valley and building the massive walls of the Elliptical Building. These structures represent in a different and more permanent medium the luxury and ostentation of the court's dress and adornments. They are scarcely utilitarian and their only apparent function was to display and thus reinforce the prestige of the court and perhaps the power of the spirits or god. . . .

Trade with neighboring people was less dramatic but probably more widespread and socially more significant. There is enough evidence for one to envisage trade in copper and perhaps salt and cotton cloth with the communities which grew up in the northwest of Mashonaland and beside the Zambezi river during the fourteenth century, typified by Ingombe Illede. This may well have been carried by Swahili middlemen who were also bringing their own goods from the coast up the Zambezi River valley to Great Zimbabwe. One advantage of this arrangement may have been that, as in later centuries, alien traders may have been assured of safe conduct as long as they accepted overall control by the ruler. On the return journey they would have carried, as well as their own purchases, the gold jewelry and perhaps the ironwork produced at Great Zimbabwe back to the Ingombe Ilede people. . . .

. . .

In the early fifteenth century Great Zimbabwe reached its climax. The Elliptical Building was completed. It contained the major religious focus, the Conical Tower and the platforms and monoliths around it. Behind the huge enclosing wall the ruler and his immediate circle also had their dwellings. Their mode of life did not differ from that of the rest of the court and at this time other members of the court, priests, administrators and relatives of the ruler, had sufficient resources to build enclosures for themselves in the Valley outside of the Elliptical Building, smaller but essentially little different from it in their layout, architectural elements or contents. . . .

By mid-century, Great Zimbabwe was the center of a considerable population directly dependent on the ruler's court. Its economy was dominated by the coastal trade but this was such that it did not encourage changes in the basic mode of life. The general populace was still dependent on subsistence agriculture and there was little incentive for it to develop new crafts or industries or to change its basic economy or trading pattern. For everyone, it seemed life could continue along the same paths towards enrichment of the few and expenditure on grandiose but socially unnecessary displays channelling some benefits to a wider circle. The society was mature and set in its ways. It had successfully adapted to the coastal trade and absorbed its influences so that they caused the minimal social disruption but it was not open to change and unable to envisage or adopt new economic strategies. What was happening seemed good for everyone and there was no need to look ahead at the remote consequences. But change was soon to be forced on it. However good the climate and rich the natural resources, the unnaturally large population, concentrated in one spot and tied to it by the very large size and splendor of the buildings, would sooner or later exhaust the grazing, the fertility of the soil, the timber available for building and firewood and any game that might have provided supplementary meat. The expansion of Great Zimbabwe's authority over the plateau, with settlements scattered over a wide area would not only have demonstrated that many other parts of the country were as attractive as Great Zimbabwe but would have enabled dispersal, should it be necessary, to take place with the minimum of uncertainty or pioneering effort. With considerable territory now under its control, particularly to the north and west, Great Zimbabwe may also have appeared simply too far from the center of things and unable to control any tendencies towards independent action or self-aggrandizement by provincial rulers. The Ingombe Ilede communities, prospering in the fifteenth century with their direct access to the Zambezi River and their control of the copper ores of Urungwe, may have posed a major threat to Great Zimbabwe's trade monopolies. Altogether Great Zimbabwe had become an unwieldy community threatened by the growing strength of groups that its very prosperity brought into being. It would have needed little to cause a major social disruption at the center: a minor failure of crops or rainfall or a temporary interruption of trade would have had effects and ramifications out of all proportion to the cause. The resulting strains could easily become too great for this particular community to adapt to. Dispersal and migration would have seemed obvious and not unattractive answers.

About the mid-fifteenth century this came about. Traditional accounts speak of "a severe shortage of salt" at the Mbire capital. Although salt was an essential item of the diet, a commodity greatly valued and extensively traded, one can see the shortage in this context as symbolic of both a depletion of food supplies and a disruption of trade. . . . [This] dispersed the population of Great Zimbabwe and removed the center of political and economic control from it. Without these it was inevitable that the whole fabric of society would rapidly crumble.

80 The Ottoman Empire Captures Constantinople

Kritovoulos. *History of Mehmed the Conqueror.* Translated by Charles T. Riggs. Princeton, N.J.: Princeton University Press, 1954. 60–73.

The fall of Constantinople in 1453 marked the end of the Byzantine empire. Within Europe, a schism over the interpretation of Christian texts, and the practice of the Christian religion, had severed the ties between the Western Roman Catholic church, and the Eastern Orthodox (Byzantine) church. This schism began as early as the fourth century CE, but accelerated in the eleventh century. In fact, one of the western "Crusades" to the Holy Land had actually attacked Byzantium in the thirteenth century. In 1453, the leader of the Seljuk Turks, Mehmed, laid siege to the city for two months and finally conquered it. Thus the center of the Eastern Empire was brought within the sphere of the Islamic Ottoman Empire. The following account is taken from the contemporary chronicle of Kritovoulos, a Greek adviser in Mehmed's court.

ADDRESS OF THE SULTAN MEHMED BEFORE THE BATTLE

"My friends and my comrades in the present struggle! I have called you together here, not because I would accuse you of any laziness or carelessness in this business, nor try to make you more eager in the present struggle. For a long time past I have noted some of you showing such zeal and earnestness for the work that you would willingly undergo everything necessary rather than leave here without [conquering the city], and others of you not only zealous themselves but even inciting the rest of you with all their might to redouble their efforts.

So it is not for this that I have called you together, but simply in order to remind you, first of all, that whatever you have at present you have attained, not by sloth and carelessness, but by hard work and with great struggles and dangers together with us, and these things are yours as the rewards of your own valor and manliness rather than as gifts of fortune. And secondly, as to the rewards now put before you here, I wish to show you how many and how great they are and what great glory and honor accompany the winning. And I also wish that you may know well how to carry on the struggle for the very highest rewards.

First, then, there is great wealth of all sorts in this city [Constantinople], some in the royal palaces and some in the houses of the mighty, some in the homes of the common people and still other, finer and more abundant, laid up in the churches as votive offerings and treasures of all sorts, constructed of gold and silver and precious stones and costly pearls. Also there is countless wealth of magnificent furniture, without reckoning all the other articles and furnishings of the houses. Of all of these, you will be the masters!

Then too, there are very many noble and distinguished men, some of whom will be your slaves, and the rest will be put up for sale; also very many and very beautiful women, young and good-looking, and virgins lovely for marriage, noble, and of noble families, and even till now unseen by masculine eyes, some of them, evidently intended for the weddings of great men. Of these, some will be your wives for you, while others will do for servants, and others you can sell. So you will gain in many ways, in enjoyment, and service, and wealth.

And you will have boys, too, very many and very beautiful and of noble families.

Further, you will enjoy the beauty of the churches and public buildings and splendid houses and gardens, and many such things, suited to look at and enjoy and take pleasure in and profit by. But I must waste time listing all these. A great and populous city, the capital of the ancient Romans, which has attained the very pinnacle of good fortune and luck and glory, being indeed the head of the whole inhabited globe—I give it now to you for spoil and plunder—unlimited wealth, men, women, children, all other adornments and arrangements. All these you will enjoy as if at a brilliant banquet, and will be happy with them yourselves and will leave very great wealth to your children.

And the greatest of all this, that you will capture a city whose renown has gone out to all parts of the world. It is evident that to whatever extent the leadership and glory of this city has spread, to a like extent the renown of your valor and bravery will spread for having captured by assault a city such as this. But think: what deed more brilliant, what greater enjoyment, or what inheritance of wealth better than that presented to you, along with honor and glory!

And, best of all, we shall demolish a city that has been hostile to us from the beginning and is constantly growing at our expense and in every way plotting against our rule. So for the future we shall be sure of guarding our present belongings and shall live in complete and assured peace, after getting rid of our neighboring enemies. We shall also open the way to further conquest. . . ."

• • •

THE BATTLE

Then the Sultan mounted his horse and went around to all the other divisions, reviewing them and giving his orders to all in general and each in particular. . . .

Now the Romans, seeing the [Ottoman] army so quiet and more tranquil than usual, marveled at the fact and ventured on various explanations and guesses. Some—not judging it [correctly]—believed that it was a preparation for battle and an alert, things which they had been expecting in the near future. So they passed the word along and then went in silence to their own divisions and made all sorts of preparations.

The hour was already advanced, the day was declining and near evening, and the sun was at the Ottoman's backs but shining in the faces of their enemies. This was just as the Sultan had wished; accordingly he gave the order first for the trumpets to sound the battle-signal, and the other instruments, the pipes and flutes and cymbals too, as loud as they could. . . .

To begin, the archers and slingers and those in charge of the cannon given them, advanced against the wall [of the city] slowly and gradually. When they got within bowshot, they halted to fight. And first they exchanged fire with the heavier weapons, with arrows from the archers, stones from the slingers, and iron and leaden balls from the cannons and muskets. Then, as they closed with battleaxes and javelins and spears, hurling them at each other and being hurled pitilessly in rage and fierce anger. On both sides there was loud shouting and blasphemy and cursing. Many on each side were wounded, and not a few died. This kept up till sunset, a space of about two or three hours. . . .

• • •

But the Romans on their part met them stubbornly and repulsed them brilliantly. They fought bravely and proved superior to the Ottomans in battle. Indeed they showed that they were heroes, for not a one of all the things that occurred could deter them: neither the hunger attacking them, nor sleeplessness, nor continuous and ceaseless fighting, nor wounds and slaughter, nor the death of relatives before their very eyes, nor any of the other fearful things could make them give in, or diminish their previous zeal and determination. . . .

Sultan Mehmed saw that the attacking divisions were very much worn out by the battle and had not made any progress worth mentioning, and that the Romans and Italians were not only fighting stoutly but were prevailing in the battle. He was very indignant at this, considering that it ought not to be endured any longer. Immediately he brought up the divisions which he had been reserving for later on, men who were extremely well armed, daring and brave, and far in advance of the rest in experience and valor. They were the elite of the army: heavy infantry, bowmen, and lancers, and his own bodyguard, and along with them those of the division called Yenitsari [Janissaries].

Calling to them and urging them to prove themselves now as heroes, he led the attack against the wall, himself at the head until they reached the moat. . . . It was a hand-to-hand encounter, and [the Romans] stopped the attackers and prevented them from getting inside the palisade. There was much shouting on both sides—the mingled sounds of blasphemy, insults, threats, attackers, defenders, shooters, those shot at, killers and dying, of those who in anger and wrath did all sorts of terrible things. And it was a sight to see there: a hard fight going on hand-to-hand with great determination and for the greatest rewards, heroes fighting valiantly, the one party struggling with all their might to force back the defenders, get possession of the wall, enter the City, and fall upon the children and women and the treasures, the other party bravely agonizing to drive them off and guard their possessions, even if they were not to succeed in prevailing and in keeping them.

Instead, the hapless Romans were destined finally to be brought under the yoke of servitude and to suffer its horrors. For although they battled bravely, and though they lacked nothing of the willingness and daring in the contest, [Giovanni Longo di Giustinianni], an Italian military leader defending Constantinople received a mortal wound in the breast from an arrow fired by a crossbow. . . . All who were with him were scattered, being upset by their loss. They abandoned the palisade and wall where they had been fighting, and thought of only one thing— how they could carry him on to the galleons and get away safe themselves. . . .

Sultan Mehmed, who happened to be fighting quite near by, saw that the palisade and the other part of the wall that had been destroyed were now empty of men and deserted by the defenders. He noted that men were slipping away secretly and that those who remained were fighting feebly because they were so few. Realizing from this that the defenders had fled and the wall was deserted, he shouted out, "Friends, we have the City! We have it! They are already fleeing from us! They can't stand it any longer! The wall is bare of defenders! It needs just a little more effort and the City is taken! Don't weaken, but on with the work with all your might, and be men and I am with you!". . . .

81 The Early Atlantic World

John Thornton. *Africa and Africans in the Making of the Atlantic World, 1400–1680.* Cambridge, England: Cambridge University Press, 1992. 13, 15–16, 21, 36–38.

Before the fifteenth century, maritime trade between Europe and Africa
was limited by the winds and currents of the Atlantic ocean. Despite the
impressive volume of overland trade between the west African coast and the
Mediterranean, there was no maritime trade between these regions because
ships were unable to sail northward from the western African coast. In the
selection following, historian John Thornton discusses how European sailors
acquired the knowledge to sail down the African coast, and what motivation
they had for doing so. Thornton discusses the limits of European seapower as
well: although European sailors might have desired to seize African coastal
towns, indigenous maritime vessels were (at first) capable of repelling such
attacks and ensuring African control of the coastline and principal rivers.

. . . [O]ne must not simply look at a map of the Atlantic and imagine that it was
equally penetrable and that those who sailed it had equal access to all parts of the [At-
lantic] zone. In many ways, in the days of wooden sailing ships, the ocean was as much
channeled as were rivers, whose direction of flow is clearly defined. No sailor could
ignore the patterns of prevailing winds and currents on the ocean. This was crucial for
the development of Atlantic navigation, for the winds and currents created barriers to
traffic for thousands of years. They limited contact between the Mediterranean and
Africa for a very long time and thwarted whatever potential Africans might have had
for effective navigation into the Atlantic beyond their coastal waters, just as it would
act as a brake on [indigenous] American ventures to Africa and Europe.

Raymond Mauny has shown that the constant north-to-south flow of the Canary
Current along the Saharan coast made it possible for ships from the Mediterranean
to sail southward as far as West Africa but prevented a return voyage. For Mediterranean sailors, Cape Bojador, just south of the Canary Islands, represented a point
of no return, and even if voyages, intentional and unintentional, went beyond it, they
did not pioneer any route with practical significance. Arabic accounts cite several
voyages made by accident beyond this point. Al-Idrisi (1154) cites one that left from
Lisbon, ibn Sa'id heard from a Moroccan traveler named Ibn Fatima of a similar
voyage sometime before 1270, and al-'Umari heard of another from Almeira in
Spain made by Muhammad b. Raghanuh in the early fourteenth century—all were
forced to return to the Mediterranean area by overland routes. It was only in the fifteenth century, and then using routes leading back through the Canaries, Madeira,
and the Azores and risking a high-seas voyage, that Europeans were able to finally
conquer the difficulties of the Bojador on a regular basis.

If the problems with the winds and currents off the Saharan coast checked
Mediterraneans from entering the African portion of the Atlantic, a similar problem hampered African navigators. Of course, Africans would have been just as
interested in going to North Africa and Iberia by sea as the Mediterranean people
were interested in reaching Africa, given the knowledge that each area had of the
other through the overland trade, but the constant current that prevented return
trips to the Mediterranean also frustrated African efforts to go to the Mediterranean from the very start. The extent of northward sailing by African vessels
seems to have been the saltworks of Ijil on the Mauretanian coast, at least according to al-Idrisi's twelfth-century account. . . .

• • •

Europeans' experience with waterborne travel was probably the most signifi-cant factor in allowing them to be the ones who finally conquered the Atlantic. The difficulties of tackling South Atlantic navigation may explain why Africans, for their part, seem to have focused their boat-building talents on craft designed for coastal and [river] navigation and as a result had engaged in little deliberate oceanic navi-gation, leaving even fairly close islands, such as the Cape Verdes and São Tomé, uncolonized and uninhabited. Indeed, they had even eschewed long-range naviga-tion in the Gulf of Guinea . . . , which might have proved economically feasible, though hampered by the same problems of currents that prevented transatlantic navigation. . . .

• • •

Not only did the needs of [the] seaborne trade between the Mediterranean and northern Europe serve as a stimulus to Iberian shipbuilding and interest in interregional trade, but the fairly large number of ships involved increased the potential for accidental voyages of discovery. The career of Lanzaroto Malocello is a case in point. Malocello was a Genoese merchant who had commercial connec-tions with Cherbourg in northern France and Ceuta in Morocco and thus had fre-quent recourse to travel in the Atlantic both north and south of Gibraltar. On one of these voyages he discovered (or rediscovered, for they were known in Classical times), probably by accident, the Canaries in about 1312. The Canaries were the first Atlantic islands rediscovered by Europeans, and their colonization, by Malo-cello around 1335, represented an early and important step into the Atlantic.

In addition to multiplying the opportunities for accidental voyages of discov-ery, maritime travel between the Mediterranean and North Atlantic, especially because it involved bulk shipping, allowed the diffusion of shipbuilding tech-niques. Thus, the sturdy round ships of the North Sea and Baltic were blended with the long an maneuverable galleys of the Mediterranean. This eventually resulted in the creation of ships capable of carrying more cargo and sailing under a wider variety of conditions than could be found in either the Mediterranean or the North Atlantic. To these discoveries were added techniques in sailing and naviga-tion borrowed from the Moslem world, with which the Genoese and Iberians had constant commerce.

Possessing the means to make oceanic voyages and to discover new lands did not necessarily mean that extensive ocean travel or exploration would be under-taken, however. There also had to be a reasonable set of motives, and financial backers had to have some confidence that such voyages would be worth the con-siderable risks that their undertaking entailed. . . .

• • •

Of all the economic possibilities that might provide motives for Atlantic navi-gation, however, the prospect of a short route to the West African goldfields seems the most likely. The Indies, after all, were far away in anyone's conception of world geography, whereas West Africa, known to be wealthy in gold, was much closer and clearly accessible by a sea route. West Africa had been a source of gold for Mediterranean countries for centuries, perhaps since Byzantine times. Moslem writers since the ninth century at least were aware of the gold-producing areas, and a steady stream of Arabic-language descriptions of West Africa resulted, including one made famous by the famed North African al-Idrisi for the Christian king Roger

II of Sicily in 1154. These were joined by Christian accounts, especially those generated by the Catalan and Italian merchant communities of North Africa, who had been dealing in the gold (called the "gold of Palolus" in these sources) since the twelfth century.

A sea route to the goldfields seemed relatively practical, because it did not involve the circumnavigation of Africa. Many maps of the period show the "River of Gold" (probably the Senegal [River]) and, according to the legend on the map of Mecia de Villadestes (1413), where one could "obtain the gold of Palolus." Although the actual field lay upstream, the "mouth of the river is large and deep enough for the biggest ship in the river." Christians believed that Moslems regularly sailed to the river. . . .

• • •

Scholars have argued that this domination of the seas gave Europeans insuperable political and commercial advantages over local people in Africa and the Americas. This claim, although possessing some merit, overlooks the complexity of the situation, especially on the coasts of the continents, and when studied in detail is not as persuasive as it first appears. Although Europeans did make some conquests in both Africa and the Americas, it was not naval power that secured the conquests. Their failure to dominate local commerce or overwhelm coastal societies, most pronounced in Africa but also in the case in some parts of the Americas, means that we must amplify our estimation of the role played by these societies in the shaping of the Atlantic world. Domination of the high-seas commerce is significant, to be sure, but perhaps not as significant as domination of the mainlands.

. . . Europeans clearly hoped that their maritime abilities would give them military advantages that would result in large profits and perhaps conquests. They were prepared to take over territory and enslave people, and their actions in the Canary Islands bore witness to that desire. However much some visitors to the Canaries might have wanted to engage in peaceful trade, it was ultimately the slave raiders and conquerors who won out. Control of the seas allowed Europeans to land freely on the islands, resupply their forces when necessary, and concentrate large forces for their final battles—and thus maritime superiority could arguably have been the cause of their success.

The earliest sailors who reached the African coast in the fifteenth century naturally hoped to continue this tradition, as apparently did the Spanish sailors who began the conquest of the larger Caribbean islands in the late fifteenth and early sixteenth centuries. But in Africa at least, their confident approach was rebuffed. Unlike the Canarians, who possessed no boats at all, the West Africans had a well-developed specialized maritime culture that was fully capable of protecting its own waters.

One of the first expeditions to the Senegal River, led by Lançarote de Lagos in 1444, brutally seized the residents of several off-shore islands. The inhabitants, although they managed to inflict some casualties, had little other recourse than to try to flee to areas of more difficult access. Other expeditions that followed did more or less the same, but it was not long before African naval forces were alerted to the new dangers, and the Portuguese ships began to meet strong and effective resistance. For example, in 1446 a ship under Nuno Tristão attempting to land an armed force in the Senegambian region was attacked by African vessels, and the Africans succeeded in killing nearly all the raiders. Likewise, in 1447 Valarte, a Danish sailor in Portuguese service, was killed along with most of his crew when local craft attacked him near the island of Gorée.

Although African vessels were not designed for high-seas navigation, they were capable of repelling attack on the coast. They were specialized craft, designed specifically for the navigational problems of the west African coast and the associated river systems. From the Angolan coast up to Senegal, African military and commercial craft tended to be built similarly. Generally, they were carved from single logs of tropical trees and only occasionally had their sides built up. Consequently, they tended to be long and very low in the water. They were almost always powered by oars or paddles and thus were maneuverable independent of the wind. They drew little water and could operate on the coast and in rivers, creeks, and inland estuaries and lagoons. Craft that were designed to carry soldiers could, according to contemporary witnesses, carry from fifty to one hundred men.

These specialized craft presented a small, fast, and difficult target for European weapons, and they carried substantial firepower in their archers and javelinmen. However, they could not go far out to sea, and the larger, high-sided Portuguese vessels were difficult for them to storm. Alvise da Mosto, a Venetian trading in Africa with a Portuguese license, records an encounter he had with an African flotilla in the Gambia in 1456. Da Mosto was mistaken, with justice, for being another raiding party from Portugal and was immediately attacked by seventeen large craft carrying about 150 armed men. They showered his ships with arrows as they approached, and da Mosto fired his artillery (bombards) at them, without, however, hitting anything. Although the attackers were temporarily stunned by this unexpected weapon, they nevertheless pressed the attack, at which point crossbowmen in the upper rigging of the Venetian ship opened fire, inflicting some casualties. Again, although impressed by the weaponry, the Africans continued fighting until da Mosto eventually made it known he did not mean to attack them, and a cease-fire ensued.

The Africans were unable, in most circumstances, to take a European ship by storm, and the Europeans had little success in their seaborne attacks on the mainland. As a result, the Europeans had to abandon the time-honored tradition of trading and raiding and substitute a relationship based more or less completely on peaceful regulated trade. . . .

82 The Portuguese on the West African Coast

The Voyages of Cadamosto and other Documents on Western Africa in the Second Half of the Fifteenth Century. Translated and edited by G.R. Crone. London: The Hakluyt Society, 1937. 17–18, 20–21, 29–30, 35–36, 58–60.

Alvise da Ca' da Mosto was born in Venice around the 1420s. He spent about ten years, from 1454 to 1464, in Portugal, and during this time accompanied several Portuguese voyages down the coast of West Africa. He later wrote of his travels. The following excerpts illustrate the nature and variety of contacts that occurred between the Portuguese crew and the West African societies that they encountered. It also illustrates the precursor of the Atlantic slave trade.

RELATIONS WITH THE AZANAGHI

These people [the Azanaghi, who lived on the northwest coast of Africa] have no knowledge of any Christians except the Portuguese, against whom they have waged war for [thirteen or] fourteen years, many of them having been taken prisoners, as I have already said, and sold into slavery. It is asserted that when for the first time they saw . . . ships . . ., they believed that they were great sea-birds with white wings, which were flying, and had come from some strange place. . . . Others again said that they were phantoms that went by night . . . because these caravels within a short space of time appeared at many places, where attacks were delivered, especially at night, by their crews. . . . Perceiving this, they said . . . , "If these be human creatures, how can they travel so great a distance in one night, a distance which we could not go in three days?". . . . And from this it may be judged how strange many of our ways appeared to them, . . .

Beyond the said mart of Edon [Oden], six days journey further inland, there is a place called Tagaza, . . . where a very great quantity of rock-salt is mined. Every year large caravans of camels belonging to the above mentioned Arabs and Azanaghi, leaving in many parties, carry it to [Timbuktu]; thence they go to Melli [Mali], the empire of the Blacks, where, so rapidly is it sold, within eight days of its arrival all is disposed of at a price of two to three hundred mitigalli [one *mithgal* equals ⅛ oz. of gold] a load, according to the quantity: then with the gold they return to their homes.

DESCRIPTION OF CABO BIANCO

You should know that the said Lord Infante of Portugal has leased this island of Argin [a Portuguese fort constructed for trade in 1448] to Christians [for ten years], so that no one can enter the bay to trade with the Arabs save those who hold the license. These have dwellings on the island and factories where they buy and sell with the said Arabs who come to the coast to trade for merchandize of various kinds, such as woollen cloths, cotton, silver and . . . cloaks, carpets, and similar articles and above all, wheat for they are always short of food. They give in exchange slaves whom the Arabs bring from the land of the Blacks, and gold [dust]. The Lord Infante therefore caused a castle to be built on the island to protect this trade for ever. For this reason, Portuguese caravels are coming and going all the year to this island.

These Arabs also have many Berber horses, which they trade, and take to the Land of the Blacks, exchanging them with the rulers for slaves. Ten or fifteen slaves are given for one of these horses, according to their quality. The Arabs likewise take articles of Moorish silk . . . silver, and other goods, obtaining in exchange any number of these slaves, and some gold. . . . As a result every year the Portuguese carry away from Argin a thousand slaves. Note that before this traffic was organized, the Portuguese caravels . . . were wont to come armed . . . and descending on the land by night, would assail the fisher villages, and so ravage the land. Thus they took of these Arabs both men and women, and carried them to Portugal for sale: behaving in a like manner along all the rest of the coast. . . .

THE KINGDOM OF SENEGAL

[T]his King is lord of a very poor people, . . . the Kingdom, also, is very small; it extends no more than two hundred miles along the coast. . . . The king lives thus: . . . each year the lords of the country . . . present him with horses . . . forage . . . cows and goats, vegetables, millet, and the like. The King supports himself by raids, which result in many slaves from his own as well as neighboring countries. He employs these slaves . . . in cultivating the land allotted to him: but he also sells many to the Azanaghi [and Arab] merchants in return for horses and other goods, and also to Christians, since they have begun to trade with these blacks.

AMONG THE JALOF, NORTHEAST OF CAPE VERDE

I . . . sailed to the country of Bodomel [Cayor]. . . . . . . at this place I made my caravel fast, in order to converse with this ruler, for certain Portuguese who had had dealings with him had informed me that he was a notable and an upright ruler, in whom one could trust, and who paid royally for what was brought to him. Since I had with me some Spanish horses, which were in great demand in the country of the Blacks, not to mention . . . woollen cloth, Moorish silk and other goods, I made up my mind to try my fortune with this lord.

. . . This lord . . . entertained me to a great feast, and after much talk I gave him my horses, and all that he wished from me, trusting to his good faith. He besought me to go inland to his house. . . . There he would reward me richly, and I might remain for some days, for he had promised me 100 slaves in return for what he had received. I gave him the horses with their harness and other goods. . . . I therefore decided to go with him, but before I left he gave me a handsome young negress, twelve years of age, saying that he gave her to me for the service of my chamber. I accepted her and sent her to the ship. My journey inland was indeed more to see interesting sights and obtain information, than to receive my dues.

ATTACK AT THE RIVER OF GAMBIA

[H]aving sailed about four miles upstream, we suddenly perceived several canoes coming up behind us . . . as fast as they were able. Seeing this, we turned on them[;] . . . without any other salute, they all threw down their oars, and began to shoot off their arrows.

Our ships, seeing the attack, at once discharged four bombards: hearing these, amazed and confounded by the roar, they threw down their bows, and . . . stood in astonishment at the sight of the shots falling into the river about them . . . taking up their bows, [they] began afresh to shoot with much ardor. . . .

. . . [Later] the negroes drew off: we, lashing our ships together by chains, dropped anchor. . . .

After much gesticulating and shouting by our interpreters one of the canoes returned within bowshot. We asked of those in it the reason for their attack upon us notwithstanding that we were men of peace, and traders in merchandize, saying that we had peaceful and friendly relations with the negroes of the Kingdom of Senega, and that we wished to be on similar terms with them, if they were willing: further, that we had come from a distant land to offer fitting gifts to their king and lord on behalf of our king of Portugal, who desired peace and friendship with them. . . . They replied that they had had news of our coming and of our trade with the negroes of Senega, who, if they sought our friendship, could not but be bad men, for they firmly believed that we Christians ate human flesh, and that we only bought negroes to eat them: that for their part they did not want our friendship on any terms, but sought to slaughter us all, and to make a gift of our possessions to their lord. . . .

At this moment the wind freshened; realizing the ill will they bore us, we made sail towards them. They, anticipating this move, scattered in all directions for the land, and thus ended our engagement with them.

83 Visual Document: Theodore de Bry's Secota (Virginia)

Europeans were fascinated with the "New World" but in an era long before the advent of television, the only visual glimpses that they could get were from artists' renditions of what they had seen in the Americas. An English painter named John White was sent to North America in the late sixteenth century to record images of indigenous people and their societies. White accompanied the English explorer Sir Walter Raleigh to British outposts on the Atlantic coastline. In Virginia, White sketched a town he called "Secota." The drawing was later reproduced by Theodore de Bry to accompany a tract published in London in 1588. What does the organization of the town tell you about the people who live in it? What sort of activities are portrayed?

DISCUSSION QUESTIONS

1. What issues seem most prevalent in the minds of people throughout the world in the fifteenth century?

2. What events foreshadowed the Columbian exchange? What similarities and differences existed between European, African, and American peoples on the eve of their encounter?

3. How would you compare Japanese urban life with daily life in the Aztec world?

4. What was the basis of people's livelihood in Great Zimbabwe? How might this society have compared with the others you have studied thus far?

5. Looking at the societies you have explored in this chapter, what features of their identities—race, gender, social standing, etc.—seem most prominent in their daily activities?

6. How would you describe the encounters between the Portuguese and West African peoples?

PART
Four

THE WORLD SHRINKS:
1450 CE to 1750 CE

Disparate societies and regions of the world were not isolated before 1450. Regional and long-distance networks of trade, cultural contacts, and religious pilgrimage existed among different societies throughout the world. In Europe, Asia, Africa and the Americas, a wide variety of societies with distinct lifestyles, cultures, and livelihoods coexisted and interacted with each other in warfare, trade, and tributary relationships, as well as religious and cultural contacts. In the "Old World" (Europe, Asia, and Africa), exchanges occurred not only within but among continents through both land and sea transportation. Similarly, societies in the Americas participated in regional and long-distance networks of trade. However, one major watershed divides the world before the late fifteenth century from the world since: the establishment of regular contact between the Americas and the "Old World" of Europe, Asia, and Africa.

The integration of the entire world had profound consequences for societies in its component parts. Regular contact between the eastern and western hemispheres facilitated exchanges of people, plants, animals, diseases, and ideas. Exchanges of plants and animals provided populations with new food resources; new diseases ravaged indigenous populations throughout the Americas and, eventually, in the Pacific, reducing them to a fraction of what they had been.

The "discovery" by Europeans that continents existed that were not mentioned in the Bible caused a profound questioning of the dominant worldview current in Europe at the time. Encounters with American societies that were organized differently, and often characterized by more equitable distributions of wealth and better standards of living for their populations, challenged European social hierarchies. A Tupí Indian from Brazil, brought to the city of Rouen in France in the mid-sixteenth century, found the great disparity of wealth visible within the city incredible, and wondered aloud why "the poor ones did not grab the fat ones by the throat." Indigenous societies in the Americas suggested alternative methods of social organization, and, in the minds of European philosophers such as Montaigne, the possibility of forging utopias.

This last, brief section of Volume 1, is continued in the first section of Volume 2. "The Changing World Balance" presents the early voyages that began to link societies and regions in unprecedented ways, and the resulting consequences. It attempts to explain why these changes occurred when and how they did. Finally, it gauges the significance of global integration for human societies since.

Chapter 14

The Changing World Balance

Global integration, the establishment of regular contact among the world's major regions, accelerated in the fifteenth century. Europeans provided the main impetus for this process, through their search for products and trade in areas beyond Europe. In the fifteenth century, Europe was still a global backwater, producing subsistence goods and raw materials such as grain, timber, and cloth. Furthermore, Europe was chronically short of precious metals. However, Europe was a peninsula surrounded by water, and elements from several maritime traditions were incorporated to make small, swift vessels that were practical for long-distance, oceanic travel. The Portuguese combined the tradition of slow, round northern European vessels (with their large carrying capacity) with swift, oar-powered galleys, adding innovations from the Islamic Indian Ocean trade, such as the triangular lateen sail.

With the expulsion of the Moors from Iberia over the course of the fourteenth (for Portugal) and fifteenth (for Spain) centuries, Spain and Portugal completed the process of consolidation of the state earlier than northern European polities. Partly because of this, they also began explorations by sea earlier than anyone else in Europe. Iberian initiatives to break into trading networks and to establish new sea routes were an attempt to bypass other networks that controlled trade. Ottoman and Arabic-speaking middlemen did not close trade to Europeans, as is often mistakenly thought; however, their control of overland trade routes and commodities significantly raised the price of goods such as luxury goods and precious metals that were highly desired by European elites. The solution was to establish sea routes to Asia. This was attempted in several ways. The Portuguese sailed down the coast of Africa over the course of the fifteenth century, and made contact with African societies along the way, as the letters of the kings of the Kongo demonstrate. Although the Portuguese established links of trade, religious missions and military assistance to the Kongo, the taking of slaves rapidly became paramount. The slave trade accelerated in the sixteenth century, as newly-established colonies in the Americas required coerced labor to become economically viable.

Eventually Vasco da Gama reached the thriving Indian Ocean trading network. However, as the reading demonstrates, it became immediately apparent that Europe produced virtually nothing for which Asians wished to trade. This problem was solved by the Portuguese innovation of mounting guns on their ships, allowing them through military force and piracy to control the trade in which they otherwise could not participate. The Spanish Crown, attempting to outflank their Portuguese rivals, backed the voyage of Christopher Columbus, who attempted to reach China and Japan by sailing westward. Instead, he reached the Caribbean, and the excerpts of the following letter include his first impressions of the land he mistakenly thought was Cipango, or Japan. Finally, the selection by Alfred Crosby shows the disastrous consequences of disease caused by European arrival.

84 Letters from the Kings of the Kongo to the King of Portugal

Monumenta Missionaria Africana, Antonio Brasio, ed. Lisboa: Agencia Geral do Ultramar, 1952. 1: 262–263, 294–295, 335, 404, 470, 488. Translated and adapted by Linda Wimmer.

Portuguese sailors established contact with the kingdom of the Kongo in the 1480s. By 1490, King John I of the Kongo and some of his nobles were baptized into the Christian faith, and a series of letters were exchanged over the next half-century between the King of Portugal and successive kings of the Kongo, particularly Afonso I. Early letters make clear the importance of the Portuguese as military allies in a civil war that occurred in the 1490s, and again in a conflict between the king and his brother in the early sixteenth century. However, over time, as illustrated in the letters, a deterioration in relations between the Portuguese and the Kongo rulers occurred, as the Portuguese changed the balance of power in the area and established and expanded slaving operations which would characterize the area throughout the early modern era.

PORTUGUESE MILITARY AID DURING CIVIL WAR (1512)

And our brother who usurped us, and without justice occupied us, with arms and a great number of people . . . became empowered in all of our kingdom, and lordships, with which when we saw the only solution for our person we feigned sickness; and it being so with us, by a divine inspiration of our Lord, we raised and strengthened ourself, and called up our 36 men, and with them we appeared, and went with them to the main square of the city, where our Father died, and where people of infinite number were with our said brother, and . . . for our Lord Jesus Christ, and we began to fight with our adversaries . . . our 36 men, inspired by grace, and aided by God, our adversaries quickly fled . . . and chaos ensued, and with them witnessing . . . there appeared in the air a white Cross, and the blessed Apostle St. James with many men armed and on horseback, and dressed in white battle garments, and killed them, and so great was the chaos, and mortality, that it was a thing of great wonder.

In this defeat our brother was taken prisoner and with justice condemned to die, as he died, for having rebelled against us; and finally we made peace in or kingdoms . . . as it is today, with the Grace of God . . . and through the miracle made by our Lord, and we send word to the King Dom Emanuel of Portugal . . . and we send to him Dom Pedro our brother, who was one of the 36 men with us . . . and with the letters that the king sent of great works given. . . .

• • •

And as the King of Portugal saw the good example . . . followed . . . for the greater growth of our Holy Catholic Faith, he sent by our cousin Dom Pedro and by Simao da Sylva noblemen of your house who came with him, the arms pictured in this card, and the shields with insignias. . . . [A]nd as these weapons arrived a cross was seen in the sky, and so the Apostle St. James and all the other Saints fought with us, and with the help of our Lord God we were given victory, and so also as by the King sent us his [men] took part with the said arms. . . .

PROBLEMS IN CONVERSION EFFORTS (1515)

Very High and Powerful Lord,

We the King Dom Alfonso . . . Lord, much holy grace and praise I give to the Holy God the Father and the Son and the Holy Spirit . . . all good and holy things are done through the will of God, without which we can do nothing . . . our faith is still like glass in this kingdom, due to the bad examples of the men who come here to teach it, because through worldly greed for a few riches truth is destroyed, as through greed the Jews crucified the Son of God, my brother, until today he is crucified through bad examples and bad deeds . . . in our time by us who walk crying in this real valley of misery and tears.

. . . [I]n teaching the word of Our Lord [these bad priests] become bad examples and so take the key to the Celestial Kingdom that is the Doctrine of our Holy Catholic Faith, to open the hearts of our simple people . . . and by entering into a life of sin take the key to Hell . . . due to the greed of this world, do not merely take their own bodies and souls to Hell, but guide those most blind with them through their bad examples. I ask of you, Brother, to aid me in establishing our Holy Catholic Faith, because, Lord my Brother, for us it were better . . . that the souls of our relatives and brothers and cousins and nephews and grandchildren who are innocent, to see . . . good examples.

. . . I ask you to send stonemasons and house carpenters to build a school to teach our relatives and our people, because Lord, although greedy and jealous men still give bad examples . . . with the Holy Sacred Scripture we may change that, because the world of the Holy Spirit is contrary to the world, the flesh and the devil. . . .

ATTEMPTS TO BUY A CARAVEL (1517)

Very Powerful and Very High Prince and King My Brother

. . . I have several times written you of the necessity of having a ship, telling you to make me one to buy, and I don't know why Your Highness does not want to consent, because I want nothing more than . . . to use it in God's service. . . .

EFFECTS OF PORTUGUESE TRADE (1526)

Lord,

. . . [Y]our factors and officials give to the men and merchants that come to this Kingdom . . . and spread . . . so that many vassals owing us obedience . . . rebel because they have more goods [through trade with Portuguese] than us, who before had been content and subject to our . . . jurisdiction, which causes great damage. . . .

. . . And each day these merchants take our citizens, native to the land and children of our nobles and vassals, and our relations, because they are thieves and men of bad conscience, steal them with the desire to have things of this kingdom . . . take them to sell . . . our land is all spoiled . . . which is not to your service. . . . For this we have no more necessity for other than priests and educators, but [send] no more merchandise . . . nor merchants. . . .

EXPANSION AND REGULATION OF THE SLAVE TRADE (1526)

[M]any of our subjects, through the desire for merchandise and things of this Kingdoms which you bring . . . to satisfy their appetite, steal many of our free and exempt subjects. And nobles and their children and our relatives are often stolen to be sold to white men . . . hidden by night. . . . And the said white men are so powerful . . . they embark and . . . buy them, for which we want justice, restoring them to liberty. . . .

And to avoid this great evil, by law all white men in our kingdom who buy slaves . . . must make it known to three nobles and officials of our court . . . to see these slaves. . . .

85 The Portuguese Arrival in the Indian Ocean

Vasco da Gama. *A Journal of the First Voyage of Vasco da Gama, 1497–1499*. Translated by E.G. Ravenstein. London: The Hakluyt Society, 1848. 40, 46, 60–61, 75.

Vasco da Gama's voyage to India is generally taken as a watermark: the entry by sea of Europeans into Asia. However, as the following passage from his logbook confirms, da Gama did not "discover" unknown land. Rather, with the help of an Indian pilot who knew the route, his crew succeeded in reaching the rich and thriving Indian Ocean trade. While this feat was much heralded on his return to Europe, his initial voyage was far from auspicious. A global hinterland whose major products included timber and wheat, and where precious metals were scarce, Europe had little to offer Asians who produced and exchanged precious metals and spices. These commodities were greatly sought after by Europeans. Consequently, Europe suffered from an inherent negative balance of trade, which in following centuries European navigators and traders attempted to redress through military might.

On Easter Sunday [April 15] the Moors [Arab prisoners of the Portuguese crew] . . . told us that there were at this city of Melinde four vessels belonging to Christians* from India, and that if it pleased us to take them there, they would provide us, instead of them Christian pilots and all we stood in need of, including water, wood and other things. The captain-major much desired to have pilots from the country, and having discussed the matter with his Moorish prisoners, he cast anchor off the town, at a distance of about half a league from the mainland. The inhabitants of the town did not venture to come aboard our ships, for they had already learnt that we had captured a vessel and made her occupants prisoners.

• • •

On the following Sunday, the 22nd of April, the king's *zavra* [a court official] brought on board one of his confidential servants, and as two days had passed without any visitors, the captain-major had this man seized, and sent word to the king that he required the pilots whom he had promised. The king, when he received this message, sent a Christian pilot [Mallim Kanaka, native of Gujarat, an Indian state], and the captain-major allowed the gentleman, whom he had retained in his vessel, to go away.

• • •

On Tuesday [May 29] the captain got ready the following things to be sent to the king, viz. twelve pieces of lambel [striped cloth], four scarlet hoods, six

---

*Throughout this piece, Portuguese confuse Hindus with Christians because they are not Muslims. Therefore, the "Christians" in the piece are actually Hindu.

hats, four strings of coral, a case containing six wash-hand basins, a case of sugar, two casks of oil, and two of honey. And as it is the custom not to send anything to the king without the knowledge of the Moor, his factor, and of the bale [a court official], the captain informed them of his intention. They came, and when they saw the present they laughed at it, saying that it was not a thing to offer to a king, that the poorest merchant from Mecca, or any other part of India, gave more, and that if he wanted to make a present it should be in gold, as the king would not accept such things. When the captain heard this he grew sad, and said that he had brought no gold, that, moreover, he was no merchant, but an ambassador; that he gave of that which he had, which was his own [private gift] and not the king's; that if the King of Portugal ordered him to return he would entrust him with far richer presents; and that if King Camolin [the Zamarin, or ruler] would not accept these things he would send them back to the ships. Upon this they declared that they would not forward his presents, nor consent to his forwarding them himself. When they had gone there came certain Moorish merchants, and they all depreciated the present which the captain desired to be sent to the king.

When the captain saw that they were determined not to forward his present, he said . . . he would go to speak to the king, and would then return to the ships. They approved of this, and told him that if he would wait a short time they would return and accompany him to the palace. And the captain waited all day, but they never came back. The captain was very wroth at being among so phlegmatic and unreliable a people. . . .

On Wednesday morning the Moors returned, and took the captain to the palace, and us others with him. The palace was crowded with armed men. Our captain was kept waiting with his conductors for fully four long hours, outside a door, which was only opened when the king sent word to admit him. . . .

When he had entered, the king . . . said that he had told him that he came from a very rich kingdom, and yet had brought him nothing. . . . To this the captain rejoined that he had brought nothing, because the object of his voyage was merely to make discoveries but that when other ships came he would then see what they brought him. . . .

The king then asked what it was he had come to discover: stones or men? If he came to discover men, as he said, why had he brought nothing? Moreover, he had been told that he carried with him the golden image of a Santa Maria. The captain said that the Santa Maria was not of gold, and that even if she were he would not part with her, as she had guided him across the ocean, and would guide him back to his own country. . . .

The king then asked what kind of merchandise was to be found in his country. The captain said there was much corn, cloth, iron, bronze, and many other things. The king asked whether he had any merchandise with him. The captain replied that he had a little of each sort, as samples, and that if permitted . . . he would order it to be landed. . . . The king said no! He might take all his people with him, securely moor his ships, land his merchandise, and sell it to the best advantage.

• • •

When the king heard that we had sailed for Portugal . . . he forwarded a letter to the captain . . . which was intended for the King of Portugal. The tenor of this letter is as follows:

"Vasco da Gama, a gentleman of your household, came to my country, whereat I was pleased. My country is rich in cinnamon, cloves, ginger, pepper, and precious stones. That which I ask of you in exchange is gold, silver, corals and scarlet cloth."

86 The Spanish Conquest of the Aztecs

Bernal Díaz. *The Conquest of New Spain.* Translated by J.M. Cohen. New York: Penguin Books, 1963. 85–7, 216–19.

Bernal Díaz del Castillo was a soldier in Hernan Cortes' army as it traveled from the coast to the capital of the Aztec empire, Tenochtitlán. For Díaz and his compatriots, the discovery and conquest of the massive empire of the Aztecs was the ultimate achievement of the Spanish in the Americas, rivaled only by the conquest of the Inca empire one decade later. In their contacts with the indigenous peoples both in the Valle Central (Central Valley) of Mexico, the Spanish discovered an empire similar to their own. With its obvious social distinctions between lord and peasant, the Aztec world promised far more in terms of wealth than any society contained in the Caribbean. Díaz was a careful observer: through his eyes come the most vivid pictures of the Aztecs, Tlaxcalans, and others, before the conquest. In the following passages, Díaz describes the role of Doña Marina, Cortes's translator, and the arrival of the Spanish in Tenochtitlán.

DOÑA MARINA

Before speaking of the great Montezuma, and of the famous city of Mexico and the Mexicans, I should like to give an account of Doña Marina, who had been a great lady and a *Cacique* [lord, or leader] over towns and vassals since her childhood.

Her father and mother were lords and *Caciques* of a town called Paynala, which had other towns subject to it, and lay about twenty-four miles from the town of Coatzacoalcos. Her father died while she was still very young, and her mother married another *Cacique*, a young man, to whom she bore a son. The mother and father seem to have been very fond of this son, for they agreed that he should succeed to the *Caciqueship* when they were dead. To avoid any impediment, they gave Doña Marina to some Indians from Xicalango, and this they did by night in order to be unobserved. They then spread the report that the child had died; and as the daughter of one of their Indian slaves happened to die at this time, they gave it out that this was their daughter the heiress.

The Indians of Xicalango gave the child to the people of Tabasco, and the Tabascans gave her to Cortes. I myself knew her mother and her half-brother, who was then a man and ruled the town jointly with his mother, since the old lady's second husband had died. After they became Christians, the mother was called Marta and the son Lazaro. All this I know very well, because in the year 1523, after the conquest of Mexico and the other provinces and at the time of Cristobal de Olid's revolt in Honduras, I passed through the place with Cortes, and the majority of its inhabitants accompanied him also. . . .

Thus it was that mother, son, and daughter came together, and it was easy enough to see from the strong resemblance between them that Doña Marina and old lady were related. Both she and her son were very much afraid of Doña Marina; they feared that she had sent for them to put them to death, and they wept.

When Doña Marina saw her mother and half-brother in tears, she comforted them, saying that they need have no fear. She told her mother that when they handed her over to the men from Xicalango, they had not known what they were doing. She pardoned the old woman, and gave them many golden jewels and some clothes. . . .

Doña Marina knew the language of Coatzacoalcos, which is that of Mexico, and she knew the Tabascan language also. This language is common to Tabasco and Yucatan, and Jeronimo de Aguilar spoke it also. These two understood one another well, and Aguilar translated into Castilian [Spanish] for Cortes.

This was the great beginning of our conquests, and thus, praise be to God, all things prospered with us. I have made a point of telling this story, because without Doña Marina we could not have understood the language of New Spain and Mexico.

THE ARRIVAL AT IZTAPALAPA AND TENOCHTITLÁN

When we arrived at Iztapalapa we beheld the splendor of the other *Caciques* who came out to meet us, the lord of that city whose name was Cuitlahuac, and the lord of Culuacan, both of them close relations of Montezuma. And when we entered the city of Iztapalapa, the sight of the palaces in which they lodged us! They were very spacious and well built, of magnificent stone, cedar wood, and the wood of other sweet-smelling trees, with great rooms and courts, which were a wonderful sight, and all covered with awnings of woven cotton.

When we had taken a good look at all this, we went to the orchard and garden, which was a marvellous place both to see and walk in. I was never tired of noticing the diversity of trees and the various scents given off by each, and the paths choked with roses and other flowers, and the many local fruit-trees and rose-bushes, and the pond of fresh water. Another remarkable thing was that large canoes could come into the garden from the lake, through a channel they had cut, and their crews did not have to disembark. Everything was shining with lime and decorated with different kinds of stonework and paintings which were a marvel to gaze on. Then there were birds of many breeds and varieties which came to the pond. I say

again that I stood looking at it, and thought that no land like it would ever be discovered in the whole world, because at that time Peru was neither known nor
thought of. But today all that I then saw is overthrown and destroyed; nothing is
left standing.

Early next day we left Iztapalapa with a large escort of those great *Caciques*,
and followed the causeway, which is eight yards wide and goes so straight to the
city of Mexico that I do not think it curves at all. Wide though it was, it was so
crowded with people that there was hardly room for them all. Some were going to
Mexico and others coming away, besides those who had come out to see us, and we
could hardly get through the crowds that were there. For the towers and the *cues*
were full, and they came in canoes from all parts of the lake. No wonder, since they
had never seen horses or men like us before!

With such wonderful sights to gaze on we did not know what to say, or if this
was real that we saw before our eyes. On the land side there were great cities, and
on the lake many more. The lake was crowded with canoes. At intervals along the
causeway there were many bridges, and before us was the great city of Mexico. As
for us, we were scarcely four hundred strong, and we well remembered the words
and warnings of the people of Huexotzino and Tlascala and Tlamanalco, and many
other warnings we had received to beware of entering the city of Mexico, since
they would kill us as soon as they had us inside. Let the interested reader consider
whether there is not much to ponder in this narrative of mine. What men in all the
world have shown such daring? But let us go on.

We marched along our causeway to a point where another small causeway
branches off to another city called Coyoacan, and there, beside some towerlike
buildings, which were their shrines, we were met by many more *Caciques* and dig-
nitaries in very rich cloaks. The different chieftains wore different brilliant liveries,
and the causeways were full of them. Montezuma had sent these great *Caciques* in
advance to receive us, and as soon as they came before Cortes they told him in
their language that we were welcome, and as a sign of peace they touched the
ground with their hands and kissed it.

There we halted for some time while Cacamatzin, the lord of Texcoco, and the
lords of Iztapalapa, Tacuba, and Coyoacan went ahead to meet the great Montezuma, who approached in a rich litter, accompanied by the other great and feudal
Caciques who owned vassals. When we came near to Mexico, at a place where
there were some other small towers, the great Montezuma descended from his litter, and these other great *Caciques* supported him beneath a marvelously rich
canopy of green feathers, decorated with gold work, silver, pearls, and *chalchi-
huites*, which hung from a sort of border. . . .

When Cortes saw, heard, and was told that the great Montezuma was
approaching, he dismounted from his horse, and when he came near to Montezuma each bowed deeply to each other. Montezuma welcomed our Captain, and
Cortes, speaking through Doña Marina, answered by wishing him very good
health. Cortes, I think, offered Montezuma his right hand, but Montezuma
refused it and extended his own. Then Cortes brought out a necklace which he had
been holding. It was made of those elaborately worked and colored glass beads
called *margaritas,* of which I have spoken, and was strung on a gold cord and

dipped in musk to give it a good odor. This he hung round the great Montezuma's neck, and as he did so attempted to embrace him. But the great princes who stood round Montezuma grasped Cortes' arm to prevent him, for they considered this an indignity. . . .

So, with luck on our side, we boldly entered the city of Tenochtitlan or Mexico on 8 November in the year of our Lord 1519.

87 Indigenous Accounts of the Fall of the Aztec Empire

Miguel Leon-Portilla, ed. *The Broken Spears: The Aztec Account of the Conquest of Mexico.* Boston: Beacon Press, 1962. 63, 65–66, 68, 71–74, 76, 78, 84–85, 87, 92–93.

The collapse of the Aztec empire resulted from a number of factors, as the indigenous accounts compiled in *Broken Spears* demonstrate. It is sometimes claimed that the Aztec ruler, Montezuma (Motecuhzoma), believed that the leader of the Spanish force, Hernan Cortes, was a returning deity to whom the Aztecs must pay allegiance. Yet the documentary record—both the indigenous one and that of Bernal Díaz—suggest that Montezuma treated the visitors as he might have treated any other visiting lords. Ultimately, what forced the collapse of the Aztec empire was the fact that the Spanish were able to ally with Tlaxcala, a powerful city-state and nominal vassal of the Aztec empire.

The documentary collection *Broken Spears* contains an account of the Spanish conquest compiled from different indigenous chronicles. The Spaniards arrived outside of Tenochtitlan on the 8th of November 1519, where they were greeted by Montezuma himself. The newcomers were impressed by the wealth of the Aztec state, and soon demonstrated their greed by seizing Montezuma and his treasures. During the Fiesta of Toxcatl, Cortes's men—Cortes himself was away from the city—massacred a number of warriors and performers, setting off a war between Spanish soldiers and their allies on the one hand, and the Aztec nobility on the other. Although the Spanish forces escaped the city during La Noche Triste (Night of Sorrows), they did so with tremendous loss of life. Ultimately the Spanish and their allies prevailed, due in large measure to the presence of a plague that attacked the Aztec capital of Tenochtitlán.

The Spaniards arrived in Xoloco, near the entrance to Tenochtitlan. That was the end of the march, for they had reached their goal. Motecuhzoma now arrayed himself in his finery, preparing to go out to meet them. The other great princes also adorned their persons, as did the nobles and their chieftains and knights. They all went out together to meet the strangers. They brought trays heaped with the finest flowers—the flower that resembles a shield; the flower shaped like a heart; in the center, the flower with the sweetest aroma; and the fragrant yellow flower, the most precious of all. . . .

Thus Motecuhzoma went out to meet them, there in Huitzillan. He presented many gifts to the Captain and his commanders, those who had come to make war. He showered gifts upon them and hung flowers around their necks; he gave them necklaces of flowers and bands of flowers to adorn their breasts; he set garlands of flowers upon their heads. Then he hung the gold necklaces around their necks and gave them presents of every sort as gifts of welcome. . . .

• • •

When the Spaniards entered the Royal House, they placed Motecuhzoma under guard and kept him under their vigilance. . . . Then the Spaniards fired one of their cannons, and this caused great confusion in the city. The people scattered in every direction; they fled without rhyme or reason; they ran off as if they were being pursued. It was as if they had eaten the mushrooms that confuse the mind, or had seen some dreadful apparition. They were all overcome with terror, as if their hearts had fainted. And when the night fell, the panic spread through the city and their fears would not let them sleep.

In the morning the Spaniards told Motecuhzoma what they needed in the way of supplies: tortillas, fried chickens, hens' eggs, pure water, firewood and charcoal. Also: large, clean cooking pots, water jars, pitchers, dishes and other pottery. Motecuhzoma ordered that it be sent to them. The chiefs who received this order were angry with the king and no longer revered or respected him. But they furnished the Spaniards with all the provisions they needed—food, beverages and water, and fodder for the horses.

When the Spaniards were installed in the palace, they asked Motecuhzoma about the city's resources and reserves and about the warriors' ensigns and shields. They questioned him closely and then demanded gold. Motecuhzoma guided them to it. They surrounded him and crowded close with their weapons. He walked in the center, while they formed a circle around him. When they arrived at the treasure house called Teucalco, the riches of gold and feathers were brought out to them: ornaments made of quetzal feathers, richly worked shields, disks of gold, the necklaces of the idols, gold nose plugs, gold greaves [armor] and bracelets and crowns.

The Spaniards immediately stripped the feathers from the gold shields and ensigns. They gathered all the gold into a great mound and set fire to everything else, regardless of its value. Then they melted down the gold into ingots. As for the precious green stones, they took only the best of them; the rest were snatched up by the Tlaxcaltecas [the allies of the Spanish]. The Spaniards searched through the whole treasure house, questioning and quarreling, and seized every object they thought was beautiful. . . .

• • •

The Aztecs begged permission of their king to hold the fiesta of Huitzilopochtli. The Spaniards wanted to see the fiesta to learn how it was celebrated. A delegation of the celebrants came to the palace where Motecuhzoma was a prisoner, and when their spokesmen asked his permission, he granted it to them. As soon as the delegation returned, the women began to grind seeds of the chicalote. These women had fasted for a whole year. They ground the seeds in the patio of the temple. The Spaniards came out of the palace together, dressed in armor and carrying their weapons with them. They stalked among the women and looked at them one by one; they stared into the faces of the women who were grinding seeds. After this cold inspection, they went back into the palace. It is said that they planned to kill the celebrants if the men entered the patio.

On the evening before the fiesta of Toxcatl, the celebrants began to model a statue of Huitilopochtli. They gave it such a human appearance that it seemed the body of a living man. Yet they made the statue with nothing but a paste made of the ground seeds of the chicalote, which they shaped over an armature of sticks. When the statue was finished, they dressed it in rich feathers, and they painted crossbars over and under its eyes. They also clipped on its earrings of turquoise mosaic; these were in the shape of serpents, with gold rings hanging from them. Its nose plug, in the shape of an arrow, was made of gold and was inlaid with fine stones. They placed the magic headdress of hummingbird feathers on its head. They also adorned it with an *anecuyotl,* which was a belt made of feathers, with a cone at the back. Then they hung around its neck an ornament of yellow parrot feathers fringed like the locks of a young boy. Over this they put its nettle-leaf cape, which was painted black and decorated with five clusters of eagle feathers. . . .

All the young warriors were eager for the fiesta to begin. They had sworn to dance and sing with all their hearts, so that the Spaniards would marvel at the beauty of the rituals. The procession began, and the celebrants filed into the temple patio to dance the Dance of the Serpent. . . . At this moment in the fiesta, when the dance was loveliest and when song was linked to song, the Spaniards were seized with an urge to kill the celebrants. They all ran forward, armed as if for battle. They closed the entrances and passageways, all the gates of the patio. . . . They ran in among the dancers, forcing their way to the place where the drums were played. They attacked the man who was drumming and cut off his arms. Then they cut off his head, and it rolled across the floor.

They attacked all the celebrants, stabbing them, spearing them, striking them from behind, and these fell instantly to the ground with their entrails hanging out. Others they beheaded: they cut off their heads, or split their heads into pieces. They struck others in the shoulders, and their arms were torn from their bodies. . . . No matter how they tried to save themselves, they could find no escape. . . . The blood of the warriors flowed like water and gathered into pools. The pools widened, and the stench of blood and entrails filled the air. The Spaniards ran into the communal houses to kill those who were hiding. They ran everywhere and searched everywhere; they invaded every room, hunting and killing.

When news of this massacre was heard outside the Sacred Patio, a great cry went up: "Mexicans, come running! Bring your spears and shields! The strangers have murdered our warriors!"

The cry was answered with a roar of grief and anger: the people shouted and wailed and beat their palms against their mouths. The captains assembled at once, as if the hour had been determined in advance. . . . Then the battle began. The Aztecs attacked with javelins and arrows, even with the light spears that are used for hunting birds. They hurled their javelins with all their strength, and the cloud of missiles spread out over the Spaniards like a yellow cloak. The Spaniards immediately took refuge in the palace. They began to shoot at the Mexicans with their iron arrows and to fire their cannons and arquebuses.* And they shackled Motecuhzoma in chains. . . .

The royal palace was placed under siege. The Mexicans kept a close watch to prevent anyone from stealing in with food for the Spaniards. They also stopped delivering supplies: they brought them absolutely nothing, and waited for them to die of hunger. . . .

• • •

At midnight the Spaniards and Tlaxcaltecas came out in closed ranks, the Spaniards going first and the Tlaxcaltecas following. The allies kept very close behind, as if they were crowded up against a wall. The sky was overcast and rain fell all night in the darkness, but it was a gentle rain, more like a drizzle or heavy dew. The Spaniards carried portable wooden bridges to cross the canals. They set them in place, crossed over and raised them again. They were able to pass the first three canals—the Tecpantzingo, the Tzapotlan and the Atenchicalco—without being seen. But when they reached the fourth, the Mixcoatechialtitlan, their retreat was discovered.

The first alarm was raised by a woman who was drawing water at the edge of the canal. She cried: "Mexicanos, come running! They are crossing the canal! Our enemies are escaping! Then a priest of Huitzilopochtli shouted the call to arms from the temple pyramid. . . . When they heard this cry, the warriors leaped into the boats and set out in pursuit. These boats were from the garrisons of Tenochtitlan and Tlatelolco, and were protected by the warriors' shields. The boatmen paddled with all their might; they lashed the water of the lake until it boiled. Other warriors set out on foot, racing to Nonohualco and then to Tlacopan to cut off the retreat. The boats converged on the Spaniards from both sides of the causeway, and the warriors loosed a storm of arrows at the fleeing army. But the Spaniards also turned to shoot at the Aztecs; they fired their crossbows and their arquebuses. The Spaniards and Tlaxcaltecas suffered many casualties, but many of the Aztec warriors were also killed or wounded.

When the Spaniards reached the Canal of the Toltecs, in Tlaltecayohuacan, they hurled themselves headlong into the water, as if they were leaping from a cliff. The Tlaxcaltecas, the allies from Tliluhquitepec, the Spanish foot soldiers and horsemen, the few women who accompanied the army—all came to the brink and plunged over it. The canal was soon choked with the bodies of men and horses; they filled the gap in the causeway with their own drowned bodies. Those who followed crossed to the other side by walking on the corpses. . . .

---

*An arquebus is a forerunner to a musket.

. . .

When the Spaniards left Tenochtitlan, the Aztecs thought they had departed for good and would never return. Therefore they repaired and decorated the temple of their god, sweeping it clean and throwing out all the dirt and wreckage. . . .

While the Spaniards were [recovering] in Tlaxcala, a great plague broke out here in Tenochtitlan. It began to spread during the thirteenth month and lasted for seventy days, striking everywhere in the city and killing a vast number of our people. Sores erupted on our faces, our breasts, our bellies; we were covered with agonizing sores from head to foot.

The illness was so dreadful that no one could walk or move. The sick were so utterly helpless that they could only lie on their beds like corpses, unable to move their limbs or even their heads. They could not lie face down or roll from one side to the other. If they did move their bodies, they screamed with pain. A great many died from this plague, and many others died of hunger. They could not get up to search for food, and everyone else was too sick to care for them, so they starved to death in their beds.

Some people came down with a milder form of the disease; they suffered less than the others and made a good recovery. But they could escape entirely. Their looks were ravaged, for wherever a sore broke out, it gouged an ugly pockmark in the skin. And a few survivors were left completely blind. The first cases were reported in Cuatlan. By the time the danger was recognized, the plague was so well established that nothing could halt it, and eventually it spread all the way to Chalco. . . .

88 The First Voyage of Columbus

The Journal of Christopher Columbus. Translated by Cecil Jane. New York: Bonanza Books, 1989. 22–24.

Christopher Columbus was not the first European sailor to land in the Americas, but it was through his "discovery" that Europe and America were brought into sustained contact with each other. Columbus himself was a Genoese sailor and mapmaker, the inheritor of Mediterranean trading and seafaring traditions. He had lived on the Portuguese island of Porto Santo in the Atlantic and travelled as far as the gold coast of West Africa. In an attempt to discover a westward route to the riches of Asia, Columbus made landfall in the Caribbean Islands. The following excerpt is taken from an edited version of Columbus' journal of his first voyage to what Europeans came to call "the New World."

THURSDAY, 11 OCTOBER

[Columbus] navigated to the west-south-west; they had a rougher sea than they had experienced during the whole voyage. They saw petrels [birds] and a green reed near the ship. Those in the caravel *Pinta* saw a cane and a stick, and they secured another small stick, carved, as it appeared, with iron, and other vegetation which grows on land, and a small board. Those in the caravel *Niña* also saw other indications of land and a stick loaded with barnacles. At these signs, all breathed again and rejoiced. . . . [S]ince the caravel *Pinta* was swifter and went ahead of the admiral [Columbus], she found land and made the signals which the admiral had commanded. This land was first sighted by Rodrigo de Triana, although the admiral, at ten o'clock at night, being on the sterncastle, saw a light. . . . Two hours after midnight land appeared, at a distance of about two leagues from them. They took in all sail, remaining with the mainsail, which is the great sail without bonnets, and kept jogging, waiting for a day, a Friday, on which they reached the small island of the Lucayos, which is called in the language of the Indians, "Guanahaní." Immediately they saw naked people, and the admiral went ashore in the armed boat, and Martin Alonso Pinzón and Vicente Yañez, his brother, who was captain of the Niña. The admiral brought out the royal standard, and the captains went with two banners of the Green Cross, which the admiral flew on all the ships as a flag, with an F and a Y, and over each letter their crown, one being on one side of the [cross] and the other on the other. When they had landed, they saw very green trees and much water and fruit of various kinds. The admiral called the two captains and the others who had landed, and Rodrigo de Escobedo, secretary of the whole fleet, and Rodrigo Sanchez de Segovia, and said that they should bear witness and testimony how he, before them all, took possession of the island, as in fact he did, for the King and Queen, his Sovereigns, making the declarations which are required. . . . What follows are the actual words of the admiral, in his book of the first voyage and discovery of these Indies.

"I," he said, "in order that they might feel great amity towards us, because I knew that they were a people to be delivered and converted to our holy faith rather than by love than by force, gave to some among them red caps and glass beads, which they hung round their necks, and many other things of little value. At this they were greatly pleased and became so entirely our friends that it was a wonder to see. Afterwards they came swimming to the ships' boats, where we were, and brought us parrots and cotton thread in balls, and spears and many other things, and we exchanged for them other things, such as small glass beads and hawks' bells, which we gave to them. In fact, they took all and gave all, such as they had, with good will, but it seemed to me that they were a people very deficient in everything. They all go naked as their mothers bore them, and the women also, although I saw only one very young girl. And all those whom I did see were youths, so that I did not see one who was over thirty years of age; they were very well built, with very handsome bodies and very good faces. Their hair is coarse almost like the hair of a horse's tail and short; they wear their hair down over their eyebrows, except for a few strands behind, which they wear long and never cut. Some of them are painted black, and they are the color of the people of the Canaries, neither black nor white, and some of them are painted white and some red and some in any color that they find. Some of them paint their faces, some their whole bodies, some only the eyes, and some only the nose. They do not bear arms or know them, for I showed to them swords and they took them by the blade and cut themselves through ignorance. They have no iron. Their spears are certain reeds, without iron, and some of these have a fish tooth at the end, while others are pointed in various ways. They are all generally fairly tall, good looking and well proportioned. I saw some who bore marks of wounds on their bodies, and I made signs to ask how this came about, and they indicated to me that people came from other islands, which are near, and wished to capture them, and they defended themselves. And I believed and still believe that they come here from the mainland to take them for slaves. They should be good servants and of quick intelligence, since I see that they very soon say all that is said to them, and I believe that they would easily be made Christians, for it appeared to me that they had no creed. Our Lord willing, at the time of my departure I will bring back six of them to Your Highnesses, that they may learn to talk. I saw no beast of any kind on this island, except parrots." All these are the words of the admiral.

89 The Impact of Disease on American Societies

Alfred W. Crosby, Jr. "Conquistador y Pestilencia: The First New World Pandemic and the Fall of the Great Indian Empires." *Hispanic American Historical Review*, vol. 43, no. 3 (August 1967): 321–327.

The establishment of regular contact between Europe and the Americas implied more than the meeting of peoples. In this reading, Alfred W. Crosby, Jr., points out that this contact also made possible an exchange of diseases, plants, animals and ideas that had profound consequences for peoples' lives and livelihoods. In particular, the impact of diseases previously unknown in the Americas upon indigenous populations was immense, and greatly facilitated the process of European conquest in the sixteenth century.

During the millenia before the European brought together the compass and the three-masted vessel to revolutionize world history, men moved slowly, seldom over long distances and rarely across the great oceans. Men lived in the same continents where their great-grandfathers had lived and seldom caused

Figure 14.1
Plants of the Columbian Exchange and their origin. 1. Avocado: New World. 2. Potato: New World. 3. Sugar cane: Old World. 4. Watermelon: New World. 5. Cocoa: New World. 6. Cotton: New and Old Worlds. 7. Tobacco: New World. 8. Coffee: Old World. 9. Cashew: New World. 10. Peanut: New World. 11. Maize [corn]: New World. 12. Manioc: New World. 13. Banana: Old World. 14. Pineapple: Old World.

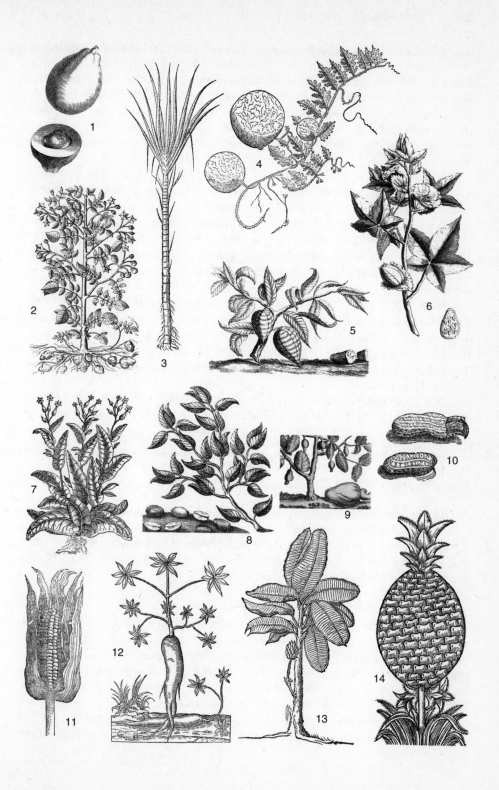

violent and rapid changes in the delicate balance between themselves and their environments. Diseases tended to be endemic rather than epidemic. It is true that man did not achieve perfect accommodation with his microscopic parasites. Mutation, ecological changes, and migration brought the Black Death to Europe. . . . Yet ecological stability did tend to create a crude kind of mutual toleration between human host and parasite. Most Europeans, for instance, survived measles and tuberculosis, and most West Africans survived yellow fever and malaria.

Migration of man and his maladies is the chief cause of epidemics. And when migration takes place, those creatures who have been longest in isolation suffer most, for their genetic material has been least tempered by the variety of world diseases. Among the major divisions of the species homo sapiens, with the possible exception of the Australian aborigine, the American Indian probably had the dangerous privilege of longest isolation from the rest of mankind. Medical historians guess that few of the first rank killers among the diseases are native to the Americas.

These killers came to the New World with the explorers and the conquistadors. The fatal diseases of the Old World killed more effectively in the New, and the comparatively benign diseases of the Old World turned killer in the New. There is little exaggeration in the statement of a German missionary in 1699 that "the indians die so easily that the bare look and smell of a Spaniard causes them to give up the ghost."

The most spectacular period of mortality among the American Indians occurred during the first hundred years of contact with the Europeans and Africans. Almost all of the contemporary historians of the early settlements, from Bartolome de las Casas to William Bradford of Plymouth Plantation, were awed by the ravages of epidemic disease among the native populations of the Americas. . . .

. . .

The victims of disease were probably greatest in number in the heavily populated highlands of New Spain (Mexico) and Peru but, as a percentage of the resident population, were probably greatest in the hot, wet lowlands. By the 1580s disease, ably assisted by Spanish brutality, had killed or driven away most of the peoples of the Antilles and the lowlands of New Spain, Peru, and the Caribbean littoral. . . .

. . .

The record shows that several generations of Indian contact with Europeans and Africans seemed to lead not to the total destruction of the Indians, but only to a sharp diminution of numbers, which was then followed by renewed population growth among the aborigines. The relationships between these phenomena are too complex to be explained by any one theory. However, their sequence is perfectly compatible with the theory that the Indians with the weakest resistance to those maladies had died, interbreeding with the hardy survivors, and, to some measured extent, with the immigrants, led to the beginning of population recovery.

90 Visual Document: An Afro-Portuguese Salt Cellar

From the fifteenth century forward, Portuguese and West African societies maintained trading relationships. This contact facilitated cultural exchange between them. one of the art forms that resulted were Afro-Portuguese ivories: forks, spoons, dagger handles, and salt cellars that were commissioned by Portuguese officials resident in West Africa and carved by African artists.

The salt cellar shown here was carved in Benin during the sixteenth century. It has two chambers and is extensively decorated by carved figures. Four Portuguese in sixteenth-century dress are clustered around the sides of the container. The lid is formed by a ship on the sea, with a figure peering out of the crows' nest. What features identify the figures as Portuguese? What features identify the artist as African rather than European? In what ways may artwork be useful for historical study?

DISCUSSION QUESTIONS

1. How did global integration occur? Why did Europeans, rather than peoples of other regions, begin the initiatives that resulted in the establishment of regular contact among all the world's regions?

2. What were the effects of global integration? What facets of our daily lives today exist because of global integration?

3. What were the advantages and disadvantages of global integration?

4. What range of possible relationships existed in contact between Europeans and societies in other parts of the world? What factors seem to determine the shape that relations take in each case?

5. What are the origins of European desires to expand their sphere of influence?

6. What evidence of the Columbian Exchange can you find in *Broken Spears?*

7. What similarities and differences existed in the experience of the Kings of the Kongo with that of the Aztecs? What factors determined the shape of each?

Credits

Grateful acknowledgment is extended to the following for permission to reprint selections from copyrighted materials:

Page 4: From Oodgeroo Nunukul, *Stadbroke Dreamtime*. Copyright © 1972. Reprinted by permission of HarperCollins Publishers Australia.

Page 5: Adapted from Juliet Piggott, *Japanese Mythology*. Copyright © 1969. Used by permission of Hamlyn, Reed Books.

Page 6: New English Bible © Oxford University Press and Cambridge University Press 1961, 1970. Reprinted by permission.

Page 10: From *A Treasury of African Folklore*, by Harold Courlander. Copyright 1975 by Harold Courlander. Reprinted by permission of Marlowe & Company.

Page 16: From "The Dawn of Humans: The Farthest Horizon," by Maeve Leakey, *National Geographic*, September 1995, pp. 38-51. Used by permission of the author.

Page 19: From *Archaeology of the Dreamtime: The Story of Prehistoric Australia and Its People*, revised edition, by Josephine Flood. Copyright © 1990. Reprinted by permission of the publisher, Yale University Press.

Page 22: From James Mellaart, *Çatal Hüyük: A Neolithic Town in Anatolia*. Copyright © 1967. Reprinted by permission of the author.

Page 24: Excerpts from "The Shang City at Cheng-chou and Related Problems," by An Chin-huai, in *Studies of Shang Archaeology*, edited by K.C. Chang. Copyright © 1986. Reprinted by permission of the publisher, Yale University Press.

Page 26: Paul G. Bahn, "50,000 Year Old Americans of Pedra Furada." Reprinted by permission from *Nature* Vol. 362, p. 114. Copyright © 1993 Macmillan Magazines Ltd.

Page 28: From Glynn Ll. Isaac, *Olorgesailie: Archaeological Studies of a Middle Pleistocene Lake Basin in Kenya*. © 1977 by The University of Chicago. All rights reserved. Reprinted by permission of the publisher, The University of Chicago Press.

Page 33: Reprinted with the permission of The Free Press, a division of Simon & Schuster, from *Chinese Civilization: A Sourcebook*, Second Edition, Revised and Expanded by

Patricia Buckley Ebrey. Copyright © 1993 by Patricia Buckley Ebrey. Copyright © 1981 by The Free Press.

Page 34: Chinese oracle bones, from the collection of C.V. Starr East Asian Library, Columbia University. Reproduced by permission.

Page 35: From *Sources of Indian Tradition*, by William Theodore de Bary. Copyright © 1958 by Columbia University Press. Reprinted with permission of the publisher.

Page 38: Reprinted from *The Babylonian Laws* edited by G.R. Driver and John C. Miles, vol.2 (1955) by permission of Oxford University Press.

Page 39: Stone tablet of Hammurabi, Giraudon/Art Resource, New York. Reproduced by permission.

Page 43: Pritchard, James B. (ed.), *Ancient Near Eastern Texts*, 3rd edition. Copyright © 1969 Princeton University Press. Reprinted by permission of Princeton University Press.

Page 52: Excerpts from Thomas J. Barfield, "The Hsiung-nu Imperial Confederacy: Organization and Foreign Policy," *The Journal of Asian Studies*, XLI, No. 1, November 1981, pp. 45-63. Reprinted with permission of the Association for Asian Studies, Inc.

Page 55: Excerpts from Joshua 6:1-26 from the Revised Standard Edition of the Bible, copyright 1946, 1952, 1971 by the Division of Christian Education of the National Council of the Churches of Christ in the USA. Used by permission.

Page 56: From *The Changing Past: Farmers, Kings and Traders in Southern Africa, 200-1860*. Copyright © 1987. Reprinted by permission of David Philip Publishers, Cape Town, South Africa.

Page 59: From Michael D. Coe, *The Maya*. Copyright © 1966. Reprinted by permission of the publisher, Thames & Hudson Ltd.

Page 61: From *The Book of Songs* translated by Arthur Waley. Copyright © 1937 by Arthur Waley. Used by permission of Grove/Atlantic, Inc.

Page 62: Herbert D.G. Maschner, "The Emergence of Cultural Complexity on the Northern Northwest Coast," *Antiquities*, 65, 1991, pp. 924-931. Copyright © 1991. Reprinted by permission of the author.

Page 67: From *The Ramayana* by R. K. Narayan. Copyright © 1972 by R. K. Narayan. Used by permission of Viking Penguin, a division of Penguin Books USA Inc.

Page 70: From Homer, *The Iliad*, translated by S.O. Andrew and M.J. Oakley. Copyright © 1955. Used by permission of Everyman's Library, David Campbell Publishers Ltd.

Page 72: Reprinted with the permission of Simon & Schuster from *Africa in History*, Revised and Expanded Edition by Basil Davidson. Copyright ©1966, 1968, 1974, 1984, 1991 by Basil Davidson.

Page 74: From B.O. Foster, Ph.D. (translator), *Livy in Fourteen Volumes*, Volume V. Books XXI-XXUU (Loeb Classical Library 233). Copyright © 1929. Reprinted by permission of the publisher, Harvard University Press.

Page 77: From *Sources of Chinese Tradition* by William Theodore de Bary. Copyright © 1960 by Columbia University Press. Reprinted with permission of the publisher.

Page 78: Michael C. Rogers, *Chronicle of Fu Chien: A Case of Exemplar History*. Copyright © 1968 The Regents of the University of California. Reprinted by permission of The University of California Press.

Page 81: Adapted from *Prehistory of the Americas* by Stuart J. Fiedel. Reprinted with the permission of Cambridge University Press.

Page 85: Reprinted with the permission of Pocket Books, a Division of Simon & Schuster Inc., from *Popol Vuh* by Dennis Tedlock. Copyright © 1985 by Dennis Tedlock.

Page 87: From *Sources of Indian Tradition* by William Theodore de Bary. Copyright © 1958 by Columbia University Press. Reprinted with permission of the publisher.

Page 89: From Robert Allen Mitchell, *The Buddha: His Life Retold*. Copyright © 1989. Reprinted by permission of Paragon House.

Page 94: From *Sources of Chinese Tradition* by William Theodore de Bary. Copyright © 1960 by Columbia University Press. Reprinted with permission of the publisher.

Page 98: *The New English Bible* © Oxford University Press and Cambridge University Press 1961, 1970. Reprinted by permission.

Page 104: From Colin Renfrew, *Archaeology and Language: The Puzzle of Indo-European Origins*. Copyright © 1987 by the publisher, Jonathan Cape. Reprinted by permission.

Page 106: From Philip Curtin et al, *African History*. Copyright © 1978. Reprinted by permission of the publishers, Longman Group Ltd.

Page 109: From *The Drunken King* by Luc de Heusch, translated by Roy Willis. Copyright © 1982. Reprinted by permission of the publisher, Indiana University Press.

Pages 111 and 113: From Irving Rouse, *Migrations in Prehistory* . Copyright © 1986. Reprinted by permission of the publisher, Yale University Press.

Page 122: From *Medieval Trade in the Mediterranean World* by Robert S. Lopez and Irving W. Raymond. Copyright © 1955 by Columbia University Press. Reprinted with permission of the publisher.

Page 126: From *Royal Commentaries of the Incas and General History of Peru* by Garcilaso de la Vega, translated by Harold V. Livermore, Copyright © 1966. By permission of the University of Texas Press.

Page 128: Goitein, S.D., *Letters of Medieval Jewish Traders*. Copyright © 1973 by Princeton University Press. Reprinted by permission of Princeton University Press.

Page 133: From G.S.P. Freeman-Grenville, *The East African Coast: Select Documents from the First to the Earlier Nineteenth Century*. Copyright © 1962. Reprinted by permission of the author.

Page 139: Map of Abraham de Cresques, Bibliotheque Nationale de France. Reproduced by permission.

Page 142: From Ma Huan, Ying-Yai Sheng-Lan, *The Overall Survey of the Ocean's Shores*, translated by J.V.G. Mills. © Cambridge University Press 1970. Reprinted with the permission of Cambridge University Press.

Page 147: From William Longland (translated by J.F. Goodridge), *Piers the Ploughman*. Copyright © 1959, 1966 by J.F. Goodridge. Reproduced by permission of Penguin Books Ltd.

Page 150: From Walter L. Wakefield, *Heresy, Crusade and Inquisition in Southern France 1100-1250*, pp. 209-213, 219. Copyright © 1974. Reprinted by permission of the author.

Page 152: Excerpt from *The Tale of Genji* by Lady Murasaki, translated by Arthur Waley. Copyright, 1929. Reprinted by permission of Houghton Mifflin Co. and HarperCollins Publishers Limited. All rights reserved.

Page 154: From *Letter to a King* by Huamán Poma, edited by Christopher Dilke. Copyright © 1978. Reprinted by permission of A.P. Watt Ltd. on behalf of The Estate of Christopher Dilke.

Page 159: *Codex Mendoza*. Reproduced courtesy of Frances F. Berdan and Patricia Rieff Anawalt.

Page 165: Reprinted, by permission, from *The Florentine Codex: General History of the Things in Spain by Fray Bernardino de Sahagun, Book 2: The Ceremonies*, pp. 197, 216-217. Translated by Arthur J.O. Anderson and Charles E. Dibble. Copyright 1981 by the School of American Research, Santa Fe.

Page 166: From James A. Brundage, Ph.D., *The Crusades, A Documentary Survey*. Copyright © 1962. Reprinted by permission of Marquette University Press.

Page 168: Francesco Gabrieli, translated/edited by E.J. Costello, *Arab Historians of the Crusades—Selected and Translated from the Arabic Sources*. Copyright © 1969 The Regents of the University of California. Reprinted by permission of The University of California Press.

Page 169: *Saladin Conquers Jerusalem*. Reproduced courtesy of Masters and Fellows of Corpus Christi College, Cambridge University.

Page 171: J.F.P. Hopkins (trans.), *Corpus of Early Arabic Sources for West African History*. © University of Ghana, International Academic Union, Cambridge University Press 1981. Reprinted with the permission of Cambridge University Press.

Page 175: Female Buddha (Fujiyan Province, late 17th c.), Guanyin, Goddess of Mercy. Gift of Mrs. R. Henry Norweb, The Cleveland Museum of Art. Reproduced by permission.

Page 178: From George Vernadsky (trans.), *Medieval Russian Laws*. Copyright © 1965. Reprinted by permission of Octagon Books, A Division of Hippocrene Books, Inc.

Page 182: Khaldun, Ibn, (Franz Rosenthal, trans.), *The Muqaddimah* (vol. 2). Copyright © 1958 renewed Princeton University Press. Reprinted by permission of Princeton University Press.

Page 185: Frances F. Berdan and Patricia Rieff Anawalt, *The Codex Mendoza*. Copyright © 1992 The Regents of the University of California. Reprinted by permission of The University of California Press.

Page 186: From H.M. Wright, translator, *Daily Life in China* by Jacques Gernet. English translation copyright © 1962 by George & Allen Unwin Ltd. Copyright © 1959 by Librairie Hachette. Used by permission of Georges Borchardt, Inc.

Page 188: Reprinted with the permission of The Free Press, an imprint of Simon & Schuster, from *Chinese Civilization and Society* by Patricia Buckley Ebrey. Copyright © 1981 by The Free Press.

Page 189: From *The Peasants' Revolt of 1381* by R.B. Dobson, pp. 64-67. Copyright © 1970. Reprinted by permission of Macmillan Ltd.

Page 192: Weaving in China. Gest Oriental Library and East Asian Collections, Princeton University. Reproduced by permission.

Page 193: Plowing in China. Reproduced courtesy of Dr. and Mrs. Gerd Wallenstein.

Page 195: Khaldun, Ibn, (Franz Rosenthal, trans.), *The Muqaddimah* (vol. 2). Copyright © 1958 renewed Princeton University Press. Reprinted by permission of Princeton University Press.

Page 197: *Wise Women of the Dreamtime* by Johanna Lambert, published by Inner Traditions International, Rochester, Vt. © by Johanna Lambert. Used by permission.

Page 201: From *The Decameron* by Giovanni Boccaccio, translated by Mark Musa and Peter Bondanella. Translation copyright © 1982 by Mark Musa and Peter Bondanella. Introduction copyright © 1981, 1982 by Thomas Bergin. Used by permission of Dutton Signet, a division of Penguin Books USA Inc.

Page 204: From *The Travels of an Alchemist*, by Li Chih-Ch'ang, translated by Arthur Waley. Copyright © 1931. Reprinted by permission of the publisher, Routledge and Sons, Ltd.

Page 207: From *The Columbia Anthology of Traditional Chinese Literature* by Victor H. Mair. Copyright © 1994 by Columbia University Press. Reprinted with permission of the publisher.

Page 208: Ibn Battuta, *Travels in Asia and Africa*, pp. 305-306. Copyright © 1929. Reprinted by permission of International Thomson Publishing Services Ltd.

Page 210: Durer, *Scène de l'Apocalypse.* Giraudon/Art Resource, New York. Reproduced by permission.

Page 213: Reprinted, by permission, from *The Florentine Codex: General History of the Things in Spain by Fray Bernardino de Sahagun, Book 6: Rhetoric and Moral Philosophy.* Translated by Arthur J.O. Anderson and Charles E. Dibble. Reprinted courtesy of the School of American Research and the University of Utah Press. Reprinted by permission.

Page 216: Reprinted from *The Ordeal of the Longhouse: The Peoples of the Iroquois League in the Era of European Colonization*, by Daniel K. Richter. Published for the Institute of Early American History and Culture. Copyright © 1992 by the University of North Carolina Press. Used by permission of the publisher.

Page 219: Mary Elizabeth Berry, *The Culture of Civil War in Kyoto.* Copyright © 1994 The Regents of the University of California. Reprinted by permission of The University of California Press.

Page 221: From P.S. Garlake, *Great Zimbabwe.* Copyright © 1973. Reprinted by permission of Thames and Hudson Ltd.

Page 222: Elliptical Building at Great Zimbabwe. © Jason Lure. Reproduced by permission.

Page 224: Kritovoulos, translated by Charles T. Riggs; *History of Mehmed the Conqueror.* Copyright © 1954, renewed 1982 by Princeton University Press. Reprinted by permission of Princeton University Press.

Page 227: From *Africa and Africans in the Making of the Atlantic World, 1400-1680* by John Thornton. Reprinted with the permission of Cambridge University Press.

Page 235: Theodore De Bry's Secota. North Wind Picture Archives. Reproduced by permission.

Page 243: From E.G. Ravenstein, F.R.G.S. (ed.), *A Journal of the First Voyage of Vasco da Gama.* Reprinted by permission of Hakluyt Society.

Page 245: From *The Conquest of New Spain* by Bernal Díaz, translated by J.M. Cohen, pp. 84-87, 215-219. Copyright © 1963. Reproduced by permission of Penguin Books Ltd.

Page 248: From *The Broken Spears* by Miguel Leon-Portilla. Copyright © 1962 by Beacon Press. Reprinted by permission of Beacon Press.

Page 252: From *The Journal of Christopher Columbus*, translated by Cecil Jane. Copyright © 1960 Clarkson N. Potter, Inc. Reprinted by permission of Clarkson N. Potter, Inc., a division of Crown Publishers, Inc.

Page 254: Alfred W. Crosby, Jr., *"Conquistador y Pestilencia*: The First New World Pandemic and the Fall of the Great Indian Empires," *Hispanic American Historical Review*, 47:3 (August 1967), pp. 321-27. Copyright Duke University Press, 1967. Reprinted with permission.

Page 255: Plants of the Columbian Exchange. James Ford Bell Library, University of Minnesota. Reproduced by permission.

Page 257: Afro-Portuguese Salt Cellar. Metropolitan Museum of Art, Bell and Rogers Fund, 1972. Reproduced by permission.